# TRADITIONAL JAPANESE MUSIC

*and*

## MUSICAL INSTRUMENTS

# TRADITIONAL JAPANESE MUSIC and MUSICAL INSTRUMENTS

THE NEW EDITION

WILLIAM P. MALM

KODANSHA INTERNATIONAL
Tokyo • New York • London

THE YAMAGUCHI KAN SERIES

Publication of this book was assisted by a generous grant provided by Ms. Yamaguchi Kan of Tsuchiura City, Japan. A select number of interesting works in English on Japan have been given such assistance.

Funding for the production of the CD was provided in part by the University of Michigan Office of the Associate Provost for Academic Affairs, as well as the Center for Japanese Studies. Thanks are also due to the Henry Luce Foundation.

Originally published in 1959 by Charles E. Tuttle Company under the title *Japanese Music and Musical Instruments*.

Distributed in the United States by Kodansha America, Inc., 575 Lexington Avenue, New York, NY 10022, and in the United Kingdom and continental Europe by Kodansha Europe Ltd., 95 Aldwych, London WC2B 4JF. Published by Kodansha International Ltd., 17–14 Otowa 1-chome, Bunkyo-ku, Tokyo 112–8652, and Kodansha America, Inc. Copyright © 2000 by Kodansha International Ltd. All rights reserved. Printed in Japan.

ISBN 4–7700–2395–2

First edition, 2000

00 01 02 03 04 05   10 9 8 7 6 5 4 3 2 1

Dedicated to the traditional musicians of Japan.

*May their art flourish
ten thousand years.*

ONE

## The Present and Past of Japanese Music

TWO

## Religious Music

# LIST OF PLATES

1. The dance pantomime "Okame" accompanied by this folk *hayashi* is seen frequently during fall festivals in Japan.   24

FOLLOWING PAGE 80

2. Some tomb figurines (*haniwa*) evoke the music, song, and dance of ancient Japan.
3. An outdoor performance on the *wagon* zither. Note the high bridges.
4. The *kagura azuma asobi* dance costume shown in the *Bugakuzu* (1905).
5. On the right, a dancer-priestess (*miko*) with *suzu*.
6. A *shirabyōshi* dancer from *Kabu ongaku ryakushi* (1888).
7. A young festival ensemble travels on a *yatai* cart during the Sanja festival in Asakusa, Tokyo.
8. The *atarigane* is played inside the gong.
9. The devil dancers of the Yasurai festival in Kyoto use a gong called the *surigane*. They also carry *taiko* drums.
10. A *satokagura* performance of the white fox in Asakusa, Tokyo. Note the *suzu* bell tree in his hand and the accompanying *daibyōshi* drum.
11. A lion dance (*shishi mai*) is popular in Japanese festivals whether done by two dancers or only one.
12. Drums, rattles, a flute, and a giant flowered hat are part of a *dengaku* ceremony at the Kasuga shrine in Nara. From *Kasuga ōmiya wakamiya gosaireizu* (1716).
13. The opening procession of the *yuki matsuri* in the mountain village of Niino in Nagano prefecture, 1956. Two firemen in uniform protect the box of dance masks.
14. The *binzasara* rattle and drums on the *kaguraden* at the *yuki matsuri* reflect old traditions seen in Plate 12.
15. Shinto chanting (*semmyō*) with drum and bell tree accompaniment at the *yuki matsuri*.
16. The "Modoki" is one of a series of dances performed in the all-night celebration of the *yuki matsuri*.
17. A large wooden fish-mouthed gong (*mokugyo*) sits ready for use as Buddhist priests chant while circling the altar.
18. Buddhist *wasan* singing is often accompanied by the *ōdaiko* drum.
19. A print from the *Seikyoku ruisan*, vol. 5 (1839), showing various types of street music of Edo. *Ōgibyōshi*, top left, *saimon*, top right, and *nembutsu* priests.
20. Edo period *kado sekkyō*, *utabikuni*, and *yotsudake* performers from the *Seikyoku ruisan*.
21. A *chindonya* trio in action, Tokyo 1956.
22. An itinerant priest on Enoshima chants prayers to the accompaniment of an *uchiwadaiko* drum.
23. Members of a Buddhist congregation of the Jōdo sect performing *goeika* music and dancing.
24. *Bon odori*, such as this 1956 example from Miyakejima, are common Buddhist-inspired folk dances in Japan.
25. The Iwate deer dance is one of the most spectacular folk theatricals (*geinō*) in Japan.
26. This eighteenth-century screen painting of the great Buddha ceremony held at the Tōdaiji in the eighth century shows *bugaku* musicians and dancers performing before the temple.
27. *Rinyūgaku*, an exotic form of court music still shown in the fourteenth-century *Shinzeikogakuzu* scroll.

11

28. The "Genjōraku" dance as pictured in the *Shinzeikogakuzu* scroll.

29. The rare *gogenbiwa* from the Shōsōin shows floral designs on its back and a Central Asian scene on the front.

30. Drawings copied in the *Kabu ongaku ryakushi* (1888) from the fourteenth-century *Shinzeikogakuzu* include the *biwa* lute and *shō* mouth organ along with instruments no longer heard in Japan such as the *kugo* harp and the *hōkyō* rack of metal plates.

31. A courtly ensemble scene in the fourteenth-century *Sumiyoshi monogatari* scroll.

32. The imperial *gagaku* orchestra in the palace music hall. They represent one of the oldest orchestral traditions in the world.

33. A *bugaku* ensemble accompanying dance at the Gion shrine in Kyoto. Note the lack of stringed instruments.

34. The *bugaku* dance "Taiheiraku."

35. Four kinds of flutes: (from the top) the *komabue*, *kagurabue*, *ryūteki*, and *nōkan*.

36. A giant *dadaiko* drum being played during a cherry blossom festival at the Gion shrine in Kyoto.

37. A large *shōko* gong with an elaborate stand at the Gion shrine in Kyoto.

FOLLOWING PAGE 176

38. A full *noh* ensemble is seen in this 1956 performance of the play *Takasago*.

39. The *mibu kyōgen* pantomime plays in Kyoto resemble ancient European morality plays and retain the style of the early folk theatricals that inspired the creators of *noh*.

40. The *nōkan* is the only melodic instrument in the *noh* ensemble. Note that the holes are covered by the middle joints of the fingers, producing the half-holed effects characteristic of its music.

41. Before every *noh* performance, the musicians play the warm-up piece "Shirabe," while the lead actor absorbs his role in a mirror.

42. Traditional Japanese music is taught piece by piece through rote methods. Here the teacher beats out the pattern of the *tsuzumi* drum with two leather-covered fans on a "rhythm box" (*hyōshiban*) while singing the vocal or the flute melody.

43. The *kotsuzumi* hand position allows the player to squeeze the ropes and hence change the tone.

44. The *kotsuzumi* is reassembled at every performance so that the rope tensions will be correct for weather and stage conditions.

45. The *taiko* drummer is executing the *kashira* pattern in the play *Hagoromo*. The white costume and mixed genders suggest an amateur recital.

46. Heian-period gentry often courted their ladies by playing the *gakubiwa*, as seen in this famous scroll of *The Tale of Genji*.

47. A *mōsōbiwa* performer chants prayers or stories.

48. Imai Tsutomu carries on the blind *heikebiwa* tradition of reciting the *Tale of the Heike*.

49. Hirata Kyokushū (1905–64) taught *chikuzenbiwa* only to those who first prayed all night beneath the waterspout at the Kiyomizu temple in Kyoto.

50. This *satsumabiwa* performer looks like a traditional blind priest narrator, but his eyes are closed only to better envision the dramatic scene he is describing.

51. *Biwa* makers still use traditional tools to carve the body out of one piece of wood. Potential *biwa* soundboards are seen stacked on the shelf behind him.

52. The *shakuhachi* is best heard in solo performances.

53. A priest and two gentlemen enjoying sweet *hitoyogiri* melodies in this drawing from the early nineteenth-century *Shichiku kokinshū*.

54. *Komusō* musicians used to collect temple funds in the box hanging around their neck and information with their eyes and ears inside a basket hat.

55. An idealized picture of a 1950s Japanese family enjoying Japanese culture.

56. A *sankyoku* performance, 1977 (*koto*, Fujii Chiyoga; *shamisen*, Ambiru Hiroka; *shakuhachi*, Aoki Reibo).

57. The *koto* hand position for the Yamada school. Note the placement of the picks.

58. The *kokyū*, Japan's only bowed instrument, being played by Miyagi Michio.

59. The Ryukyu *sanshin* is the predecessor of the Japanese *shamisen*.

60. Female *gidayū* performers have been popular in little theaters for over a century.

61. Male *gidayū* performers are best heard in the *bunraku* theater.

62–73. The intense concentration and dramatic expressions of the *tayū* narrator are clearly seen in this sequence of photographs of the late Takemoto Tsudayū performing in a 1956 puppet theater.

74. A *nagauta* ensemble is the major lyrical music of the *kabuki* but here is performing in concert.

75. The *gidayū shamisen* is much more heavily built than the *nagauta* one. The three plectrums shown are (left to right) used for *jiuta*, *nagauta*, and *gidayū*.

76. The *hanamichi* ramp from the back of the theater to the stage is the major entranceway for actors. The *geza* musicians see them through slats in the scenery wall where the ramp meets the stage.

77. Onstage music is called *debayashi*. In this scene from *Kanjinchō* the musicians are in their usual position, though scenery may change matters.

78. Behind the bamboo blind the offstage *geza* musicians provide all kinds of special music and sound effects. Here the play requires the sound of a *noh hayashi*.

79. In this scene from *Momijigari* the *tokiwazu* musicians are placed on a dais at the foot of the *hanamichi*, the *nagauta* are stage left, and the *gidayū* are barely visible above the stage left entrance. Such mixtures of music are called *kakeai*.

FOLLOWING PAGE 256

80. The thunder god appears complete with local raincoat during the ancient *ameagari* rain dance from Kumamoto prefecture.

81. The Ainu *tonkori* lute is plucked with both hands.

82. Ainu throat game performers create strange effects by singing into each other's mouths.

83. A 1956 *kamishibai* man selling candy before he illustrates his story with paper pictures in a frame on the back of his bicycle.

84. A 1957 street vendor of hand puppets demonstrating his wares in Kyoto, as was done in ancient times.

85. The Awaji tradition of puppet performances continues, now with female musicians.

86. A performance of Gifu puppets at an outside stage before an interested but chilled audience.

87. Regional *noh* from Mizuumi in Fukui prefecture performing *Takasago* as part of a temple fund raiser. The same play is seen on a *noh* stage in Plate 38.

88. Children's *kabuki* in Shiga in one of several youth troupes in Japan.

89. *Yamabushi kagura* in Iwate prefecture continues to perform old ritual dances in costumes designed centuries ago.

# LIST OF FIGURES

## LIST OF CD CONTENTS

Track 1. The *kagura* song "Sakaki."
Track 2. The Tokyo festival piece "Shichōme."
Track 3. Dance music from the *yuki matsuri*.
Track 4. A Buddhist chant.
Track 5. The *gagaku* piece "Etenraku" in the *hyōjō* mode.
Track 6. An *ageuta* from the *noh* drama *Matsukaze*.
Track 7. The finale of the *noh* drama *Takasago*.
Track 8. A *mōsōbiwa* Buddhist chant.
Track 9. The opening of the *heikebiwa* narration of *Tale of the Heike*.
Track 10. The opening of the *satsumabiwa* narration "Atsumori."
Track 11. Excerpt from the *chikuzenbiwa* narration "Ōgi no mato."
Track 12. The opening of the *shakuhachi* piece "Hifumi hachigaeshi."
Track 13. Opening song and interlude from Yamada *koto* piece "Matsukaze."
Track 14. *Gidayū* excerpt from the puppet play scene "Sakaya no dan."
Track 15. The *kouta* piece "Tomete mo kaeru."
Track 16. Excerpt from the *nagauta* piece "Gorō Tokimune."
Track 17. The opening of the *kabuki* play *Momijigari*.
Track 18. The Japanese folk song "Tsugaru jongarabushi."
Track 19. A *bon odori* song, "Kawasaki."

My wife and I were having dinner with Donald Richie, January 9, 1956. Late in the meal, he mentioned that Merideth Weatherby of Charles E. Tuttle Company wanted to know if I was interested in writing a book on Japanese music. The fact that I was a graduate student aged twenty-eight who had only been in Japan four months and that I had never published anything did not seem to be a problem. Rather, the challenge seemed to be that, among all the books on Japanese flower arranging, the tea ceremony, judo, sumo, cooking, and theater, there was almost nothing on music. Thus in February of 1956 I began writing. My innocence and youthful enthusiasm were such that I turned in the draft in July 1957. Weatherby told me it was the first time in his career that he had ever got a manuscript in on time.

The traditional role of an editor is to get a draft manuscript into shape but, in Weatherby's case, he was primarily concerned with designing a publication that would be handsome enough for a coffee table. At his suggestion, drawings of all the instruments were added along the top of pages, as were the forbidden fruit of most publications, color pictures! Toward the end of production I asked for a bilingual glossary index using yet another luxury, Japanese characters. Since the book was printed in Japan, this presented no problem and was included. Without Weatherby's help, the work of a graduate student would never have made *The New York Times*, nor remained on the market from 1959 until 1993. I have always been grateful to him for this exceptional help.

In that context, I now thank Stephen Shaw and Moriyasu Machiko of Kodansha International, as well as Judith Ravin, for editing the complicated combination of text, drawings, music, plates, and a CD into a new book. I also appreciate Christopher Blasdel's helpful critical reading, and Waseda Misako's assistance with index romanization, *kanji*, and definitions.

Though I have written several books since the first one, none has been reviewed in *The New York Times*, nor have they been as expensive, with color prints and a hard cover. Still, the information in the original *Japanese Music and Musical Instruments* does seem to have established it as a standard reference work which, to my surprise, is even used in Japan as a textbook. The function of this new edition is to create a more accessible book for the student and the intellectually curious. It also attempts to correct some of the errors that were never removed by the previous publisher.

When rewriting it after nearly forty years, I did not want to destroy the book's youthful flavor with emeritus professor prose. Some of its naiveté has therefore been left as a historical record of the way in which researchers viewed exotic music in the 1950s, and I accept full responsibility for what might now be considered as misconceptions. Japanese colleagues have also requested that I keep many of the original pictures, as they show how things were in the 1950s and who the performers of that decade were.

Reliving an experience that has been part of my life for over four decades has been difficult but a pleasure. I look forward to sharing it with you.

William P. Malm
March 2000

# FOREWORD

Basil Hall Chamberlain, in his introduction to Konakamura Kiyonori's *Kabu ongaku ryakushi* (A Short History of Song and Dance Music, 1888), ended his remarks by saying: "The result of his labours is a work which will be the despair of future investigators, leaving to them, as it would seem to do, nothing further to discover." Since that time, there has actually been quite a lot to discover about Japanese music, not only as it relates to dancing or singing, but also in its instrumental development. Sir Francis Piggott was much wiser when he said that his book on Japanese music, published in 1893, was only an introduction to the topic.

Until the mid-twentieth century, further attempts in Western languages to survey Japanese music were rare, the few papers on the subject being restricted to specialized aspects. By the end of the century, new Western studies flourished, as did translations of books and articles by Japanese authors. Still, many excellent studies remain hidden from Western readers, being only in Japanese. Both the past and present editions of this book were written so that the Western world should know the basic facts about the various forms of traditional Japanese music and musical instruments and their place in the overall history of Japan. Like Piggott's book, this too can be no more than an introduction to a most complex subject. I am fortunate, however, in having had many more sources to draw upon than Piggott did.

I have tried to offer as much general information as possible for the layman, but, for the musicologist, have included brief paragraphs and suggestions concerning more technical matters. For those who wish to pursue the matter further, I have also added at the end of the book an outline of musical notations, a list of audio-visual materials, a Bibliography, and a bilingual Glossary Index. An important new addition is a CD with examples of all the major musics discussed. The fine drawings of musical instruments that enriched pages throughout the 1959 edition, done by Kuwata Masakazu of Tuttle Company, have been replaced by the equally effective renderings of Robin Wilt, a talented Ann Arbor artist. Plates 2, 4, 6, and 29 are also her work, as are Figures 23 and 27.

In general, the book has three main orientations: the history of Japanese music, the construction of the instruments, and the music itself. The materials for the history section are drawn primarily from the sources listed in the Bibliography. The musical analyses are for the most part based on my own research. I have tried to make each chapter a self-contained unit. This has necessitated some slight repetition of information. The organization is, however, as chronological as possible, and reading straight through the book should give one a grasp of the overall evolution of Japanese music. Thus, whether one's interest is in a special form of Japanese music, music in general, theater, Japanese culture, or simply intellectual curiosity, it is hoped that this book will prove both informative and entertaining.

As to editorial matters, macrons have been used for all Japanese words and names, but not for places. Names are written in the Japanese order, surname first. Japanese characters and short definitions of musical terms are found in the Glossary Index. The traditional Hepburn Romanization for Japanese has been used; the only exception is the French Romanization *noh*, as it is easier on the eye than *no* or *nō* for English readers. In the same context, the linguistically "correct" *kunrei* system is not used, as nonspeakers of Japanese find that *shakuhachi* is easier to pronounce than *syakuhati*.

Credits and permissions for plates and notations are as follows: Tōdaiji temple: Plate 26; Tokyo National Museum of Art: Plate 31; Tokyo National University of Fine Arts and Music Archive: Plates 27, 28; Iwanami Motion Picture Production Company: Plates 17, 41, 43, 78; the Tokugawa Reimeikai Foundation: Plate 46; the *Mainichi* newspaper: Plate 51; Miyagi Michio Memorial Hall: Plate 58; Yoshida Chiaki: Plates 76, 78, 79; Kaneko Keizō: Plates 86, 88; Hōgakusha for Japanese notation: Figures 52–57; and Nōgaku Shorin for Japanese notation: Figures 18, 42. Shiba Tsukeyasu gave permission to use his Western notation as a basis for Figures 3 and 10. My thanks to Carter Pann, who designed these added figures and all other new notations, on a Sibelius computer program. Tom Haar is thanked for his permission to use his own photographs in Plates 87 and 89, and the work of the late Francis Haar in Plate 77. Plates 81 and 82 were given to me by the late Professor Kurosawa Ito. Plates 3, 42, and 55 came originally from the Japan Tourist Bureau. All other photographs and transcriptions are by the author.

In the 1959 book, I thanked Howard Hibbett, Richard Lane, and members of the Japanese Folk Theatrical Institute for their help, as well as Takemoto Kazuyo as an ever-efficient and courteous *arbeiter*. That book was the result of two years of research (1955–57) done under a grant from the Ford Foundation, to whom I expressed my sincere gratitude, adding that the opinions expressed in the book were my own and did not necessarily reflect those of the Foundation or its officers. In this new book I wish to add my special thanks for over thirty years of support from the Center for Japanese Studies of the University of Michigan (Ann Arbor) in both travel to Japan and in research assistance. Once more I must state that the opinions in the new text are my own and not necessarily those of the Center or its officers.

Dr. Kishibe Shigeo deserves special gratitude. He chose my Japanese music teachers and guided me through both books! A true Japanese mentor and friend. Fukushima Kazuo and the Research Archives for Japanese Music at Ueno Gakuen University also provided some much-appreciated assistance. I add my thanks to George Gish and David Hughes, whose thesis work at the University of Michigan made new information available to me. Dr. Kikkawa Eishi, Edward Seidensticker, and Richard Emmert were also most helpful and are thanked along with the dozens of Western and Japanese colleagues who have contributed so much to my understanding of Japanese music over the four decades between the two books.

Finally, I want to thank the men and women to whom this book is dedicated: the traditional musicians of Japan. Without their cooperation, an effective book on Japanese music would be impossible. I only hope that I have been able to do their profession full justice.

# TRADITIONAL JAPANESE MUSIC

## *and*

# MUSICAL INSTRUMENTS

*Both music and dance
are voices of the Way.*
Hakuin Zenji (1686–1769)

1. The dance pantomime "Okame" accompanied by this folk *hayashi* is seen frequently during fall festivals in Japan.

In a tiny restaurant, the young lady on the television screen who was dancing to "Indian Love Call" was given sudden competition. A red-faced, golden-eyed lion rushed in, clacking his wooden jaws and shaking his stringy hair in a violent and determined effort to bring good luck to the shop and good fortune to himself. An elderly man in kimono and derby hat stood outside nonchalantly playing a lively accompaniment on his bamboo flute. A more prosperous lion might have had a drummer as well, but this was the time of the *omatsuri*—the local festival—and the drummers were all busy. Three of them were only a block away, sitting on a newly built stage next to the neighborhood shrine beating out a highly syncopated accompaniment to the flute strains of *edobayashi*, a music as gay and lively as Dixieland.

The crowd that had gathered at the sound of the deep-toned temple drum was not paying conscious attention to all this joyous music. Nevertheless, caught up in the spirit of the music, they were happily providing vocal counterpoint to the flute's tessitura flights. Children in gaily colored kimono were mainly concerned with buying little squid and octopuses dipped in soy sauce, trying to move goldfish with a thin paper net from large pans to plastic bags, or hiding their doll-like faces in clouds of cotton candy.

The lion pranced on to the next store, and a new set of musicians arrived to do battle with the hapless young lady on the television set: the entrance curtain was suddenly pushed aside, and in came three girls of rice-fed proportions who struck up a folk song inviting the patrons to the festivities at the shrine. Even the noise of Japanese noodle-eating couldn't drown out their song, which announced the beginning of what in effect was the Japanese equivalent of a church canvass. But even the most friendly, well-dressed vestryman could never tear a parishioner from his gastronomical pursuits half as easily as these three plump girls could with their music and dancing. The rhythmic strumming of the three strings of the *shamisen* gave an effect surprisingly similar to American mountain banjo music, though the drum and the dance of simple beckoning gestures added a distinctly Japanese flavor.

Having firmly defeated the ballet of the Indian maiden, the three blue-and-white kimono went out again into the street. Here was a riot of color and sound to rival the carnival scene in Stravinsky's *Petrushka*. The young men and boys were all dressed in blue *happi* coats with a large red character on the back, their hair tied back with blue-and-white towels and their faces painted white with rice powder. They stood milling around the shrine shed wanting to start the procession, which was the main focus of the festivities. One young boy was doing his best to add to the merry confusion by straddling the high shrine drum in its cart and beating out a rather unimaginative "pom, pom, pom-pom-pom," quite out of synchronization with the rhythm and meter of the nearby stage musicians.

In the midst of this whirl of people and sounds, to which was added the cacophony of car horns and impatient three-wheeled motorcycle trucks, a somber priest with a high basket-like hat completely covering his head appeared. Apparently oblivious to the surrounding competition, he wandered from door to door playing soft, woody melodies on his vertical bamboo flute, stained by myriad dusty fingers and the neglect endemic in the life of a dying profession. His windy tune ended. A coin dropped into the white box hung around his neck, and he went on to the next store, seemingly indifferent to the anachronism of his profession, his fate, or the function his guild once performed throughout Japan.

Any thoughts of lugubrious sentimentality, however, were soon pushed aside by a great shout that came from the men as they brought the portable shrine out of its shed. It was a highly ornamented black-and-gold miniature temple, and on its roof stood a golden phoenix, flashing and flapping its wings in the sun as the shrine was jostled about by the youthful shoulders that supported it on its wooden beams.

A group of boys assigned to pull the drum wagon took up their positions, and the girls fell in behind as the procession began. Older men led the procession, setting a majestic cadence by striking the pavement with poles topped by rattling metal rings. A much faster rhythm was heard in the short-breathed chant of the young shrine-carriers who trotted behind them. But what a way to carry a shrine!

This was a folk festival, and the dignity Westerners usually associate with processions was very much out of place in the crowded, narrow streets of Yoyogi-Uehara in Tokyo. The custom has always been that the shrine is carried to every street, bringing more good luck than even the busy lion can provide, and at a dearer price. However, the transportation of the shrine from place to place was not so much a procession as a tug-of-war. First one line of bearers and then the other would take the offensive, and the poor phoenix flapped wildly as the shrine canted perilously from one side of the road to the other. Needless to say, there were plenty of extra bearers to give the contestants a rest.

The big shrine was followed by smaller ones so that the younger boys could get some early training in shrine-carrying in addition to getting in on the fun, of course. Off they went, much as their fathers and grandfathers had before them, with a police escort who stopped the traffic and considerately blew their whistles in time with the chanting....

This is not an imaginary scene but an accurate description of Tokyo on September 22, 1955, when I first experienced Japanese music in Japan. Such scenes have been part of every September in Japan for decades, and there seems to be little doubt that they will continue for many decades to come. Though television antennas were beginning to cover the slate-tiled roofs and I heard jazz echoing across Lake Chuzenji in Nikko, the vitality and popularity of traditional music still seemed to be firmly rooted in the daily lives of most people. In Meiji Stadium, the afternoon crowd cheered and sang school songs much as any American sports crowd would, but, when evening came, fires were lit in the adjacent park and people gathered to dance *bon odori* in celebration of the autumnal equinox. The man who repaired your automobile might also sing *yōkyoku*, the music of the *noh* drama dating from the fifteenth century, while the businessman and fellow straphanger in the fast-moving subway could be seen poring over the words of a *kouta* song in preparation for a lesson at the end of a day selling textile machinery. One could go on indefinitely citing examples of such traditional music existing in modern surroundings. The systematic presentation of these genres of music, along with the exposition of their historical backgrounds and musical characteristics, is the theme of this book. This is the world of *hōgaku*, the traditional music of Japan.

# CHAPTER ONE
# THE PRESENT AND PAST OF JAPANESE MUSIC

## 1. Japan's Musical Life (1957)

Japan is presently attempting to support two musical cultures at one time: Western music and traditional music. Of these the former is easily understood by the Westerner because it is part of his own heritage. If one wishes, one can spend a busy season attending symphony concerts, lieder programs, and piano recitals. There is even a fairly wide choice of opera companies, and such operas as *William Tell* and *Hary Janos* have a better chance of being seen in Tokyo than in the United States. At the same time, those of more modern tastes can join the Society for Contemporary Music or attend concerts given by Japanese composers of *musique concrète*. There are also the new works by Japanese composers that are played at every concert of the Tokyo Symphony. Traveling artists now make Japan a regular part of their itinerary, and one need seldom feel starved for Western music in Japan. The popular music business also expands, local products competing with Euro-American hits for the market.

At the same time, there is an equally large part of the nation's musical life called *hōgaku*, music that is uniquely Japanese. Unfortunately, this traditional music is often incomprehensible to Westerners and Western-trained Japanese because there have been few guidebooks to lead one through *hōgaku* as a highly evolved art form, a music that has as many facets and approaches to beauty as the music of the West or other Asian musics.

The scope of *hōgaku* includes orchestral music, chamber music, music drama, and a host of vocal forms. The approach may be different from that of Western music, but the aesthetic goals are essentially the same. This very difference is one of the best reasons for studying Japanese music or, for that matter, the music of any non-European country. Such studies provide an opportunity to view an equally logical but different system of musical organization. This, in turn, may give us a new view of our own music. In addition, there is the sheer hedonistic desire to increase our response to unfamiliar artistic media. If one appreciates Schubert songs, enjoyment of *kouta* takes only a little reorientation, and a lover of opera should find Japanese narrative singing tremendously exciting.

There is really a third world in musical Japan, one might call it a limbo, and this is music by modern Japanese composers that uses traditional materials in a new manner. In some cases it is a concerto for *koto*, in others, a string quartet using Japanese folk songs as themes. This fascinating subject, however, is the topic for a different book. The dramatic rise of Western music in Japan is yet another theme that is not part of this book. We are concerned here primarily with the indigenous music from its beginnings to its present condition.

One of the reasons why the study of *hōgaku* is so interesting is that it conveniently symbolizes the position of the traditional in Japan today. Though Japan is called the most Westernized country in the Orient, it is carrying many burdens of the past while attempting to assimilate and create within the new patterns of the West. Some of these traditions will be dropped and others will change their shape in order to fit into their new environment. Still others appear to be important enough to be kept intact despite their different surroundings. Within the boundaries of Japanese music, all three of these reactions can be found. The reasons for the continued vitality of one form and the decline of another can be ascertained by a more detailed study of each case. In such studies, the form must be evaluated both as music and also as a manifestation of the artistic needs of a certain social class. In general, we can say that those forms that survive today have been able to maintain the public's interest musically and fulfill certain social needs. However, before one can understand clearly *hōgaku*'s position in modern society, one must first have some idea of its place in the general history of Japan.

# 2. Music and Japanese History

The exact ethnological origins of the Japanese are not clearly known. However, from ancient times there have been waves of migrating cultures applying pressure on whatever indigenous culture there may have been. It is characteristic of the Japanese, even today, to be able to sustain the most intense cultural invasions and yet maintain enough independence to make use of these foreign cultures in a different way. It is impossible to tell how much of this was true in prehistoric times, but in addition to the Chinese, Korean, Mongolian, and Southeast Asian influences found in archaeological remains, there seems to be something that can be explained only as indigenously Japanese. Of course, technically, we cannot speak of the prehistoric Japanese in any national sense, for the inhabitants of the islands were divided into many small clans which showed little signs of merging until around the first century A.D.

Tradition claims that the Yamato people were the first to foster the concept of an imperial clan to which other groups owed allegiance. The strength of this Yamato clan began in Kyushu, the southernmost of Japan's main islands, and the next few centuries of Japanese history are basically concerned with the gradual extension of imperial Yamato power in a northerly direction.

Musically, this age represents the period of primitive forms, primarily folk music. Where the music appears to have been more complex, it probably came from isolated Chinese or Korean colonies and was not native music as such. In fact, to learn more about ancient Japanese music we must turn to Chinese sources, as Japanese was not as yet a written language.

In the chronicles of the Wei dynasty of third-century China, we find an account of a visit to the islands of Japan that includes a mention of music, dancing, and singing as part of a funeral wake. A sixth-century chronicle tells of a group of Chinese scholars sent to Japan from Paekche, an ancient kingdom in southwestern Korea. Among these men of learning were listed several musicians. From such scraps of information we get the impression that music was an important thread in the general fabric of Japanese life from the earliest times.

The first native literary products, the *Kojiki* (A.D. 712) and the *Nihon shoki* (A.D. 720), give us some indication of music's place in early mythology. The most famous tale is that of the sun goddess, who was insulted by her brother—the newly appointed guardian of Hell—and retired into a cave, leaving the world in darkness. It was in order to coax the sun goddess to return that Ama no Uzume danced her lewd and humorous dance before the other gods, who were assembled at the mouth of the cave. Since the music, dancing, and resultant laughter aroused the sun goddess's curiosity enough to bring her out of hiding, the theatrical arts got off to a good functional start even in Japanese mythology.[1] In addition to such myths, the *Kojiki* and *Nihon shoki* contain some two hundred poems, many of which were clearly sung.

*Dōtaku*

By the time of these writings, we have come to the end of what is called the ancient period of Japanese music history. The other major sources concerning early music are archaeological. *Haniwa* tomb statues are particularly interesting, for some show zithers, drums, and groups of singers (Plate 2). Thin bronze bells (*dōtaku*) of a unique shape were also found, but their function is unknown. The only kind of actual music that is attributed to this period is *kumeuta*, songs for an association (called the *kume*) of palace guards supposedly connected with Jimmu, the legendary first emperor of Japan.

The first major historic period in Japan, the Nara period (710–794), saw the initial struggles to establish a national government and an attempt to impose a Chinese social and intellectual order on the rustic clans of Japan. The period name comes from the city of Nara, which was laid out in 710 in accordance with the plans of a famous Chinese city. One can imagine what a Mecca of miracles China must have seemed to the Japanese, who were without a written language, permanent cities, a centralized govern-

1. See *Kojiki*, trans. by Donald L. Philippi (Princeton, NJ: Princeton University Press, 1969), Book 1, Chap. 17.

ment, or any religious concepts beyond a rather indefinite pantheism. In every category of life Chinese models were used, often with little thought given to their suitability. Some of the results were a polysyllabic language being forced into a monosyllabic script, the planning of cities too large to populate, and sweeping reform edicts without the power to execute them. There was also a wholehearted embracing of the doctrines of Buddhism and Confucianism.

When the imperial household was weary of its web of intrigue and insurrection, or when a nobleman sought rest from his struggles with Chinese philosophy, edifying relaxation was provided by the government bureau of music. Much as early American classical musicians had to be from Europe, the Nara court musicians were all from China or Korea. There is even a tale, said to date from the third century, of Korean musicians instructing the Japanese to save the timber from wrecked ships because it was properly seasoned for instrument construction by the salt water and the sun. Thus, foreign music and dance began to move out of the colonies and became part of the life of the new intellectual centers of Japan very early in the Nara period.

The great literary anthology of this time, the *Man'yōshū* (eighth century), contains some four thousand poems, many of which are believed to be aristocratic revisions of ancient folk song texts. The *Shoku Nihongi*, a historical chronicle of the late eighth century, tells of rituals and music performed at the dedication ceremonies of new shrines and temples. The most famous example is the founding of the Tōdaiji temple, at which hundreds of musicians and dancers are said to have performed. Music thus became an ancillary to the early development of Japanese architecture and the other fine arts.

The music of the Nara period can be classified as belonging to the first international period in Japanese music history. The court music was all of Chinese, Korean, or Indian origin and was played primarily by foreign musicians in its original style. While the poetry anthologies indicate that folk music had continued its steady pace, the historical records and relics show us a music that was primarily instrumental and often connected with dance. At the same time, the music of Buddhist ritual became known throughout Japan and exerted some influence on the native vocal style, though perhaps the influence was mutual, as in the case of Gregorian chant and early European folk songs. In sum, the main feature of the music of the Nara period was the importation of foreign musicians and music of both a sacred and secular nature. As yet, the native genius seems to have had little influence on this music, nor were the native musicians held in particular respect. The parallel with America in the early nineteenth century is quite striking.

During the Heian period (794–1185), there were signs that the Chinese influences were beginning to be assimilated and modified. Great changes occurred in the governmental system, with the position of the emperor becoming weaker and the power of the regent stronger. This strength was consolidated under the exclusive control of the Fujiwara clan. While the imperial troops did battle with the Ainu tribes in the north, the court turned more and more to the problems of etiquette and ritual. The northern frontiersmen paid little attention to the pious edicts of the distant emperor, while the noblemen, stripped of all political power, found themselves immersed in one of the most ultrarefined societies in history. The favorite courtier was the man who could improvise the best poem in Chinese, while the women made use of a phonetic script to produce Japanese literary works of great acumen and vitality, mixed with a Gothic-like sentimentality. Beneath this surface of silk and delicate lacquer flowed a writhing torrent of intrigue and suppressed desire. Fame and banishment were eternal potentials, and the distance between them was no farther than his lordship's chambers. One might tempt fate by the mere pushing aside of a bamboo curtain or by passing beyond a gilded screen that served as some semblance of privacy in this life within a jade goldfish bowl.

This was also the period of one of the most famous feuds in Japanese history, that of the Minamoto (or Genji) and the Taira (or Heike) clans. It ended with the defeat of the Taira in 1185, but out of the ruin came a legacy of legends that has provided endless inspiration for the fine arts. There also emerged the concept of the samurai, the faithful warrior, whose loyalty was more important to him than his life. Above him loomed the figure of the military dictator, who would soon find the effete court a good place to garrison his troops and issue his orders.

The most famous literary product of this age, the *Genji monogatari* (The Tale of Genji) by Lady Murasaki, is replete with scenes of music.[2] In this wonderful tale of romance, music and poetry form the very matrix in

2. See Murasaki Shikibu, *The Tale of Genji*, trans. by Edward G. Seidensticker (New York: Knopf, 1978).

which the characters are set. Every truly "refined" person in the book can play at least one or two instruments, and we find that one of Genji's fondest memories of Lady Murasaki is the music lessons he gave her on the lute. He was led to another of his amours by the sound of a *koto*, so beautiful that he was filled with passion for the unseen performer. In good romantic tradition, she was, of course, equally as lovely.

The music of the Heian period still employed a host of Chinese instruments and forms, but the musicians themselves were more often Japanese by this stage. The people of the court took up music with a passion, and it gradually developed distinctly Japanese characteristics. While one often thinks of this music as being instrumental, it must not be forgotten that almost all of it contained some poetry. The Japanese fine arts in general were inseparable from literature, taking their basic orientation from the written word. A lovely scroll may be an evocation of a Chinese poem, while the *biwa* lute always served as the supporting vehicle for poetry and sagas. Heian *gagaku* court music comes closest to a pure instrumental form, though even here a chorus is common. When there is no chorus, there is often a dancer who still links the music to some ancient myth or historical event. This court music is a block of sound; it does not move but allows other things to move through it. In this way, it has managed to survive to the present day. Some claim it is unchanged, though most scholars now realize it has been modified by centuries of Japanese creativity. Either way, such a continuous line of patronage has no parallel in the history of Western instrumental music.

In the field of purely vocal music, the Heian period produced Buddhist hymns and also many secular songs. Among these songs were those specially composed for use at the many banquets that figured so heavily in the court schedule. One can imagine the long, matted rooms filled with soft faces and clothes of every hue. As the properly attired guests partook of the properly displayed foods in the proper order, these banquet songs added just the right amount of sentimental impropriety to season the evening and the conversation.

The Heian period, then, represents the heyday of court music and the beginnings of native influence on imported music and instruments. Again it is worth reflecting for a moment that beyond the capital there must have been a great body of folk music that floated unnoticed and unrecorded over the muddy rice fields.

The Kamakura period (1185–1333) produced the military dictatorship of Minamoto no Yoritomo and the tradition of the shogun, or the man controlling the shogun, as the true ruler of Japan. The warrior became the dominant figure in the government as well as in battle. However, in order to avoid the insidious softness and maneuvering of the court in Kyoto, the military established a separate headquarters in Kamakura. All real authority now stemmed from the empirical, untutored north. The ambitious men of Kyoto were soon found at the side of the military men of Kamakura advising, administrating, and helping form a new feudal system, the effects of which are evident to this day. This system differs from the Western concept of feudalism primarily in the unusual sense of clan unity and the interlocking obligations incumbent on both lord and vassal.

During this period, Buddhism increased in popularity, especially among the common people, on whom the effects of evangelism were immense. The ethics of the warrior class had a more philosophical base, and the influence of Zen Buddhism was very strong. The contrast of the military life and the contemplative severity of Zen complemented each other to such an extent that, even as late as World War II, officer candidates were required to study Zen. Perhaps some of Zen's appeal may have been its special type of austerity, for the greatest fear of the military leaders was the loss of the Spartan pride they had engendered in their men.

One of the most famous memorials to military virtue is the *Heike monogatari* (Tale of the Heike),[3] which was written originally for recitation to the accompaniment of the *biwa*. This long saga retells the battles of the Taira and Minamoto clans, which figured so strongly in the previous period. While extolling the deeds of the past and the impermanence of life in general, it set the standard by which many a Kamakura warrior vowed to live.

Unfortunately, the disdain of court life did not last in more peaceful times, and the warriors were soon aping the manners of the courtiers they controlled. The Kamakura regency seemed in danger of falling, when the country was distracted by Kublai Khan's attempt to invade Japan. Individual valor and two truly miraculous storms destroyed the Mongolian Armada, but the days of the regency were already numbered. In 1333,

3. See *Tale of the Heike*, trans. by Helen Craig McCullough (Stanford, CA: Stanford University Press, 1988).

Kamakura and the power of the shogun disappeared in a holocaust that was a portent of the bloody days to come.

By the time of the Kamakura period, most traces of the international character of Japanese music had disappeared. Court music in general was declining, while there was a steady growth of more theatrical arts for the entertainment of both the court and the military headquarters. The comic dances of *dengaku* were so popular that certain officials were censured for neglecting their duties in order to enjoy the daily performances. Lute-accompanied sagas of military glory had a steady audience, and the form developed greatly in style and technique. Buddhist chanting, likewise, became more popular and exerted a stronger influence on the secular music of the time. Its style is said to have permeated even the drinking songs. Indeed, there was a mixture of sacred and secular elements in Kamakura music that reminds one of a similar condition in the music of Gothic Europe.

In general, the music of the Kamakura period is marked by a new emphasis on vocal and more dramatic music. This tendency will be seen to gather momentum in the periods to follow and represents the beginning of a genuinely native music movement. The days of imperial power were over, and the arts reflected the change to a feudalistic society with a style that was better suited to the new, roughshod patrons.

The Muromachi, or Ashikaga, period (1333–1568) is characterized by a degeneration of larger sociopolitical units into smaller ones. The centralized government of the Ashikaga shogun was replaced by the rule of powerful independent land barons, and the concept of clan loyalty gave way to the spirit of unity only on a family level. Under the new code, an individual no longer felt any dishonor in changing sides during one of the many feudal wars that plagued this period as long as he remained true to his immediate household.

The period began with rival emperors and a war of succession, and ended with a disastrous rivalry for the position of shogun. The warriors committed the fatal error of moving to Kyoto and were soon caught up in a life of luxury based on the idea that the acquisition of art objects and intellectual sycophants represented success. While the local officials were busy acquiring neighboring fiefs, the Kyoto warriors were engaged in tea ceremonies or attending the many new theatrical entertainments that had been devised to amuse them.

War and revolt were rampant, and blood flowed more thickly than the ink of the many painters who found patronage with the military or the temple. When the blood had dried, the social system of Japan was found to be completely changed, with the family now as the central unit. When the ink had likewise dried, there remained a legacy of art, permeated with Zen and new Chinese influences, but full of vigor and independence. The brilliance of the famous Golden Pavilion in Kyoto makes us forget the sordid struggles that formed a background for the gentle conversations that went on within its serene walls.

In this period, the court became so impoverished that one emperor had to sell his autograph to subsist. The military class, on the other hand, luxuriated in a manner often in excess of their treasuries. Due to an increase in foreign trade, the first signs of a strong merchant class also appeared. Meanwhile, the history of individual families is replete with tales of rapid expansions and sudden demises. This left many a samurai without a master and hence without a conscience. This uneasy balance of classes needed only a few more drops of insurrectional blood to tip the scale and pour the entire society into a new mold in the following century.

The outstanding feature of the Muromachi period's music is the growth of the theatrical arts. Public and private performances of dance-dramas and acrobatics became increasingly popular and prepared the way for the development of the *noh* drama. This timeless and subtle art was gently fashioned by Kan'ami (1333–84) and his son Zeami (1363–1444). At court, the traditional music suffered greatly, though it is recorded that even during the period of the terrible Ōnin War (1467–77) the court managed to keep up the annual *kagura* dances at the shrines. Some references to folk music appear, especially in regard to its influence on performances at the shogun's palace in the Muromachi district of Kyoto. Short ditties (*kouta*) are recorded, as are an ever-increasing number of narrative songs. Itinerant storytellers wove their tales on the street corners, often with only the beating of a fan for accompaniment, little realizing that they were preparing the way for one of Japan's greatest musical forms, the *jōruri*.

At the same time, a simple bamboo *shakuhachi* flute began to be heard, played by wandering priests who were gentle heralds of a greater music to come. In short, the Muromachi period was a time of musical potential, a material and psychological buildup for a flood of activities that was soon to burst upon the artistic world in a torrent of color and sound.

The first break in the dam occurred at the end of the Muromachi period, often called the Azuchi-Momoyama period (1568–1600). This new stream of music came from the *noh* drama, which emerged as a refinement of the many entertainments mentioned earlier. A broken and blood-soaked Japan was hammered back together by a final set of wars under the leadership of Oda Nobunaga and his associate Toyotomi Hideyoshi. It was Hideyoshi who first sounded a warning to the newly arrived Christian missionaries that Japan was tolerant of all religions as long as they did not threaten the uneasy security of the state. Disdain for this warning and the foreigner's overconcern with mercantile rather than spiritual advancement brought about the martyrdom of many a simple follower of the cross.

Hideyoshi also sacrificed numerous Buddhist soldiers in his unsuccessful attempts to invade Korea. With greater success, however, a three-stringed guitar called the *sanshin* was invading the southern part of Japan and adding further potential to the gathering musical forces. This coincided with an improvement in instrument construction. The *sanshin* was transformed into the shape of the *shamisen*, and the art of drum-making was raised to such a level that a Momoyama drum is prized in Japan much as a Stradivarius violin is in the West.

The Tokugawa, or Edo, period (1600–1868) represents one of the most singleminded attempts to maintain a status quo in all world history. The first Tokugawa shogun, Ieyasu, instigated a system of government that was based on the principle of immobility in every class. The court was subsidized but reduced to a life of ceremonies; the feudal lords were relocated so as to neutralize their power and prevent conspiracy, while the warriors' great perquisites were contingent on obedience to the shogun. The power of religion was broken forever, first by splitting up the dangerous Buddhist sects and, secondly, by ruthlessly suppressing the Christian movement. The final hymn of the slaughtered Christians of Shimabara was also the swan song of Western influences in Japan for more than two hundred years. A tiny Dutch colony called Dejima, in the harbor of Nagasaki, remained as Japan's only legitimate contact with the West. The country deliberately shut out the world and sought peace and stability under a military dictatorship that had no wars to fight but waged a constant, if finally unsuccessful, battle against change.

Beneath the stolid, unchanging letter of the Tokugawa law, however, there was a swift current of new forces that eventually overflowed its confines and revolutionized Japan's entire social structure. The major turbulence was found in the lowest class in the Tokugawa hierarchy, the merchants. When the capital was moved to Edo, now known as Tokyo, a new concept in cities was begun in Japan. Here was the new seat of government and an important new commercial center. It was filled with the pensioned-warrior class and the hostages held by the shogun to ensure the loyalty of the country lords, all of whom were restless, repressed, and in need of distraction. The latter was provided by the greatest flourishing of the entertainment world in Japanese history.

Such a large city had many needs, and the merchants were quick to provide the necessary services, at an almost unnecessarily high profit. The Tokugawa law had effectively immobilized the feudal and warrior class, but the despised merchants found that circumventing the law lost them no prestige (since they had none) and often made them very rich. The whole period presents a picture of the gradual decay of the samurai and the covert rule of the moneylender. At the lowest level of the social strata were the rice farmers. They were called upon to provide the basic wealth, but were given no share in it; in fact, at one time they were even forbidden to eat the rice they grew. When these lower classes moved out from underneath the rigid upper layers, the entire structure collapsed. The history of the Tokugawa era is the fascinating saga of an attempt to change an agricultural society into a commercial society despite government resistance and the lack of one of the vital components of commerce, foreign trade.

Throughout this tale, however, we find a secondary theme, the development of a bourgeois art. As was noticeable in the previous period, there was an increasing interest in the theatrical arts in Japan. This reached its zenith in a segment of the Tokugawa period known as the Genroku era (1688–1704), during which the pleasure districts of Tokyo, Osaka, and Kyoto became the very centers of Japanese life. Here the class distinctions had less meaning. The merchant could openly display his newfound wealth, while the samurai could forget his recent poverty in the blandishments of paid companions, wine, and the distractions of a host of *kabuki* and puppet theaters. This was the famous *ukiyo*, the "floating world" in which Japanese society drifted until the sheer weight of pleasure-seekers burst the entire structure wide open. However, despite the upheaval engendered by the re-entry of Western culture in the late nineteenth century, many of the patterns of thought and action drilled into the people of

Edo by the shogunate are still firmly entrenched in the modern population of Tokyo, as in the rest of Japan.

Musically, the Tokugawa period saw the rise of *shamisen* music, the flourishing of the *koto* and *shakuhachi*, and a vast development in music for drama; in short, an advance in all that one usually thinks of being the traditional music of Japan. The period can be compared favorably with the early nineteenth century in Europe, when the symphony, the opera, and chamber music were in their prime. The ancient *noh* plays found refuge in the patronage of a few conservative officials and eventually gained a following among a section of the middle class. However, the new dramatic genres of puppet and *kabuki* theater dominated the age. Great playwrights like Chikamatsu Monzaemon created a host of new plays. In the *bunraku* puppet theater, *jōruri* singers declaimed them with exceptional intensity, while the flamboyant costumes and acting styles of *kabuki* actors provoked shouts of approval from townsfolk and ruling classes alike. In Edo theater, audience participation and a good cry were as essential as they were to Italian operas of the same centuries.

Thus, we have in the Tokugawa period a manifestation of almost every type of music known in Japan. The court musicians set the leisurely pace for the ceremonies that were the major raison d'être of the imperial court. The blind priests continued to recount past glories to the accompaniment of the *biwa* lute, and basket-hatted priests solicited alms by means of the bamboo flute. For blind laymen there was the teaching of the *koto*, which had become popular among the leisured ladies who served as political hostages in Edo. The tottering aristocracy took solace in the *noh* drama, while many of the samurai fled to the entertainment quarters. Meanwhile, the townsfolk luxuriated in a new sense of power, which included access to an immense variety of dramatic and erotic music, and the music of the farmer, traditionally considered an ignorant but all-providing drone, flowed on as always. The placid river of folk music showed signs of branching into regional styles, but it remained basically undisturbed, primarily because it was ignored. The tales of Edo, like the romantic novels of Europe, paint scenes of rustic festivals and peasant merrymaking, but as in the case of their European counterparts, their authors often chose to disregard the despairing eyes that belied many a farmer's smile.

Although the traditional arts of this period thrived as never before or since, the fabric of Edo society was tenuous and, rather than growing stronger, merely became bloated until it was fatally punctured by the masts of the black ships of Commodore Perry.

The following Meiji period (1868–1912) can best be summarized by saying that the floodgates opened. Western culture inundated the land, and the outlines of tradition were only dimly discernible in the torrent of new ideas. The Japanese endemic weakness for being "modern" or "smart" was never more apparent than in the late nineteenth century. From the Heian to the Momoyama periods, familiarity with some element of Chinese culture had always been considered "chic," and in the Tokugawa period, fashions and language were guided by the leading actors and geisha of the day. In the Meiji era, however, it was one's knowledge of steam engines and anatomy or an ability to do second-rate oil paintings that seemed to count.

The samurai class made one last show of strength but was crushed by an army trained along Western lines. The shogunate had been caught in its own propaganda, for the emperor rose to power on the prestige they had provided, plus the backing of those who saw the danger behind the approaching black ships. Many felt that the country could only be saved from Western dominance by overhauling its outdated social structure and by adopting Western techniques of warfare and administration.

It is significant that the first Western music in the Meiji era was military. Bandmasters were part of the cadre of foreigners solicited by the regime, and the gentle nuances of the *koto* were drowned out by the brassy heralds of a new age. Though music education of the period was originally designed to include Japanese music, Western music soon dominated the scene.[4] The most fatal intrusion for traditional music, however, was the cold, opaque moon of harmony that eclipsed *hōgaku*'s source of life. The beauty of Japanese music lay in an extremely subtle melodic style, which became leadened and deadened by the addition of factual tonic and dominant chords. Those musicians who resisted the trend were called old-fashioned and fell on evil days. Thus the beginning of the Meiji period presented a picture of the traditional arts on the defensive in what appeared to be a losing battle. Japan began to change from a mercantile nation into an industrial and colonial power. It learned to run its trains on time and

4. See William P. Malm, "The Modern Music of the Meiji Era" in *Modernization and Japan in the Humanities*, ed. D. Shively (Princeton: Princeton University Press, 1971).

taught its children to sing "Annie Laurie," but still found the Western attitude toward it rather patronizing until it discovered the key to esteem in the West: war. Its battles with China were considered an inter-Asian affair, but the West took sudden notice of Japan when it thoroughly defeated its nearest Caucasian nation, Russia. Japan learned its lesson well, but the bones of thousands of soldiers that are scattered over the Pacific are symbols of its failure in the final test.

Militant nationalism in the twentieth century created a mass of marches and patriotic songs. However, the rise of national pride had certain salubrious effects on traditional music. *Hōgaku* music fitted the jingoism of the times, and performers were sent to entertain at military hospitals and even at the front. Court music was opened to the public for the first time as a type of cultural propaganda. Whatever the motives, traditional music showed a steady resurgence of strength, except for those unhappy years of the great debacle when theaters were closed and some music was banned because it was not thought to be contributing to the war effort.

The impact of the West left its mark, but the exact degree of influence is not yet apparent. Again, past history might give us some clues. As was mentioned earlier, Japan completely adopted the ways of eighth-century China during the Heian period. Along with Chinese literature, architecture, government, and religion, it coveted Chinese music. As a matter of fact, the best surviving examples of Tang Chinese music are found today in the *tōgaku* music of the court orchestra of Japan and the *tangak* of Korea. What Japan had wholeheartedly adopted it gradually began to adapt, and in time arts that were built on Chinese models yet different and distinctly Japanese emerged.

One is tempted to make a comparison of this medieval situation with the Meiji Restoration of 1868. There is perhaps some justification for supposing that Japan may again slowly bend these foreign ways to the inclinations of its native genius, but there is one important factor that must not be overlooked. Japan took on the manners of China at a time when it had scarcely developed a culture of its own. The ways of the West, however, were superimposed on a highly developed culture with hundreds of years of growth behind it. The first reaction to this foreign catalyst was the complete subjugation of the native arts, but today both styles seem to be growing in strength and stature. How malleable each will become is one of the most interesting questions in Japan today. For our purpose, the important thing to note is that the traditional arts do still flourish and give some indication of preparing to advance again with restored self-confidence and with an audience of enthusiastic listeners.

Now that our rapid survey is finished, what general trends can be found in the growth of Japanese music? First, there is the dominant position of vocal music. Every instrument developed under the aegis of the human voice. The first instrumental solos were created to serve as interludes between the verses of songs. One could even study Japanese music as an ancillary to literature, for so much of the time it serves primarily as a vehicle for words.

This leads to the second main observation, which is that Japanese music history is marked by a steady growth of theatrical music. A seventh-century census lists a special clan dedicated to the telling of stories, and ancient records show the function of Shinto priests as being primarily ceremonial. This early concern with the theatrical side of entertainment and religion grew in ever-increasing importance, until it was completely out of proportion during the Tokugawa period. A sense of balance has returned since then, but a visitor cannot but be struck by the innate theatricality of much of Japanese public life.

In our discussion of the development of the clan and family spirit we neglected to note its effect on the teacher-student relationship, which is also a special characteristic of the Japanese music system. Education at any level is an extension (or contraction, if you will) of the obligations between the lord and vassal. Even in the cynical present day, a music teacher has a right to expect loyalty from his pupils, and the student instinctively feels a certain veneration toward the master. The word *sensei* in Japanese has far greater implications than the word "teacher" does in English. *Sensei* is one's mentor, and even if his teaching seems inadequate for one's needs, it would be a gross breach of etiquette to look for someone new. Not only would this be discourteous but one would lose the fellowship of the fraternity of other students and earn the suspicion of any new group into which one tried to enter. Not to "belong" is one of the greatest tragedies in Japanese life. The intensity of this social pressure in Japan is far greater than in the West. This was the great legacy of the Tokugawa period, and even the humble *shamisen* teacher and his pupils were and, to a great extent, still are bound by these unwritten laws.

As the center of Japan's political history slowly moved northward from Kyushu to Kyoto, to Kamakura, then to Edo, there was an equally steady development in independent musical forms and instruments. In general, the pattern was that an instrument be introduced in the south via Korea or the Ryukyu Islands and would then gradually change as it moved further north. The most complete metamorphosis occurred with the *shamisen*, but the music of the *koto*, *shakuhachi*, *biwa*, and the court also became more original while traveling the well-worn Tokaido road from Kyoto to Edo.

Now, standing on the shore of the present, we are able to view the currents of musical progress as they pass by the major landmarks of Japanese history. If water seems to have been used here frequently as an analogy, it is because water is such an important factor in Japan's existence. The Japanese live on a strip of land crowded between the mountains and the sea. They must depend on the rain and mountain streams for the cultivation of their rice; they rely on the ocean for their fish and, in modern times, their international trade. Many Japanese students express a desire to go to America just so they can see with their own eyes a vista of land in every direction. Before launching into a detailed study of the many forms that make up Japanese music, it is wise to reflect that a feeling of confinement has been inbred into the Japanese character by the very geography of the land. Japanese history is the story of throngs of people jostling up and down this narrow strip of preferred land. Japanese arts likewise present an attempt to move within very prescribed boundaries. Given these rather rigid limits, one must be willing to appreciate the consummate skill with which Japanese artists have been able to refine rather than expand their techniques. Music is not an international language, and the sonic treasurers of one culture may not appeal to everyone's personal taste. Still, with sensitive listening and a little guidance, one can learn to respect the highly developed organization and moments of genius that are integral parts of the finer products from a distant, exotic music world. One of those worlds is the kaleidoscope of sounds in *hōgaku*, the traditional music of Japan.

# CHAPTER TWO

# RELIGIOUS MUSIC

## 1. Shinto Music

### INTRODUCTION

Shinto, "the way of the gods," is Japan's indigenous form of religious expression. Since the days of its mythical origin, Shinto has experienced a continual fluctuation between heydays and dogdays, but it has never had and probably never will have a total eclipse in the land of the rising sun. Shinto shrines are still a part of every village scene as well as most big-city wards. Though they have no regular weekly services and sometimes not even a full-time priest, there is a daily stream of workmen and housewives who may be seen dropping by to toss a coin in the offering box, rattle the shrine gong, bring the spirits to attention with a clap of the hands, and say a short prayer. Besides the prayers of thanks or supplication, there are often prayers of remembrance. These are usually directed toward some recently departed relative, but such prayers are not so much forms of ancestor worship as they are an overt recognition that there is an inde-structible link between the generations past and the generation present. Shinto is based on the concept that this present generation owes the past an eternal cultural and spiritual debt. This debt is paid with remembrance, and the Shinto shrine is constructed of symbols that are meant to help recall the past, whether it is last year or two thousand years ago.

The business of blessing or purifying is one of the main functions of most Shinto ceremonies. In ancient times the Shinto priests seemed to have been primarily concerned with the problem of purification and keeping sacred places free of defilement. Today, one will still see on the site of new buildings a sacred square formed by ropes strung between four small trees. In the center of the square, offerings are placed much in the same manner as was done centuries ago. Even fire engines, airplanes, and new atomic reactors require some form of Shinto benediction.

Shinto became an instrument of nationalism during the 1930s and suffered correspondingly with the end of World War II. However, the thousands of modest shrines that dot the rice fields or occupy a shelf in stores, restaurants, and homes attest to the fact that Shinto has become embedded in Japanese life not so much by government policy or evangelism but by its very antiquity and perhaps by its convenience. For example, in the countryside it serves as a form of fertility rite, whereas in the city it becomes a kind of personal spiritual lobbyist much like the patron saints of Christianity. There have been no religious wars over Shinto because there are really no theological issues to fight about. The Buddhist religious leaders were wise enough to recognize its usefulness to the people and harmlessness to the temple with the net result that, at one time, Buddhist priests also served in Shinto ceremonies. Indeed, any study of things religious in Japan is complicated by the fact that Shintoism and Buddhism are tremendously intermingled.

From the musical standpoint, the problem is even more acute. The most virile form of religious music in Japan is that used in various folk festivals, but it is not always possible to say which music is Buddhist and which is Shinto. In fact, sometimes the same piece is used by both, with only the words changed. The lion dancer who opened the prologue of this book is a very lively example of the continuous influence of Shinto music on everyday Japanese life. This same lion, however, may turn out to be Buddhist on a different day. With a reminder that any categorical discussion of religious music in Japan is a semi-artificial organizational device and does not always represent actual musical or historical distinctions, let us look at the main styles of Shinto music.


KAGURA IN THE PALACE

The word *kagura*, "god music," is a generic term for all Shinto music and dances. Technically it can be divided into the forms that are featured at imperial palace Shinto functions (*mikagura*) or large national shrines (*okagura*) and those involved in local shrine events (*satokagura*). However, academic terms are not always those of the performers themselves. One can see dances called *mikagura* in village ceremonies or regional shrines, and the term *satokagura* is seldom heard in local conversations where the term *okagura* might be used with a sense of local respect. For general use, just the word *kagura* is sufficient. We will discuss the palace and large shrine events first.

The famous dance by Ama no Uzume before the cave of the sun goddess is considered to be the origin of Shinto music as well as everything else musical and choreographic in Japan. From the very beginning this music was associated with dancing, a connection that has remained firm to the present day. Thus, any discussion of *kagura* music automatically is concerned with dance as well.

The ancient records contain accounts of *kagura* from very early times, and many of the poems that have survived are the texts of *kagura* songs. Besides the story of *kagura*'s origin and the song texts, the *Kojiki* contains tales that identify music as part of the communication between mankind and the gods. Here is an example:[1]

> When the Emperor Chūai [circa A.D. 200] was preparing to go to war he went to the Ashibi shrine in Kyushu and performed for the gods on his zither. Through the empress as oracle a deity promised great success in land to the West but the emperor rejected the prophesy as false for he had seen only ocean in that direction.[2] He stopped playing and the deity condemned him. The empress then heard the zither playing again and when it stopped she found the emperor, dead.

This custom of an imperial performance as a prelude to the pronouncements of an oracle was retained for many generations until professional musicians fell heir to the duty. Even then, music was still considered a necessary attribute for the emperor as well as his court.

Shinto ceremonial music falls into eight repertoires, derived from sources as far back as the eighth century. One is simply called *kagurauta* (*kagura* songs). *Azuma asobi* (eastern entertainment) contains special dances to be discussed later. *Onaibiuta* (night duty songs), *yamatouta* (Yamato[3] songs), and *ōuta* (big songs) are performed before certain festival days. The list is completed with *ruika* (funeral songs), *kumeuta* (palace guard songs, men-

1. See *Kojiki*, Book 2, Chap. 92.
2. Actually Korea was beyond the ocean.
3. Yamato is claimed to be the name of the first major clan in Japan.

tioned earlier), and *tauta* (field songs). The latter are for agriculture-related ceremonies. There is still the tradition of an annual planting of rice by the emperor.

Poetry is an important part of each *kagura* piece. Its topics fall into two basic types: (1) *torimono*, songs meant to praise the gods or seek their aid, and (2) *saibari*,[4] songs used to entertain the gods. In both cases the accompaniment is basically the same. It is analogous to Bach's sacred and secular cantatas, in which the musical style is quite similar but the words are different. The following two poems show the difference more clearly.[5]

> I. A *torimono* poem from the *kagurauta* repertory (CD track 1)
> Throngs of people are enthralled
> by the fragrance of the *sakaki* leaves.
> In the land of the gods
> their home is in the mountains.
> Here, before the deities
> the *sakaki* leaves flourish abundantly.

> II. A *saibari* poem from the *kumeuta* repertory
> At the high castle of Uda
> I stretch out a line (to catch) a snipe.
> I wait. I don't catch a snipe.
> With great skill and courage
> I catch a whale!

Many of the *kagura* genres include dance. Plate 4 shows an *azuma asobi* common in *mikagura*. Note that the male dancer (*ninjō*) is holding the *sakaki* branch mentioned in the first poem. The circle attached to the branch represents the mirror that helped to bring the sun goddess out of her cave. The two poems given above are typical of styles that were popular in the Japanese court. However, it should be added that among the *saibari* poems many pieces can be found that apparently came directly from Japanese folk music. Today all the ancient texts are sung in a drawn-out, formal style. They generally open with a soloist who may be joined

4. *Saibari* is different from *saibara*. See p. 100.
5. For the Japanese texts and transcriptions see Biblio. ref. 3·2, 63–69 and 269–71.

later by a unison chorus. All the performers are male. When accompanied, a small ensemble is used consisting of one to four instruments whose names are found in the ancient texts. There are also instrumental solos, duets, and trios. These are used as preludes to songs or for special events like the lighting of a sacred fire in the garden of the palace or a large shrine.[6]

Let us look first at the two most characteristic *kagura* instruments.

## SHINTO INSTRUMENTS AND TONE SYSTEMS

Sections of a text or form may be marked off by the *shakubyōshi*; this is a small wooden set of clappers that produces a sharp, thin sound when the edge of one is struck at right angles by the side of the other. A single clap is common but, as seen in Figure 3, two claps may also be used in a call/response manner or as separate patterns for different verses. The instrument is derived from an ancient Chinese tradition, though its shape and manner of performance are quite Japanese.[7]

*Shakubyōshi*

Early *wagon*

*Wagon*

The next most common instrument is a six-stringed zither called the *wagon* (pronounced with a soft "a") or *yamatogoto* (Plate 3). It is claimed as one of the few completely indigenous instruments of Japan. Replicas found in prehistoric figurines (Plate 2) support this theory, though the shapes of these instruments resemble certain Korean forms. The remains of a *wagon* prototype were found recently in the excavations of an ancient house site, further proving its antiquity.[8]

By the end of the Nara period, we have fairly definite information as to how the *wagon* was tuned and played. By this time, though, the influence of Chinese music theory was very strong, and it is difficult to tell how much of the original character of the *wagon* had survived except for the fact that

6. The latter are called *niwabi no kyoku* and are a category of *kagurauta*.
7. Examples of its continental roots can be heard in ancient Korean music and in Confucian ceremonies in Taiwan.
8. See David Hughes, "Music archaeology of Japan," in *The archaeology of early music cultures*. Bonn: Verlag für systematische Musikwissenschaft, 1988, 55–87.

its musical style seems quite distinct from that of imported Chinese zithers.

The tuning of the *wagon* is done by placing an inverted V-shaped bridge under each string and moving the bridges so as to make the strings the proper length to produce a given pitch. The bridges were originally the forked branches of trees, hence their shape.

The basic tuning of the *wagon* is shown in Figure 1.[9] Note that it uses a five-tone (pentatonic) scale derived from the first pitches created naturally in the so-called acoustical overtone series. This scale is found in music all over the world. The numbers below the notation represent the strings, starting with the one nearest to the player. Figure 2 shows that the melodic lines use a richer vocabulary in a seven-toned scale with two variation tones.[10]

FIGURE 1. The standard tuning and scale of the *wagon*

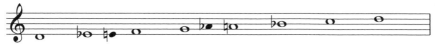

FIGURE 2. The tonal vocabulary of *kagura* melodic lines

The most interesting musical features of the *wagon* are its tuning and its melodic structure. The Western harp, the zither, and the modern Japanese *koto* (except the first two strings) are usually tuned so that a sweep across the strings will produce a scale and thus make the playing of melodies relatively easy. The *wagon*, however, is tuned more like a guitar; that is, the notes of adjacent strings are some distance apart. The unique difference in the case of the *wagon* is that the tones, unlike those of the guitar, do not progress in a regular order from low to high. This makes it difficult to play a melody. In Western music we would say that it made harmony easy to play, but Japanese music uses no Western-style chords at all. Why such an arrangement? The answer is found in the function of the *wagon*: rather than playing melody or harmony, it performs arpeggiated patterns.

Figure 3 is the opening phrase of the *kagura* song "Sakaki" translated

9. Figures 1, 2, and 4 are written one octave higher than actual pitch for convenience in comparisons with other examples in this book.
10. See also the *gagaku* tone system in Chapter Three, p. 114.

earlier and heard on CD track 1. It contains the four basic named patterns used in *wagon* music: *zan, ji, oru*, and *tsumu. Zan* is played by a fast sweep toward the player, starting at string 6, and *ji* is played with a sweep away from the player, starting on string 1. The left hand stops the sound of all but the last string immediately after the sweep so the short-lived cluster of tones is basically a color rather than harmony in the Western sense. A majority of *wagon* music consists of these two patterns only. The patterns *oru* and *tsumu* are equally non-melodic and are played softly; they may vary in pitch and rhythm.

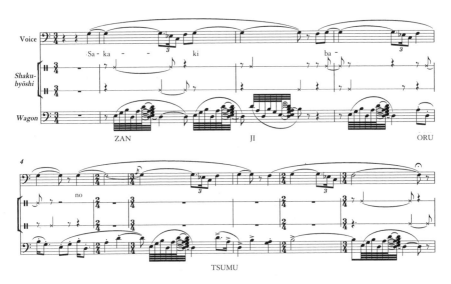

FIGURE 3. The opening of the *kagura* song "Sakaki"

The tuning and the patterns obviously are related. However, as seen in Figure 3, none of the patterns relates directly to the vocal melody; rather, they function as time markers and tone color. Since this is our first example in Western notation, it is important to know that, unlike most Western classical music, all performances are not essentially the same. Compare this notation with track 1 of the accompanying CD. It would seem that the overall tone color is more important than the exact location of each pattern in relation to the vocal line. This may be due in part to the Japanese tradition of regional or guild variations in performance practice. The *wagon* patterns also illustrate a horizontal (linear) rather than vertical (harmonic) orientation, which is characteristic of all Japanese music.

*Kagurabue*

The flute used in *kagura* is the six-holed *kagurabue* or *yamatobue* (Plate 35). Today its characteristic tone quality is seldom heard in performances outside the imperial palace. The *ryūteki* or *nōkan* shown in the same plate may be substituted for it. The other melodic instrument of *kagura* is the double reed instrument called the *hichiriki* (see Chapter Three, p. 107). When the flute and *hichiriki* are used together, they perform the melody heterophonically; that is, they play variations of the tune simultaneously with the vocal line.

Figure 4 shows that in *azuma asobi* music the *wagon* is tuned to a different pitch from other genres. Its music tends to use only the *ji* pattern. The exact origin of the dance is not clear but there are references to it as far back as 763.

**FIGURE 4.** The *wagon* tuning and scale for *azuma asobi* music

KAGURA IN LARGE SHRINES

Female Shinto officiants (*miko*) are part of most larger shrine staff. They can be seen performing a dance (*mikomai*) most often in Kyoto, Nara, Izumo, at the imperial shrine in Ise, and the Meiji shrine in Tokyo. However, as shown in Plate 5, there can be local *mikomai* as well. It was pointed out earlier that sacred dancing had its mythological beginning in the performance of a female goddess. This tradition of female dancers and shamans continues to the present day in smaller, regional temples. Among shamans, who still function as soothsayers or spiritualists, the most exotic are probably the *mikanko* who beat a musical bow over a tub while chanting, and the blind *itako* who rub Buddhist rosaries together to enter into spirits. Male shamans also exist.

The *mikomai*, originally a boy's dance, is now performed in traditional Shinto female robes, with white powdered faces and the hair dressed in the style of the Heian period. The main musical comment to make about *mikomai* is that the dancers usually carry a small tree of bells called a *suzu* (Plate 5). This instrument is still in great use in folk dances and ceremonies, particularly Shinto ones. The classic *mikomai* accompaniment remains the *wagon*, flute, and *hichiriki*, to which may be added a few drums or other instruments borrowed from court music.

*Suzu*

The second main type of female Shinto dance is the *shirabyōshi*. This dance was performed by girls who received special training and were called *shirabyōshi* after the name of their dance and their white (*shira*) costume (Plate 6). These dancers could boast of a very long and occasionally lurid past. During the Heian period there were regular schools in the court for the training of dancing girls for the shrine (and the palace) as well as other schools for male dancers and musicians. The *shirabyōshi*, however, seem to have been particularly popular. Many classic love affairs in Japanese literature involve these comely and apparently many-talented young ladies. For example, Giō, in *Tale of the Heike*, and Shizuka, the sweetheart of Japan's military hero, Yoshitsune, were both *shirabyōshi*.

The music used by these girls was generally a form of song known as *imayō* (see Chapter Three, p. 100). Besides the use of *imayō*, which in its final form evolved into a sort of court "popular" music, the instrumental accompaniment for the *shirabyōshi* also showed the early secularization of these temple dancers. Instead of the traditional Shinto trio, an hourglass-shaped drum called a *tsuzumi* (Plate 6) formed the mainstay of the rhythmic background, while a flute and occasionally other drums were also used. These dancers had their heyday in the Heian period and suffered a steady decline thereafter, but they have left behind a legacy of romantic tales and song-poems which help us recapture some of the flavor of the opulent age in which they lived and loved.

At present, *okagura* is restricted primarily to Kyoto, Nara, Ise, and Tokyo, although various simplified versions are found elsewhere. Before passing on to the folk styles of Shinto music, certain characteristics of Japanese music that already appeared in these early forms should be noted. For example, there are the stereotyped melodic patterns used in the music of the *wagon* —a convention that will be found at work throughout this survey of Japanese music and seems to have appeared even before the arrival of Chinese and Indian influences. Another characteristic is that instrumental music is functional and concert music rare. In Shintoism, services are often performed today with unaccompanied prayers called *norito* or *semmyō*,[11] and instrumental music is used for ceremonial events like processions or dances. From the very start, music in Japan appears to have been connected with literature, dancing, or ceremonial activities. This is a link that remained intact for centuries and is one of the keys to an understanding of it.

## LOCAL *KAGURA* AND FESTIVAL MUSIC

In agricultural societies, the seasons and the main agrarian events are marked by official ceremonies and sacred sanctions. The same is true in Japan. The New Year, the spring, the midsummer growth, the autumn harvest, and the winter snow are all greeted by a festival. These occur at temples large or small as seen in Plate 12, in which a "field music" (*dengaku*) ceremony for the rice-planting season is being performed at the main shrine in Nara. Wherever the festival is, it is called a *matsuri*, or more politely *omatsuri*. The generic term for its music is *matsuri bayashi*. The local forms of festival dances or pantomimes are called *satokagura* (village *kagura*) or *minzoku geinō* (folk theatricals).

While these basic events are found throughout Japan, the particular form that each local festival takes is quite varied. By looking at a few, we can learn what to expect from any future encounters with similar folk events.

Perhaps the most frequently seen folk festivals are in the fall, occurring in late September or early November, and in the New Year's events.[12] The fall festivals are the most readily accessible because they are celebrated in the large cities as well as in the country. The prologue to this book was a description of a Tokyo *matsuri*, giving a picture of the shrine procession and its surrounding festivities, but now it is time to look at the music in greater detail.

The main source of music for such festivals is a small band of musicians called the *hayashi*. This is a generic term for percussion ensembles, with or without melodic instruments. In city festivals, the *hayashi* usually consists of three drums, a hand gong, and a flute (Plates 1 and 7).[13] One drummer

11. For distinctions see Donald L. Philippi, *Norito* (Princeton, N.J.: Princeton University Press, 1990), 2–3.
12. Japan changed from a lunar to a solar calendar in the Meiji period. Some festival dates are calculated on the old system and some on the new.
13. In Plate 1 the gong player is absent. He is the dancer.

*Ōdaiko*

*Taiko*

is assigned to the big *ōdaiko* while the other two play on rough-hewn versions of the smaller *taiko*. The festival *taiko* heads are lashed together with rope and tightened by a second encircling rope, though many of them nowadays are tightened by means of metal nuts and bolts. Their structure is like that of the *taiko* used in the *noh* drama, except that the skins are thicker, as are the ropes and wood. The playing method also differs. Instead of the delicate stand used for *noh* drums, the folk *taiko* is tipped up in front by means of a stick that is shoved into the ropes. Sometimes the drum is merely placed on a wooden crate (see the *ōdaiko* in Plate 5) or suspended on a frame (Plate 7). If these drums seem rather un-Japanese in their relative crudeness it must be remembered that, originally, many were homemade,[14] and that they are subject to the rough handling of folk musicians and severe weather changes on open-air stages.

The generic term for all Japanese drumsticks is *bachi*. The festival *taiko* are played with slimmer *bachi* than those used for the *ōdaiko* and for the *taiko* in *noh*. Most Japanese drumsticks are made of light cypress (*hinoki*) wood so that their size does not impede the lively rhythms they may play.

The *ōdaiko* has a convex wooden body and two tacked heads. Two thick sticks are used on either one or both heads as well as on the rim or even the body. Plates 1, 5, and 7 show that its placement varies. The folk *hayashi* in general is open to considerable variation, and other styles of drums can be used together with singers or special percussion instruments. The most unusual drum is the *daibyōshi* (Plate 10 and p. 246). This is used to accompany the *satokagura* pantomime plays, many of which are based on the ancient *Kojiki* mythologies. In order to be out of the way on stage, the drums and

14. With the rise of Japan's economy since the 1959 edition of this book, along with the popularization of Japanese percussion ensembles at home and abroad, the professional percussion and festival equipment manufacturers have flourished. Visit the stores on the corners of Kaminarimon 1-chōme near the Tawaramachi subway stop in Tokyo.

flute are set to the side rather than at the back. The *daibyōshi* player sits on one side of the drum and plays with two long bamboo sticks, the left one striking the head with a backward motion of the hand. This way he can follow the actions of the performer while playing the drum. It is a unique but practical arrangement.

The standard brass gong (*kane*) in festival *hayashi* is the *atarigane* (Plate 8 and p. 246). This can be suspended but is more often held in the hand and played with a bone mallet set on a stick, striking at the cup or the inner edge. The middle three fingers of the left hand may touch the gong to deaden the sound when hitting the edge. The basic mnemonics with which its rhythms are taught are *chon* (hitting in the middle), *chi* (hitting the inside edge), and *ki* (reversing the stroke to another part of the edge). As we shall see, the teaching of music through sounds that imitate those of the instrument (*shōga*, onomatopoeic mnemonics) is characteristic of Japanese music. The *kane* also comes in other sizes, such as the *surigane* seen in the procession of Plate 9.

*Takebue*

The flute used in folk *hayashi* groups is usually a simple bamboo pipe with six or seven holes called a *takebue* or *shinobue*. Not only do the length and number of holes vary from group to group but the manner of playing may also differ. There are some Japanese folk flutists who, unaware of the belief that all Japanese are right-handed, play their flutes to the left (Plate 1).[15] The *kagurabue* or the *nōkan* may accompany *satokagura* pantomime plays.

Festival ensembles are often named after the particular district from which they come or the specific type of music they play. For example, there is a *kandabayashi* from the Kanda district of Tokyo, and the popular ensemble from the Asakusa area of Tokyo is called the *edobayashi*, for it is the repository for much of the festival music of old Tokyo (Edo), as is the district in which it is played. *Matsuri bayashi* music is considered as a folk form though it is often played by professionals. It has been discussed in this chapter on religious music, however, because of its close connection with Shinto festivals. For one thing, it is often used to accompany folk *kagura* dances. During *omatsuri*, one can see many of the most common *satokagura*

15. This picture is from the first roll of film I ever used in Japan. Looking at the flute player, I thought it was printed backward until I read the signs on stage.

characters: the comic female (Plate 1), the country bumpkin (*hyottoko*), the dog (*nimba*), and the always popular lion (*shishi*, Plate 11). Plate 10 shows the magic white fox (*kitsune*) with proper Shinto paraphernalia, the bell tree (*suzu*) and magic wand (*gohei*).

Both the dances and the music are repetitive, and each section is performed many times before any contrast is presented. Frequently these repeats are in sets of three or nine, as three is considered a lucky number. City *kagura* dances are more like performances for public entertainment than most of those seen in the country, although they still retain the fundamental choreographic concept of the efficacy of the magic numbers three, five, and seven. Though the spirit may be lost, the tradition remains. Such prolonged repetitions become boring if one follows the dance too closely, and it is only the gods, perhaps, who are meant to watch them continuously. For the onlooker, casual observation mixed with conversation is the best approach to the enjoyment of such performances. The same can be said for many Oriental theatricals and folk events, such as Chinese operas, Javanese shadow plays, and Edo-period Japanese *kabuki* (when tickets were cheaper). The idea of mixing attention with subliminal awareness is the key, I believe, to both the organization and appreciation of many such stage productions.

Since the music for an *omatsuri* is not directly related to special ceremonies, its form is different from that of the usual religious music. There are a certain number of set pieces that are played in a given order and then repeated in that order as often as necessary. The exact pieces used vary from one *hayashi* group to another, but the most common sequence is "Yatai," "Kamakura," "Shōten," "Shichōme," and again "Yatai."[16] (Note that five pieces being played by five musicians increases one's luck.) Viewing these pieces on a countrywide basis, one will find that, although the titles may be the same, the melodies are often different. The names merely seem to designate broad divisions in the traditional festivals rather than specific tunes, though they do have meanings. (A *yatai* is the cart on which festival ensembles are pulled through the streets [Plate 7]; *shōten* [or *shōden*] can mean anything from a place of prayer or a sacred spirit to the privilege of submitting a petition to the imperial court; and *shichōme* means "fourth avenue." Judging from CD track 2, it must be a lively place.)

16. Traditional notation and cassettes of all these pieces are found in Biblio. ref. 2·14.

Many village ensembles as well as the modern stage groups tend to produce steady rhythmic drones over which independent rhythms are played to create tension and forward motion. The modern groups are Western-influenced in their approaches to form, with calls and responses between drums and loud and soft contrasts.[17] In the *edobayashi* version of "Shichōme" on CD track 2, you can hear the more sophisticated style of traditional urban *hayashi* as well as some of the roots of the new styles that have become popular internationally.

**FIGURE 5.** Rhythmic patterns in "Yatai"

The excerpt from the festival piece "Yatai" in Figure 5 illustrates one special feature of Japanese music that could be called the "sliding door" effect. Both the flute and the drums are playing phrases of eight-beat lengths but, like Japanese sliding doors (*fusuma*) of equal length, when used they may not begin at the same place. Just play or sing the melody and have someone else beat the drum patterns and you will feel the tension created by this deliberate out-of-phase timing. It is an important factor in giving the music a strong sense of moving forward. A resolving cadence is created when things "even out" at the next-to-last drum pattern,

17. The fad began in the late 1960s when some young Japanese, influenced by Western traditions and commune movements, set up a community on Sado Island whose major activity was learning to play Japanese-style drums (which were never used in Japanese schools). The group, called Kodō, now does international tours and has world drum festivals on Sado regularly.

which has ten beats instead of eight. This "sliding door" device will be seen several times in the chapters ahead. It is seldom heard in the new *hayashi* ensembles that are found both in Japan and around the world because they are more Western-oriented in form and rhythm.[18] Another derivative from the Japanese folk *hayashi* in modern groups is the use of spectacular physical movement patterns in drumming.

*Hayashi* music in an actual festival environment can be a casual affair and should be considered in the same light as the tailgate band at a New Orleans funeral. It is both fun and musical. It is meant to entertain both gods and men and seems to do well in both capacities.

If one travels further into the backwoods of Japan, one can find some of the most ancient forms of Japanese folk music. A goodly portion of this music is reserved for use in the various seasonal religious festivals. These festivals, while replete with entertaining dances, are also quite seriously connected with ritual and magic numbers. Speaking in broad terms, the program for most such events will include a procession, a purification ceremony, sacred dances, a symbolic or real banquet, secular dances, and a climactic event or benediction.

## A SNOW FESTIVAL IN NAGANO

In the mountain fastness of the small village of Niino in Nagano, there occurs one of the most famous of the *kagura* festivals, the *yuki matsuri*, or "snow festival." It takes place every year on January 14 as an act of supplication that spring fertility will once again follow the winter barrenness. For several days before, special purification ceremonies and banquets are held, but the festival itself officially begins on the afternoon of the fourteenth with a procession from a temple on one side of the village to the main shrine on the other side. The function of the procession is to carry the masks of the *kamisama*, the spirits, to the main shrine (Plate 13). In traditional fashion, this shrine is on a hill in a forest. The music for this procession consists of a short flute melody played over and over with the beating of an *ōdaiko* drum for accompaniment. One should add that the drunken shouts of some of the participants are also part of the music, as is

18. Naturally, the author's ensemble at the University of Michigan played in the old-fashioned style, and the "sliding door" effect was frequently employed.

a flourish from the local firemen's bugle corps which forms part of the entourage.

On arriving at the shrine, the sacred dances are immediately begun on the special *kagura* stage (*kaguraden*), which forms part of most shrine compounds. To the accompaniment of flute and drum, groups of men and boys move through the stately measures of the dances, making sure that everything is repeated three times on all sides. The men carry serpentine

*Binzasara*

Japanese rattles (*binzasara*) while the boys carry drums (Plate 14). A similar combination of instruments is seen in an eighteenth-century ceremony at the more famous Kasuga shrine in Nara (Plate 12). The *binzasara* is one of a variety of rattles (*sasara*) used in Japanese folk music. Folk rattles can be made of split bamboo, but the *binzasara* consists of plates of wood that are strung together to produce a sharper tone. The men at the *yuki matsuri* dance to the "jat, jat, jat" of their *binzasara*, always played three times and always left-right-left (CD track 3). In the 1956 performances I first saw, the boys merely carried the drums without playing them (Plate 14). These dances take over an hour and, though the crowd drifts off to buy souvenirs or saké, the dances are scrupulously repeated the proper number of times to ensure the cooperation of the gods. There is little apparent awe of the spirits, for the dancers talk and even smoke and drink during the performance, but the superstition of the magic numbers still has a great hold on this rural population.

The next set of sacred dances takes place within the shrine itself. These are interesting because they are dedicated to Kannon, the Buddhist goddess of mercy, providing an excellent illustration of the mixing of the Buddhist and Shinto religions mentioned earlier.

The symbolic banquet at this festival consists of the opening of the sanctuary and the placing of proper offerings within it. All the participants in the festival are then blessed with the special *gohei* wand, brought from the inner sanctum. The music of the prayers that follow is of interest: it consists of chanting done to the accompaniment of the large drum and the rattling of *suzu* bell trees (Plate 15), a music called *semmyō* that is closely related to a style of Buddhist hymn singing (*wasan*) to be studied later.

The climactic event of the festival occurs around 1:00 A.M. when a tall column of pine branches is lit. The bonfire is started by means of a sacred boat that is lofted nine times before it finally touches the branches. The pine burns with a pitchy intensity. Suddenly, through the shower of sparks the first god appears. Standing in the orange glare of the fire and surrounded by shouting men and waving lanterns, the dancer truly gives the impression of something supernatural. From their position under the eaves of the shrine roof, the flutist and drummer strike up the tune of "Saihō," and the gods themselves begin to dance. This dance consists of a series of movements, each done three times. The entire dance is repeated nine times, with only the ending changing. This is altered so that the dancer may bless different parts of the shrine at the end of each repeat. The last repetition includes an interlude performed by the drum and the rattle dancers who appeared earlier.

The next dance, "Modoki" (Plate 16), is exactly the same as "Saihō," only the mask is different. This is one of the most interesting characteristics of Shinto festivals. A farmer explained to me that this redundancy was necessary to ensure that the gods really saw and fully appreciated their dances.

As the night progresses toward dawn, a further series of dancers plunge through the smoke to do their bit to entertain the gods. More secular entertainments appear, including short, masked comedy skits. There is an extremely interesting dance by two men wearing model horses which may be an imitation of the ancient imperial custom of having horse races and archery contests on festival days. Another dance, more directly related to the fertility overtones of the festival, is an amorous pantomime between an old lady and an old man, both played by masked children. Finally, at dawn, three devils (*oni*) appear who perform a slow stylized fight. One curious element of this dance is that the dancers cannot see out of their masks, and hence each man is moved about by an assistant much in the manner of Japanese puppets.

There is a comic horse dance, which is then repeated as a lion dance; another comic skit; and the festival draws to a close with the singing of a final chant by a group of men gathered around an upturned drum on which offerings have been placed. The masks are put away, the souvenir sellers fold up their booths, the remaining saké is drunk, and the population wanders home for a good sleep, content in the knowledge that the gods are on their side for another season.

A videotape of a 1994 performance[19] shows the villagers in better clothes and some newer buildings as compared to those seen in our 1956 photos, but the ceremony is basically the same. One joy in Japan seems to be that while traditions may change, they do not stop.

FIGURE 6. Dance music from the *yuki matsuri*

The music for the *yuki matsuri* is played by a flute and a drum with the occasional addition of the *binzasara* or the *suzu*. Figure 6 (CD track 3) is the music used for the devil dance ("Oni no mai") mentioned above. It is typical Japanese folk music for flute and illustrates one of the common folk scales. This scale, known as the *yō* scale, and its companion, the *in* scale, are said to have developed out of the *ritsu* scale (compare Figures 7 and 21). The musical characteristics of this melody are discussed in Chapter Ten. It is included here to help capture the ponderous, primitive spirit of this folk devil dance.

The *yuki matsuri* displays all the characteristics of a Shinto festival, as listed earlier. If one travels about the country, one will see a host of festivals using a variety of masks, dances, and ceremonies; the basic outline,

19. See Appendix III, *Nihon rekishi to geinō*, Vol. 3.

however, will remain roughly the same. It is the pleasant task of future anthropologists and ethnomusicologists to ferret out the many fascinating details that remain undiscovered in the world of Shinto folk festivals. For the more casual observer, they provide a colorful spectacle and a pleasant memory of Japan.

MODERN SHINTO

Before closing the topic of Shinto music one should note that new, neo-Shinto sects continued to appear throughout the nineteenth and twentieth centuries. With them often came eclectic mixtures of music. For example, in 1814 the Kurozumikyō was founded by Kurozumi Munetada at an Inari shrine in Okayama. Kurozumikyō expanded greatly and even received government encouragement as national Shintoism grew in the Meiji period. Its music was called *kibigaku*, *kibi* being the old name for the Okayama area, and it was created by Kishimoto Yoshihide, a regional *gagaku* musician dropped from his position by Meiji reforms. He combined some *gagaku* wind and percussion instruments with the modern *koto*. This mixture of courtly and modern sounds in the music of many new Japanese religions perhaps explains the modern tendency to use the *gagaku* piece "Etenraku" along with Mendelssohn and Wagner march music in most Japanese marriage ceremonies whether at a shrine, temple, church, or a commercial wedding building. Another sect—Tenrikyō, founded by Nakayama Miki in 1838—used a kind of *kagura* in its services, accompanied by a variety of instruments, and *gagaku* became important in many of its rites. The "score" notation of Figure 43 is, in fact, a Tenrikyō publication. Movements that included hand gestures like those of Buddhist mudras also became part of its practice, though not to the extent of the newer, so-called "dancing religion," whose followers express their faith in real dance movements.[20] But while the many new religions that made their appearance after World War II offer interesting studies in syncretism and spiritual diversity, musically one must still look to the classic Shinto and Buddhist traditions for the significant religious musical heritage of Japan.

20. The Tenshō Kōtaijingūkyō, founded by Kitamura Sayo in 1947.

# 2. Buddhist Music

Western music is based on two great traditions, the music theories of ancient Greece and the extension of these theories by the Catholic Church. Its scales, modes, notations, and concepts of consonance and dissonance are all deeply rooted in this background, though the present-day products may seem to be very distant indeed. By the same token, Japanese music is based on two equally great theoretical foundations, the music of ancient China and the music of Buddhism.

Buddhism entered Japan in the Nara period and continued to grow in influence and power during the subsequent Heian and Kamakura periods. Coming primarily from Chinese sources, Buddhism became an important purveyor of Chinese culture and ideas. Among the intellectual accouterments of this Chinese Buddhism was the theory and practice of singing and composing chants based on sacred texts (sutras) and hymns. This art became known in Japan as *shōmyō*. Year after year, Japanese monks would set out on the perilous journey to China to sit at the feet of the great singing masters of the Chinese monastery of Yushan (or Gyozan in Japanese) in order to be able to instruct their brethren in the proper manner of praising the Lord Buddha in song. Yushan must have been the musical Mecca of the Orient, the Rome of ninth-century Buddhism, where Japanese, Chinese, Tibetan, and Indian knelt together to read commentaries on the Diamond and Lotus sutras or to raise their voices in praise of the Buddha, whose serene smile could be seen dimly through the clouds of burning incense.

Buddhism began in India, and the art of *shōmyō* is also said to have originated in the singing of the ancient Hindu Vedic hymns. Perhaps the Japanese monks met Indian teachers of this style during their stay at Yushan. It is said that some Indian priests actually came to Japan to teach. In any event, there is some basis for believing that part of this Indian tradition was also absorbed into the music of Japanese Buddhist rites. However, the organized theory of music, as learned by the Japanese, is based on Chinese texts and Chinese teachers. This theory was not the exclusive property of the clergy, for the music of the court also originated from Chinese models. There, the theory was kept fairly intact, while the Buddhist monks, perhaps because they had more time and inclination for commentaries, extended some of the basic ideas. But for our purposes one can say that the music theory of *shōmyō* and that of court music (*gagaku*) are basically the same and that they have a common origin in Chinese music theory. Some of the ideas they incorporate will be presented here and some in the following chapter, but it must be remembered that they are all basically of one piece.

Buddhism, like Christianity, is fraught with sectarianism. These theological schisms are reflected in turn by various music styles, each responding to the beliefs and ceremonial requirements of a particular sect. For example, in speaking of Christian music, one must differentiate between Catholic, Orthodox, Anglican, American Protestant, and many other styles. Likewise, in Japanese Buddhism differences exist in the music of the Shingon, Tendai, Jōdo, Nichiren, and a host of other sects.[21] However, if our discussion is organized around musical types rather than sectarian styles, a better idea can be formed of the general scope of Buddhist music.

Since *shōmyō* began as the chanting of Buddhist texts in India and went from there to China before coming to Japan, it is now sung in three different languages. Those songs sung in the ancient Indian dialect are called *bonsan* (CD track 4), those in Chinese are called *kansan*, and the songs in Japanese are *wasan*. Because the Japanese adopted Chinese ideographs for their written language, giving them Japanese pronunciations, it is possible for them to sing Chinese songs with their own pronunciation. This form of *shōmyō* developed into a distinct style called *kōshiki*.

When we want to know about the background and origins of Western music, we turn to the ancient collections of Gregorian chant or refer to the theories of Odo of Cluny, Guido d'Arezzo (the inventor of *do*, *re*, *mi*), and a legion of other clerical scholars. If we seek a similar heritage in Japanese music, we must look to such works as the *Shōmyō yōjinshū* by Tanchi (1163–1237), of the Tendai sect, or the main codex of the Shingon sect, the *Gyozan taikaishū* (1496), with its important theoretical appendices by Chōkei. By distilling certain major facts from these important works, a basis can be formed on which to build a study of all subsequent Japanese music.

First in any music theory, East or West, is the problem of scales and modes. In *shōmyō* there are two basic scales and a third one over which there are sectarian differences. Ignoring some historical variations in nomenclature, the two basic scales can be called *ryo* and *ritsu* (Figure 7). Each has

21. Recordings of each can be purchased from Buddhist supply stores.

FIGURE 7. The *ryo* and *ritsu* scales [22]

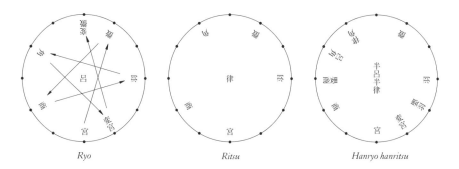

Ryo                     Ritsu                    Hanryo hanritsu

FIGURE 8. A circular design for Buddhist scales

five basic notes called *kyū*, *shō*, *kaku*, *chi*, and *u*. Notice that each scale has two auxiliary tones. The prefix *ei*, like the Western sharp, raises a tone a half step, while the word *hen*, like the Western flat, indicates that a note should be lowered a half step. These auxiliary tones are known collectively as *hen'on*, literally "changing tones," and are used primarily for modulation.

The third scale is meant to be a combination of the above two, thus its usual name is *hanryo hanritsu*, "half *ryo* and half *ritsu*." Which half goes where is the bone of contention between the various theorists. Figure 8 shows the three theoretical scales set in circles. This book is about music, not theology, but it is tempting to consider that Figure 8 reflects the Buddhist concept of cyclical rebirth in contrast to the linear, horizontal rendering of scales found in the music theory books of Christianity, in which birth and death are thought of as a straight-line, one-time event.

22. Early studies often wrote *ryosen* and *ritsusen*, adding the word "scale" (*sen*) to the term. It was usually dropped in later writings.

In Western music the space of one octave contains twelve possible pitches. Played in succession, they are called a chromatic scale. These notes also exist in Japanese (or Chinese) music theory. In Western music, seven of these twelve notes are chosen to form a normal scale. The Japanese scales also consist of seven notes, but only five of them are considered vital. In Western music one can take a given scale structure (for example, a major scale) and start it on any one of the twelve notes. It is in this way that C major, E-flat major, F-sharp major, etc. are constructed. In Chinese music theory such a process is also possible, but one standard Japanese theory (unfortunately there is more than one due to sectarianism) allows scales to begin on only five pitches out of the twelve. *Ryo*-type scales can be started only on the note D or G. *Ritsu* scales should begin on E and B, and the mixed scale should start only on A. Notice that these starting notes are the five basic pitches of the *ritsu* scale shown in Figure 7. Also bear in mind that this *ritsu* scale is the classic pentatonic scale mentioned earlier (see Figure 1). As for the problems of modes within each scale, modulations, and other transpositions, all that need be said here is that these topics are also covered in the theory books. These Buddhist tomes are replete with charts, diagrams (like Figure 8), and tables—the symbols of authority for music theorists all over the world. As in the case of many such theoretical works, the charts and diagrams do not always coincide with actual performance practices.

Before leaving the subject of scales, one more thing should be noted. The essential difference between the *ryo* and *ritsu* scales is the placement of the *kaku* note. It is a half step lower in the *ryo* scale. This is somewhat analogous to the situation in Western music, in which the important difference between major and minor is the lowered third note in minor. One might call the *ritsu* a major-type scale and the *ryo* a minor-type, though it is not safe to carry the analogy too far.

Into these scale molds Buddhist music is poured. As the chanting in Buddhist rites developed, certain standard musical phrases and ornamentations appeared. These were given special names, the exact meaning of which often varies with the particular scale being used and the sect using them. Thus, certain patterns were reserved for use only in the *ritsu* or the *ryo* scale, though they had the same name. The most common type of ornamentation is called *yuri*, or "swinging." There are many kinds of *yuri* but their basic technique is the use of a waver or slight change in pitch that colors the line and provides the melody with a small sense of rhythm (listen to CD track 4).

Rhythm is less discussed in Buddhist theory books. There are studies on the seven-five syllable construction of texts and the names of certain rhythmic patterns. There are hymns and chants (particularly *wasan*) that are sung in a steady, one-syllable-per-beat manner, but CD track 4 demonstrates the standard style of *shōmyō* performance. Syllables are elongated in what could be called deep breath rhythms. In the opening solo passage, one hears not only the liquid, sliding movement between pitches but also the space for ornamentation and for subtle changes in the tone quality of the voice. These are characteristics of much of Japanese music, particularly that of the *shakuhachi*. They could likewise be compared with the aesthetics of other Japanese arts, such as ink painting or flower arranging. There must be time and space to savor an art form.

Given the fluid nature of the music, *shōmyō* notation looks indefinite though, as the unison chorus performance shows, it is quite specific (compare CD track 4 with Appendix I, Figure 40). Given the dominance of Buddhism in Japan, however, there are naturally sectarian variations in ceremonies and their music, making it impossible to provide an all-encompassing example of performance practice. One specific case will be used to infer the general style of many of the other sects and to study the instruments used in such services.

## A BUDDHIST CEREMONY AND ITS MUSICAL INSTRUMENTS

The main Tendai temple in the Asakusa amusement area of Tokyo is well known for its hidden image of the goddess Kannon. The following is an account of a morning service at that temple in the winter of 1956.[23] As in the Christian tradition, the faithful and the priests are called to the ceremony by means of a large bell. The Buddhist bell (*hanshō*), however, does not have a clapper but is struck on the outside with a wooden hammer in a loud and rapid manner that is associated in the West with country fire alarms. The processional accompaniment is rendered on a large hidden drum of the

*Hanshō*

23. At 6:00 A.M., only a cleaning lady and myself were in attendance.

*ōdaiko* type. The ponderous beats echo through the main hall and produce an atmosphere of solemnity equal to that created by the chanting entrance of Christian monks.

The general term for Buddhist ceremonies is *hōe* and the sections within them are called *hōyō*. The head priest (*dōshi*) and group of other priests (*shikishū*) will now lead us through the order (*shidai*) of an early morning Tendai rite.

The head priest kneels on a dais immediately before the image. Various offerings and sacred vessels are arranged before him, and to his right there is a small, hanging, fish-mouthed chime made of bronze called a *kei* (CD track 4, first sounds). This is used rather like the small bells of the Catholic mass, i.e., it signals certain special moments in the ceremonial movements of the head priest. For this purpose, two more bells are provided. One is a small hand bell with a clapper. It is found throughout the Orient and in Japanese is called a *rei* (p. 246). The other is a bowl-shaped bell called an *uchinarashi* or *kin*. This is set on a brightly colored cushion and struck on the edge with a mallet. The latter instrument is found commonly in home

*Kei*

*Kin*

shrines and is capable of a lovely, sustained tone. It comes in a variety of sizes from monsters of sixty centimeters in diameter to very small ones, and has become quite popular in modern Western percussion ensembles. The major sections of the ceremony may be marked off by strokes on a knobbed Oriental gong (*nyō* or *dora*, see p. 246). The rims of the cymbals (*nyōhatsu* or *nyōhachi*) heard at the end of CD track 4 clatter together in a style that is common to Buddhist rites as far away as Tibet.

When the priests are all in their places, a gong is sounded and the chanting begins. As in most religious traditions, the opening phrase is sung by a solo cantor (CD track 4), sometimes with the other priests humming softly behind him. The tempo is very slow, and rhythm seems almost nonexistent. Gradually the entire ensemble joins in as the main priest begins the ablutions and blessings requisite to the presentation of offerings to the Buddha. Musically, the point of greatest interest in this particular performance (not heard on CD track 4) is that each priest sings at his own pitch level. Some feel that this is not the intention of the original style, but, be that as it may, the effect of some twenty men chanting as many pitches is quite striking.

Similarly, one of the important parts of many Buddhist services is the *gyōdō* during which the priests chant while dropping symbolic lotus petals, sometimes as they parade around the central dais (Plate 17). The fascination of this music lies in the fact that the cantor often sings a completely different piece in Sanskrit, while the other priests chant in ancient Chinese. The Sanskrit piece (called *bai*) gives the same effect as that of a *cantus firmus* in the early polyphony of the Catholic church. The similarity in effect (though not necessarily in sound and form) is intriguing. Perhaps certain ideas concerning psychological and acoustical effects are universal in the field of religious music.

Bells and chimes continue to mark off the progress of the service. The prayers and holy scriptures are read in a simple chanting style like that used for similar sections in many Christian services. Responsive singing between the cantor and the priests occurs during the section in which the priests rise and make obeisance to their god. It is interesting to note that this ceremony, like the Shinto dances mentioned earlier, is often repeated in multiples of three. The ceremony ends with the singing of *wasan*, a chant in Japanese. As already noted, unlike the preceding *shōmyō*, it is sung in a very steady rhythm, set in this case by means of an *ōdaiko* drum (Plate 18). The verses of the *wasan* are usually in the seven-five syllable scheme but are sung in phrases of eight beats. This, as will be seen later, is a fundamental rhythmic orientation in Japanese music. When the *wasan* is finished and the final prayers are said, the *wasan* drum is given one sharp rap which signals the beginning of beating on the larger hidden drum, marking the stately measures of the recessional. The Buddhist service is now over.

This, of course, is only one ceremony of a particular type for a particular sect. Some of the musical variations that should be mentioned occur in the popular Jōdo and Nichiren sects. Both have a love of the percussive, and greater use is made of drums and gongs during their ceremonies. Among the endless battery of Buddhist percussive instruments, two are especially popular. One is the *mokugyo*, a wooden, fish-mouthed slit gong (Plate 17), known in the West as a Chinese temple block. In dance bands it is the "clippidy clop" of many a Western ballad, and in the Buddhist home it is the ostinato over which one chants the name of Buddha as a means of salvation. This persistent wooden "tat,

*Mokugyo*

tat, tat" has been heard by many a tourist who has wandered through a Japanese village in the early morning or at sunset.

One of the most striking uses of the *mokugyo* was heard during a 1956 Jōdo sect ceremony. At the end of the service the priests began their steady chanting of *wasan*. From the side of the sanctuary another priest began a slower rhythm on a very large, deep-toned *mokugyo*. This rhythm was picked up by a chorus of women who were kneeling behind him, each with a smaller instrument. They also chanted, and the rhythm of their song rose slowly until the temple was filled with an overpowering chaos of rhythm and uncoordinated chanting. It was an excellent and exciting example of psychological considerations overcoming music theory in the shaping of religious music.

The other main percussion instrument of Buddhist music is practically the trademark of the Nichiren sect: the *uchiwadaiko*, the fan drum (Plate 22). A single head is stretched over an iron ring and then attached to a wooden handle. The drum is beaten with a wooden stick, and religious slogans are often written on the head. The Nichiren sect is quite evangelistic, and one can sometimes see one of its followers tramping down the street, pounding an *uchiwadaiko* as a means of calling all sinners to repent. These drums are also used in the Nichiren services, the congregation beating out the prayers while an acolyte provides syncopation on an *ōdaiko*. Under such conditions, it is not difficult to see that vocal technique suffers. In any event, there is little chance of drowsing during a Nichiren service. In the more important services of many different sects, court instruments are added, but the battery mentioned above is the center of most branches of the Buddhist instrumental tradition.

*Uchiwadaiko*

The life of the Buddhist monastery, like that of the Catholic, is filled with many hours of office and has a concomitant number of special gongs and bells to assist in the marking of these hours. In the cloisters of the famous Zen sect of meditative Buddhism one can find some twenty-odd instruments used to regulate the monk's daily life. Among them, only two will be mentioned here. One is the *bangi* (or *hangi*), a large wooden board that is beaten with a mallet to

*Bangi*

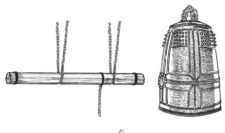

*Ōgane*

call the monks to the central hall for periods of meditation. This board (found in other sects too) is often inscribed with a religious poem. Another instrument must be mentioned because it is the very symbol of the Buddhist temple as pictured in poetry and remembered by the foreign visitor. This is the *ōgane* (or *bonshō*), a large bell that hangs in a separate bell tower within the temple compound. It is struck by means of a long, horizontally suspended pole. Its deep, rich tone marks off the hours of the day, and on New Year's Eve, *ōgane* from every part of the city slowly mark the passing year. The great Japanese classic, *Tale of the Heike*, begins and ends with the solemn tolling of such a bell, for it amply symbolizes the Buddhist concept of the impermanence of this world and the inextricable unity of life, death, and time.[24] One might say that *shōmyō* destroys time in the sense that any deep religious meditation seems to escape temporality, but the *ōgane* symbolically restores a sequential regularity to life.

The Buddhist tradition is rich in such ritualistic and artistic abstractions of its various religious precepts. Plate 26 shows that elaborate ceremonies can even include court music (*gagaku*) and court dance (*bugaku*). During such occasions, the chanting and the instrumental music perform simultaneously two unrelated musics, creating a multisonic texture more powerful than any the American composer Charles Ives had ever dreamed of.

For the music lover, the art of Buddhist music certainly provides ample testimony to the grandeur of the Japanese Buddhist heritage. The study of this music not only provides a basis for the understanding of many subsequent styles but also gives one an indirect glimpse of what might have been the musical traditions of ancient India and China.

24. The opening text is found in the translation for CD track 9 in Appendix II.

## BUDDHIST FOLK MUSIC AND FESTIVALS

Buddhism has a long and distinguished history of evangelism. Its priests traversed vast deserts, mountains, and oceans to bring the message of Śākyamuni to the Orient and eventually the entire world. Like all evangelists, they found music very helpful in the process of conversion. Also, like the Christian missionaries, they realized that the words of their standard ceremonial music were in too foreign a tongue to be of much help in reaching the common people. In the Heian period, Buddhist priests and nuns took to the streets as well in their efforts to spread the message of the sutras beyond the temple, as is shown in the lower left-hand corner of Plate 20 where two "singing nuns" (*utabikuni*) from the early Edo period are pictured. The box seen under the arm of one of the nuns contains picture scrolls that were shown as the nun narrated and sang about the life of Buddha and its meaning in terms of salvation. Such religious narratives were known as *sekkyō* and their musical version as *utasekkyō*. Sometimes the narrations were accompanied by a small *sasara* rattle (like the one being played by a different musician in the upper left-hand corner of the same plate). The *sekkyō* tradition was one of the roots of the many secular narrative musics discussed in Chapter Eight and also in Biblio. ref. 5·7. By the eighteenth century, secular forms of *sekkyō* could be heard from other itinerant storytellers, in the street, in tea houses, or in the theater, and the term is still found in pieces of *shamisen* or *biwa* music.

Other hymns were written for rural populations. This began with *wasan*, the Buddhist chants that already existed in Japanese. Both the melodic style and the texts of *wasan* were changed in order to capture the attention of new, less sophisticated congregations. One group of priests created sets of simple *wasan* which were taught to the large population of the capital. This form of music became one of the main contributing factors in the *imayō* music of the Shinto dancing girls mentioned earlier. Other hymns that were written for more rustic populations were absorbed quickly into the local folk-music tradition. Hence, many of the older folk songs existing today have a Buddhist overtone to their texts and sometimes a distinct *shōmyō* quality in their melodies. One example, heard in 1957 on a small island called Miyakejima, comes to mind. During a recording session held on the island, one of the old ladies dragged out of her memory a song in which each syllable was separated by a long melisma in almost a classic Buddhist chanting style. Some of these religious folk songs are still called *wasan* by the folk singers, though frequently they are designated as *bushi*, a generic term used as a suffix with a wide variety of folk songs. One characteristic of the older Buddhist folk songs, besides the influence of chant, is the fact that accompaniment is seldom used. Hand clapping or an occasional drum may be added, but music of this category, which uses the *shamisen*, is usually of much later origin.

One of the more violent transfers of music from the sacred to the secular occurred with a type of hymn known as *saimon*. These hymns were used in Buddhist, Shinto, and Confucian rites and were later incorporated into the structure of the various theatrical predecessors of the *noh* drama. In the late Muromachi period, they again became popular, but by then the secular influence of the above-mentioned theatricals had become too strong. Instead of praising Buddha, the songs were used to satirize current events and people, rather like Carribean Calypso music. These lampoons were invented primarily by traveling priests called *yamabushi*, seen in Plate 19, carrying a Buddhist *shakujō* rattle. Like some of the early European friars, these men had only a very loose connection with the temple or its morals. They soon took to recounting dramatized versions of the latest love affairs around town, especially those ending in double suicides. Such music might be called a fifteenth-century musical tabloid. This type of *saimon* was eventually coupled with the *shamisen* and became known as *utazaimon*, an important predecessor of a genre of narrative music to be studied later (see *jōruri*, Chapter Eight). The only remains of the old *saimon* are found in certain dirty ditties used in folk theatricals and dances. The religious forms of this music have disappeared. Its real significance, however, lies in its relation to *utazaimon* and the *shamisen* genres that followed.

Another form of Buddhist folk music is *goeika*. These hymns also originated in *wasan* and attained their greatest popularity in the Muromachi period. They were particularly popular as pilgrims' songs and are still used during sacred processions to various temples. A hand bell and a small gong set on three legs (*hitotsugane*) or an *atarigane* are often used as accompanying instruments. Plate 23 shows *goeika* in use as part of an important ceremony of the Jōdo sect. Notice that, as in some of the ceremonies of the newer Japanese religions, a form of religious dancing has been added.

The *goeika* songs were also contributing factors in the creation of a type of folk song known as *ondo*. The word *ondo* has become a generic term for various types of folk songs. Usually these songs are antiphonal, with a soloist being answered by a chorus. Like the word *bushi*, *ondo* is used as a suffix: for example, there is *akitaondo* from the Akita district and *fukuchiyamaondo* from the Fukuchiyama area.

Among the most common types of *ondo* are those used to accompany the dances of the *obon* festival. This is perhaps the best known of all Buddhist festivals. It is a sort of All Souls' Day and occurs in mid-July or mid-August, depending on the locality. The dances of this festival, the *bon odori*, are the most widespread not only in Japan but also among Japanese communities overseas and come in a great variety of styles. Like the folk songs mentioned earlier, the older dances use no instrumental accompaniment; instead there is a chorus of singers, with the dancers themselves sometimes entering into the song (Plate 24). Those pieces dating from the Edo period, however, frequently use flute, drum, and *shamisen* or, more recently, cassette recordings with modern arrangements. *Bon odori* are usually done in a circle with the musicians (or tape machine) in the center, often on a tower (*yagura*) festooned with a red-and-white cloth. The most common style of these dances is rather easygoing, perhaps in keeping with the languid mood of the summer evenings on which they are performed. Plate 24 shows a characteristic movement of both the feet and the rest of the body. Fans are often used along with simple hand gestures. Both men and women dance *bon odori*, and there is usually no difference in choreography between them. In fact, like other styles of Japanese dance, *bon odori* can be described as "hermaphroditic." Like many a Buddhist statue, it seems sexless, although this does not mean that it is not sensual. Such eroticism as may arise from the mass movement of a circle of Japanese girls and boys in summer kimono, however, is more cumulative than direct. Though there are some very lively *bon odori*, most of them are rather restrained, a form of simple community dancing in which the steps are easy enough for anyone to join in.

Among the more specialized Buddhist folk dances, the best known are the *nembutsuodori*. These are said to have derived from the *nembutsu* section (literally, the calling of the name of Buddha) of some Buddhist ceremonies. In old paintings one can see groups of priests prancing about and beating gongs while performing *nembutsu*. Such priests also wandered the streets (Plate 19). A popularization of a *nembutsuodori* is said to have been the first dance by the founder of *kabuki*. As this form evolved among ordinary people it took on several interesting characteristics. Unlike *bon odori*, these dances are not done by mixed groups but by men or women separately, the men often carrying drums and the women wearing straw hats, with their sleeves tied back, moving not in a circle but usually in a procession. The accompaniment was originally *wasan* or *nembutsu* music, but various percussion instruments and a flute were added later, and nowadays the *shamisen* is also sometimes used. The *nembutsuodori* itself has become quite mixed into the general field of folk theatricals so that it is no longer always possible to say that a certain dance is "authentic."

In addition to Buddhist folk music and dances there are many festivals based on Buddhist themes. One of the most colorful is the birthday of Nichiren (November 12). On this day, the followers of that sect form great processions, with everyone dressed in white, and large floats and umbrellas festooned with paper flowers carried through the streets. The striking musical element is a massed band of flutes and fan drums (*uchiwadaiko*). The whole event is strongly reminiscent of the processions pictured on the bas-reliefs found in the ruins of ancient civilizations of the Middle East.

For those who are able to explore the countryside, there are a host of special local festival events to see. One of the most spectacular Buddhist dances is the *shikaodori*, the deer dance, from Iwate prefecture (see Plate 25). There are many kinds of lion and deer dances in which the dancers also beat drums, but few can match this one in dramatic movement. With two plumes towering out of their backs, a large drum in front, and a fearsome mask covering their faces, the dancers stride about with forbidding dignity. Suddenly, one will bend forward and the two plumes will smash against the ground in a whirl of dust. The thin melody of a bamboo flute seems hardly adequate to keep these awesome creatures under control. They look so belligerent that one almost expects them to begin fighting each other. This *shikaodori* is an excellent example of the more virile type of Japanese dancing that is often unknown to the cosmopolitan student of Japanese culture.

The above survey has only scratched the surface of the immense field of Japanese religious folk music. However, even in such a cursory study one can see how thoroughly the religious traditions have impregnated the folk field. Buddhist folk music equals Buddhist classical music theory as one of the most fruitful areas of study in Japanese music.

## 3. Christian Music

Catholic Portuguese priests first came to Japan in 1594, and as part of their missionary work, Western chant and hymn singing was taught. The first printing of Western music in Japan, in fact, was a 1605 edition of the *Cantus Gregorianus* in Nagasaki. Christianity, however, was suppressed in the early seventeenth century by the Tokugawa shogunate, which saw it as a potential danger to its own power. Still, there were congregations on some of the smaller Japanese islands and in the mountain villages that remained untouched and continued to practice their new religion as best they could remember it, in the absence of any priests to serve them. These "hidden Christians" (*kakure kirishitan*) were not discovered until 1865, when religious tolerance returned. After more than two hundred years of secret services, the oral tradition of these congregations had changed the original rites and music almost completely. It is fascinating to listen to the men[25] chant nonsense syllables which occasionally contain such combinations as "Maria," "deus," or "sanctus."

Before the Jesuit priests left centuries ago, they had warned the converts to avoid false priests (i.e. Protestants and other Catholic orders). Thus, most congregations did not join the "new" religions of the Meiji period, and remain a separate sect to the present day.

Protestant missionaries were not active until the late nineteenth century. Their music was much the same as Christian music elsewhere and had little effect on indigenous music. The latter in turn did not have much effect on this imported religious music. There are a few folk songs which are claimed to be based on old Christian hymns or Catholic chant, and there may be hymns based on Japanese folk songs. In the latter case, the debilitating effect of harmony has rather destroyed any charm the tunes may have had originally. In general, the relatively late arrival of Christian music, its suppression, and its revival in the wake of Japan's modernization kept it outside the world of traditional Japanese music. As an example of the way it kept its distance, one missionary proudly wrote in as late as 1921 that Japan was turning to civilized Western music and away from those "old-fashioned strumming oddities."[26] There is plenty of reputable Christian music in Japan, but there is nothing particularly Japanese about it. The *Messiah* in Japanese is still the *Messiah*.

Christianity, however, has had other effects on contemporary Bud-

---

25. No women sing though they are present in the circle around an altar that has crosses, Virgin Marys, Buddhas, and other religious icons on it.
26. Isabelle McCausland. "Music in Japan Today," *Musician*, XXVI (Nov. 1921), p. 4.

dhism. There are organs in several major temples. Fighting fire with fire, some branches of Buddhism have begun to issue hymn books with special editions for their expanding foreign missions. In the missionary context, one can point to the fact that in many Japanese hotel rooms one can now find English / Japanese Buddhist tracts, often next to or in lieu of Gideon bibles.

## 4. Summary

Looking back over our entire discussion of religious music, it can be seen that the various forms of Japanese religious folk music share many musical characteristics. The choreography, location, costume, and *raison d'être* of each event may be different, but the accompaniment is still built around singing, the flute, and some percussion. The later entrance of the *shamisen* has also been noted. From this study the tremendous intermingling of Buddhist and Shinto elements in all regions of art and life can be seen. The point was made that frequently the same pieces are used for Buddhist and Shinto ceremonies, with only the words changed.

On the classical music level, the adoption of the standard Shinto trios of *wagon*, *hichiriki*, and *kagurabue* was mentioned. The close connection of the various Shinto dance forms with court ceremonies and with the secular theatrical entertainments of the nobility should be remembered.

Finally, the importance of early Buddhist music theory and practice must be emphasized once more. *Shōmyō*, *wasan*, and their Chinese-inspired methodologies form a base from which one can watch the world of Japanese music blossom into the host of more familiar forms by which it is known today.

2. Some tomb figurines (*haniwa*) evoke the music, song, and dance of ancient Japan.

3. An outdoor performance o
the *wagon* zither. Note the hig
bridges.

4. The *kagura azuma asobi* dance costume shown in the *Bugakuzu* (1905).

5. On the right, a dancer-priestess (*miko*) with *suzu*.

6. A *shirabyōshi* dancer from *Kabu ongaku ryakushi* (1888).

A young festival ensemble travels on
*yatai* cart during the Sanja festival
Asakusa, Tokyo.

8. The *atarigane* is played inside the gong.

9. The devil dancers of the Yasurai festival in Kyoto use a gong called the *surigane*. They also carry *taiko* drums.

10. A *satokagura* performance of the white fox in Asakusa, Tokyo. Note the *suzu* bell tree in his hand and the accompanying *daibyōshi* drum.

1. A lion dance (*shishi mai*) is popular in Japanese festivals whether done by two dancers or only one.

85

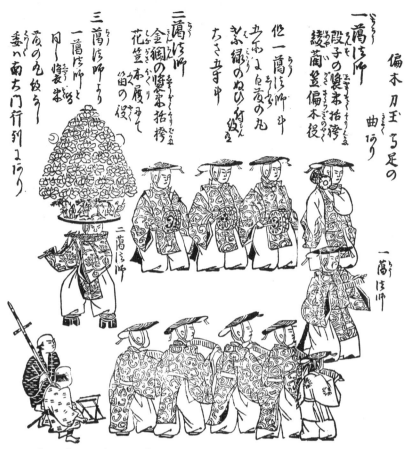

12. Drums, rattles, a flute, and a giant flowered hat are part of a *dengaku* ceremony at the Kasuga shrine in Nara. From *Kasuga ōmiya wakamiya gosaireizu* (1716).

13. The opening procession of the *yuki matsuri* in the mountain village of Niino in Nagano prefecture, 1956. Two firemen in uniform protect the box of dance masks.

14. The *binzasara* rattle and drums on the *kaguraden* at the *yuki matsuri* reflect old traditions seen in Plate 12.

15. Shinto chanting (*semmyō*) with drum and bell tree accompaniment at the *yuki matsuri*.

16. The "Modoki" is one of a series of dances performed in the all-night celebration of the *yuki matsuri*.

17. A large wooden fish-mouthed gong *(mokugyo)* sits ready for use as Buddhist priests chant while circling the altar.

18. Buddhist *wasan* singing is often accompanied by the *ōdaiko* drum.

19. A print from the *Seikyoku ruisan*, vol. 5 (1839), showing various types of street music of Edo. *Ōgibyōshi*, top left, *saimon*, top right, and *nembutsu* priests.

20. Edo period *kado sekkyō*, *utabikuni*, and *yotsudake* performers from the *Seikyoku ruisan*.

21. A *chindonya* trio in action, Tokyo 1956.

22. An itinerant priest on Enoshima chants prayers to the accompaniment of an *uchiwadaiko* drum.

23. Members of a Buddhist congregation of the Jōdo sect performing *goeika* music and dancing.

24. *Bon odori*, such as this 1956 example from Miyakejima, are common Buddhist-inspired folk dances in Japan.

5. The Iwate deer dance
one of the most spectac-
lar folk theatricals (*geinō*)
Japan.

6. This eighteenth-century screen painting of the great Buddha ceremony held at the Tōdaiji in the eighth century shows *bugaku* musicians
nd dancers performing before the temple.

27. *Rinyūgaku*, an exotic form of court music still shown in the four-teenth-century *Shinzeikogakuzu* scroll.

28. The "Genjōraku" dance as pictured in the *Shinzeikogakuzu* scroll.

29. The rare *gogenbiwa* from the Shōsōin shows floral designs on its back and a Central Asian scene on the front.

1. Drawings copied in the *Kabu ngaku ryakushi* (1888) from the ourteenth-century *Shinzeikogaku- i* include the *biwa* lute and *shō* outh organ along with instru- ents no longer heard in Japan ich as the *kugo* harp and the 5*kyō* rack of metal plates.

箜篌

琵琶

方啓

笒笙

1. A courtly ensemble scene in the fourteenth-century *Sumiyoshi onogatari* scroll.

32. The imperial *gagaku* orchestra in the palace music hall. They represent one of the oldest orchestral traditions in the world.

33. A *bugaku* ensemble accompanying dance at the Gion shrine in Kyoto. Note the lack of stringed instruments.

. The *bugaku* dance "Taiheiraku."

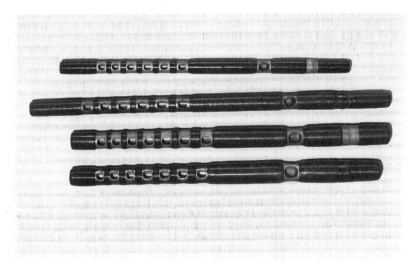

**35.** Four kinds of flutes: (from the top) the *komabue*, *kagurabue*, *ryūteki*, and *nōkan*.

36. A giant *dadaiko* drum bei
played during a cherry blosso
festival at the Gion shrine
Kyoto.

37. A large *shōko* gong with an
elaborate stand at the Gion shrine
in Kyoto.

# CHAPTER THREE

# *GAGAKU*, THE COURT MUSIC OF JAPAN

## 1. The History of Court Music

In the summer of 752, the great image of Buddha at the Tōdaiji in Nara was finally completed. To celebrate this august event, the emperor and all his court traveled to the great hall and presented their felicitations to the Buddha with all the dignity and grandeur at their command. Eloquent speeches were read by state ministers, hymns of praise were sung by large choruses of priests, and the full company of court musicians and dancers numbering in the hundreds provided regal spectacles suitable for both the rulers of heaven and of earth (see Plate 26). The music for this performance was *gagaku*, the court music of Japan. We noted earlier that *gagaku* is still part of some Buddhist ceremonies, but we will now follow its path through the halls of emperors' palaces and the mansions of noblemen and warriors.

The word *gagaku* means "elegant, correct, or refined music." *Bugaku* is the term used when this music is used to accompany dances. Instrumental performance without dance is called *kangen*. Under the continual patronage of the court since the sixth century, this music is perhaps the oldest extant orchestral art music in the world. Through all the vicissitudes of Japanese imperial history, a hard core of *gagaku* music tradition has managed to survive, and because of its direct influence from the musics of the Asian continent, inferences can be made as to the type of music played in the ancient courts of India and China. In short, *gagaku* is one of the most unique forms of music in the world: a living museum for the musicologist or cultural historian and a rare and exotic delight for the general music lover. Before discussing the variety of instruments used in *gagaku* and the structure of its music, one must first review its distinguished genealogy in order to fully appreciate its right to the title of "elegant music."

There are three great continental traditions that form the beginnings of *gagaku*: the ancient music of India, China, and Korea. Korean music seems to have been the first importation. There are references to it as early as the third century, and further indications of its importation in the fifth century. The major influx of Korean music did not occur, however, until the seventh and eighth centuries, when Japan opened its mind to the cultural influences of the entire continent.

The various waves of Korean music that entered Japan went under the names of the particular kingdoms in Korea from which they came (*shiragi-gaku* in 453, *kudaragaku* in 554, later *komagaku*, etc.). However, the music was not necessarily pure Korean music, since the Korean courts were themselves under constant Chinese influence. In fact, the Chinese form known as *gigaku* (remnants of which are found in certain Japanese folk lion dances) is said to have been introduced into Japan in 612 by Mimashi, of the kingdom of Kudara in southern Korea. There is even a hint of Manchurian music coming to Japan via Korea. All this complex of music was first classified under the general term *sankangaku* (*sankan* meaning the three kingdoms of Korea). Later, it was called *komagaku* as the music derived from the kingdom of Koma came to predominate.

Another foreign style of music that entered Japan came from a land very far from Korea, India. In Chapter Two, Indian priests were mentioned as having done missionary work in Japan. According to a traditionally accepted account, an Indian and a Southeast Asian priest came to Japan in 736 and introduced the music and dances of their respective homelands. This music was named *rinyūgaku* after a kingdom in Southeast Asia. One such ensemble is seen in Plate 27. Some of these pieces survive in the modern court repertoire though most of their instruments do not. Their dances are particularly distinctive in their use of grotesque masks which seem very un-Japanese. The choreography of the "Genjōraku" dance, in which a masked dancer exorcises a snake, has even been traced by some to an ancient Indian legend (Plate 28). The accouterments and choreography of the *rinyūgaku* dances seem quite unique, and one can only wonder what traces of the original music might remain in an orchestra so thoroughly Sino-Japanese.

The paramount foreign influence in *gagaku*, as in all things Japanese, came from China. During the Nara and Heian periods Chinese music poured into Japan via returning priests, envoys, musicians, and students. In 734 the ambassador, Kibi no Makibi, brought back the ten-volume Chinese *Digest of Music Matters* (in Japanese the *Gakusho yōroku*). Like the Buddhist music materials mentioned in Chapter Two, Chinese court music sources resulted in later Japanese expansions of them. In 1233 a court dancer, Koma no Chikazane, produced the *Kyōkunshō*, a similar ten-volume set in Japanese. Also, the Japanese Imperial Music Bureau (Gagakuryō), established in 701, was filled with Tang dynasty musicians and a good number of Koreans. If compared with nineteenth-century America, these men were like the Germans and Italians who controlled American musical activities.

The Chinese music found in *gagaku* seems to have been originally developed as banquet music rather than for ceremonial purposes. The greatest source of Chinese ceremonial music was found in the Korean court, where ancient texts and contemporary practice reveal a rich tradition of Confucian ceremonies and dances quite lacking in Japan and now rare in China itself (see Biblio. ref. 1·10, II, 206).[1] Of course, some such music did come to Japan either directly or via Korea. But it makes sense that returning students, though scholars, should have been more familiar with the banquet music of their Chinese university towns than with the formalities of the Chinese court.

By the ninth century, *gagaku* had incorporated a confusion of different types of music, each with its special instrumentation and style. Music by Japanese composers, known as *wagaku*, was not deemed worthy of performance at the Imperial Music Bureau. Such "homegrown" music was relegated to a separate, less exalted area of the palace, the "big-song hall" (*ōutadokoro*).

This wide variety of music probably placed a considerable strain on the imperial coffers, and was not designed to produce polished music specialists. The need for reform was evident, and the retired emperor Saga with the aid of a group of noblemen spent the better part of the years from 833 to 850 trying to bring order to this chaotic situation. In eighteenth-century Europe it was the so-called Mannheim school of composers who standardized Western orchestral instrumentation. In ninth-century Japan it was

---

1. It is still played in Korea and Taiwan.

Saga and his followers who created the standard *gagaku* orchestra. In addition to limiting the number of instruments, they also organized the repertoire into two main categories. Indian and Chinese music was combined under the classification of *tōgaku* (also known as "music of the left"), while the many styles of Korean music and Manchurian music were classified as *komagaku* (or as "music of the right"). In addition, some of the old dance pieces were rearranged, and new Japanese pieces were commissioned. The origin of the distinction between "left" and "right" music is open to debate, but it smacks very much of the Confucian ideals in which a Japanese gentleman of that period was trained.[2] It may also have influenced the content of the two traditions. Since there were more *tōgaku* pieces available than there were *komagaku* works, some pieces were transferred and new Japanese compositions in the *tōgaku* style were also added to *komagaku* to make the categories as symmetrical as the dances performed within them. In this process, much of the original Korean flavor was lost.

By the middle of the Heian period, *gagaku* had become extremely popular at court. Not only was it a necessary element in all ceremonies, but the courtiers themselves also played it (see Plate 31). In a political system in which cloistered emperors often controlled retired emperors who in turn directed ministers who controlled the ruling emperor, there was a surfeit of smaller courts whose problem was more one of ennui than of affluence. Amateur groups, known as *miasobi* or *gyoyū*, flourished among the courts of these shadow emperors. In addition to selected Chinese pieces, new vocal forms were popular: *rōei*, chanted Chinese poems; and *saibara*, *gagaku*-patterned folk songs. The latter stand in about the same relation to folk music as do the more "folksy" Haydn symphonies. Descriptions of these amateur musicals are preserved in *The Tale of Genji* and other literary works of the period. They remind one slightly of scenes from the court of Frederick the Great of Prussia or from the Esterhazy estate in Austria.

In speaking of the *shirabyōshi* dancers in Chapter Two, mention was made of another very important form of court vocal music, *imayō*, or "contemporary songs." This music had a double origin. One beginning, mentioned earlier, is found in the simple hymns (*wasan*) that were created by evangelistic Buddhist priests for missionary work. These *imayō* might be compared in function to the Bowery hymns of the Salvation Army. The

---

2. Note the Confucian symmetry of the dance in Plate 34.

second type of *imayō* originated when someone became tired of learning the court orchestral music by solfège and decided to put poems to the melodies. This is the reverse of the instance found in Western music history in which syllables were taken out of a poem to form our solfège (*do, re, mi*). In the court form of *imayō*, many different poems were imposed on one melody (in much the same way that "John Brown's Body Lies A-Molding in His Grave" or "The Battle Hymn of the Republic" share a tune with other texts). This music was, in effect, the "popular" music of the court, and the "hit" tune was the melody of "Etenraku" (Figure 10). These so-called *etenraku imayō* were often used by female entertainers with words suited to the occasion or to the mood of their patrons. A late Heian addition to such court entertainments was a special ceremony held before the emperor where music called by the informative term *enzui*, or "poolside drunkenness," was played.

The Heian period represents the zenith of aristocratic power and affluence. During the subsequent Kamakura period, the warriors predominated and *gagaku* suffered accordingly along with the other pastimes of the courtier. In the courts of the Kamakura and Muromachi rulers, a new form of banquet or party music appeared called *enkyoku* or *sōga* ("fast songs"). Though the text of *enkyoku* recorded in anthologies seems edifying enough, the manner of performance by partying warriors is thought to have been rather different from the rigid formality one associates with the imperial court. Party music, however, tends to have a notoriously short life span, and little is known about these melodies.

Unfortunately, some of the instrumental music of *gagaku* itself was lost as well during the military periods that followed the Heian. The tradition of passing down the secrets of each instrument's music through one clan caused major losses when big orchestras were broken up and scattered by the destruction of war. In the hope of preserving the tradition, the *Taigenshō* was written in 1512 by the court musician Toyohara Muneaki; but there were few musicians who had an overall grasp of the subject, and at one time the court was hard pressed to find enough performers for a single ceremony.

Eventually, however, the military themselves found *gagaku* of use. With the founding of the Tokugawa dynasty in the seventeenth century, the remaining musicians were split into two groups, one in Kyoto with the emperor and the other in Edo with the shogun. This system remained in place throughout the Tokugawa period, and it was only with the coming of Western culture after the Meiji Restoration that *gagaku* was reduced to one ensemble at the palace in Tokyo (which also had to play Western music), plus various smaller groups at scattered temples and shrines.

Thus, the art that was the responsibility of hundreds of musicians and dancers at Tōdaiji in the eighth century lay, by the mid-twentieth century, in the hands of some twenty men at the imperial palace and their few colleagues elsewhere. However, the many unique features of *gagaku* soon attracted an international audience. There were world tours, new compositions by both Japanese and Western composers, and performance groups formed outside Japan. It is a pleasure to know that this ancient tradition will survive and change. There is an anthropological term called "marginal survival" which indicates that the oldest versions of any tradition are best found, not at their point of origin, but rather at the furthest point traveled from it. Perhaps in the near future Japanese *gagaku* will be best heard in California or Texas.

## 2. The Instruments

*Gagaku* is the earliest significant instrumental form in Japanese music. It can be called orchestral since it has instruments in each of the three basic units—percussion, strings, and winds. Collectively they produce a sound that seems ancient and grand. At the same time they can be said to use a chamber music sound idea that is characteristic of most Japanese ensemble music. No matter how large the ensemble may be, one tends to hear each type of instrument as a separate unit. Their sounds do not meld together as in Western, harmonically oriented orchestral music. Rather, the performance style and distinctive color of each type of instrument separate the lines as they move in a horizontal direction, with only the mouth organ providing some vertical sound.

The study of *gagaku* instruments has yet another special appeal. In 756, the household goods of the late emperor Shōmu and other objects from the Tōdaiji temple were placed in a storehouse called the Shōsōin. Through all the strife of history and ravages of time, forty-five musical instruments survived in this unique collection. Thus we will sometimes be able to refer to eighth-century models as we describe contemporary instruments.

## PERCUSSION

Perhaps the most impressive feature on entering the imperial *gagaku* room is the sight of the two monstrous *dadaiko* drums (Plate 36). These huge drums are used to add a ponderous quality to the choreography of certain dances. It is quite an effect when the dancer shifts his weight from his heel to his entire foot in coordination with the roof-shaking thud of the *dadaiko*.[3] This tone is produced by means of two heavy, lacquered beaters (Plate 36), which are always struck in a left-right sequence. The skin is not as immense as it appears from a distance. The area of skin beyond the rim of the body of the drum is actually a separate piece from the central playing section. The use of separate skins is necessary because a single hide could not cover such a large area and still be capable of enough tension to produce a sound. Twisting the ropes that secure the two heads with large wooden pegs affects the pitch of the drums even though each skin is not one continuous piece. The musical tone of this drum is nil, but its psychological effect is tremendous, which is why it is used only in *bugaku* dance pieces.

The next drum in size is the *taiko*. This comes in different forms, depending on whether it is to be used in a performance hall, played standing, or used in a parade. The standard *gagaku taiko* is called a *gakudaiko* or sometimes a *tsuridaiko*. The drum has two tacked heads and is suspended on a stand in front of the player (Plates 31 and 32). Only one side is struck. This is done by means of two sticks (*bachi*) with leather heads. In keeping with the mythical symbolism of *gagaku*, the left-hand beat is female and the right-hand beat male, and serves to identify the larger phrase units by means of rhythmic time marking.

*Tsuridaiko*

The bronze gong that can be seen suspended on a small stand to the left of the *taiko* in Plate 32 serves another time-marking function. This gong, called a *shōko*, also comes in three sizes, depending on where it is used. As one can see in Plate 37, it is played on the inside by means of two hard-tipped sticks. Its function is to further subdivide the musical phrase by means of single beats. In

*Shōko*

3. Only male performers are used in imperial *bugaku*, though women may take lessons and perform elsewhere.

practice, it is usually heard on the first beat of every measure, with a special added anterior stroke every four bars (listen to CD track 5). Its metallic sound supplements nicely the tone of the drums.

Whenever a group of instruments is performing, it is the custom all over the world to appoint one person as the leader. In the West it is usually the first violinist or a specialist, the conductor. In the Orient, this duty is usually given to a drummer. In *gagaku* it is the player of the *kakko*, a small horizontal drum with two lashed heads made of deerskin (Plates 32 and 33). Unlike the other drums mentioned, both heads are used.

*Kakko*

The two drumsticks employed are built more lightly because two of the three basic patterns used on the *kakko* are types of rolls. One is a slow roll (*mororai*) done with both sticks, and the other is a gradually quickening roll done on the left skin (CD track 5). The other pattern consists of a single tap with the right stick. This drum regulates the tempo of the piece by means of these various patterns and, unlike the more rigid time-marking instruments mentioned above, is used prominently in free rhythmic sections as well as just to mark off the passage of a certain number of beats or phrases. The drum is featured in *tōgaku*.

When *komagaku* music is performed, the leader does not play the *kakko* but uses the *san no tsuzumi*, a larger hourglass-shaped drum of Korean origin. The *san no tsuzumi* is also laid on its side and has two lashed heads although only one is struck. Ancient scrolls show interesting pictures of this

*San no tsuzumi*

drum which indicate that it may originally have been played with bare hands (see Plate 27). It is the only one remaining of a series of four different hourglass-shaped drums that were used in ancient times.

These are the basic percussion instruments of *gagaku*. Their notation is discussed in Appendix I. Simply stated, the systems involve a series of dots to represent the basic beats and special Japanese characters to indicate the type of strokes to be used. I should also mention again the *shakubyōshi*, two simple sticks that are beaten together by the chorus leader during *gagaku* vocal pieces. A more ancient form of clapper may be seen in the hands of the first musician on the left end of the group in Plate 27. This instrument is related to the folk *binzasara* mentioned in Chapter Two (Plate 14). Some metal plates from the *hōkyō* rack shown in Plate 30 were also found in the Shōsōin, but the use of this instrument in ancient Japan remains obscure.

STRINGS

There are only three stringed instruments used in contemporary *gagaku*. The first is the *wagon*, already discussed in the previous chapter. A comment should be added on Plate 3, which shows an example of *tachigaku*, "standing music." For such outdoor performances, extra men, called *toneri* or *kotomochi*, are added to the ensemble to hold the *wagon* for the player. This humble task does not prevent them from wearing splendid costumes.

*Gakusō*

The second *gagaku* string instrument is called the *gakusō*, *sō*, or *koto*, a thirteen-stringed predecessor of the later popular Japanese zither (Plate 55). Though it is built with all the potentialities of its successor, its use is very restricted in *gagaku*. Both finger picks (*tsume*) and bare fingers are used to play the *gakusō*, but unlike the regular *koto*, the strings are never pushed down behind the bridges to produce additional tones. Like the *koto* (and unlike the *wagon*), the strings, with the exception of the bottom one, are tuned in an ascending scale. There are different tunings for each *gagaku* mode. The use of the *gakusō* resembles the *wagon* in that it plays only a few stereotyped patterns plus occasional short melodies or graces. The two basic patterns are *shizugaki* and *hayagaki*, seen in Figure 9. Since the instrument is tuned according to the tonality of the piece being played, the actual pitches of these two patterns may vary. As seen in Figure 10 (second line from the bottom), a pattern may begin on different pitches within a piece. The choice relates to the melody, although—as the score in Figure 10 shows—its principal function is to mark off sections of the music, without being genuinely melodic.

**Figure 9.** The two *gakusō* music patterns

The remaining string instrument in *gagaku* is the *biwa* or *gakubiwa* (Plate 30), the latter term being used to differentiate it from later models. This pear-shaped lute has four strings and four frets and is played with a small plectrum. The *gakubiwa* is also used to mark off the passage of time, accomplished by means of arpeggios, which sometimes have a two- or three-note melodic fragment at the end (see Figure 10, bottom

*Gakubiwa*

line of score). Set in the matrix of the full *gagaku* ensemble sound, however, the effect of the *gakubiwa* is primarily rhythmic. Its notation is mentioned in Appendix I. In closing, it should be noted that, unlike later *biwa* techniques, the strings of the *gakubiwa* are pressed down only on the frets, not between them.

Before we leave the topic of stringed instruments, we should mention some of the treasures that survived in the Shōsōin, referred to earlier. There are five *biwa*, all inlaid with elaborate designs, many of which reflect the richness of continental Asian trade in ancient times. Outstanding in this respect is the defunct five-stringed *gogenbiwa* (Plate 29), with its inlaid motifs of a camel and palm tree oasis on the front and traditional Middle Eastern floral designs on the back. Though drawings of this instrument are found on the continent, it is literally one of its kind in East Asia.

The Shōsōin contains parts of another rare string instrument, a *kugo* harp. Its shape can be traced back to the ancient Middle East. Another design of a *kugo* is seen in Plate 30. Neither harp seems to have been used in Japan except as part of an imitation of Tang dynasty orchestras or of the angelic ensembles seen in Buddhist frescoes from Central Asia and China. An elegant Chinese *qin* zither is also to be found in excellent condition in this fascinating imperial warehouse. The *qin* was used for solo music in mansions and temples. In Chapter Seven we will note the continuance of a *qin* tradition to the present day in both China and Japan.

## WINDS

We now come to the heart of the *gagaku* orchestra. The wind section of *gagaku* plays an analogous role to that of the strings in a Western symphony orchestra. It is the winds that carry the main melodic line and add the distinctive harmonic milieu so characteristic of *gagaku* music. Because they are the mainstay of this music, they also are heir to many interesting legends and historical commentaries.

The *hichiriki* (Plates 32 and 33), a short, double-reed woodwind, is perhaps the most controversial instrument in Japanese music. The sharp-tongued Sei Shōnagon in her eleventh-century diary *The Pillow Book* has the following

Hichiriki

**FIGURE 10.** The *hyōjō* mode "Etenraku" in Western transcription

107

remarks to make about it (Biblio. ref. 1·10, II, 993): "The horrible sound of the *hichiriki* is like the noisy crickets of autumn. I can't stand to be in the same room with that sound. One festival day, when I was in the waiting room attending upon her Majesty, I was entertained by the lovely sound of someone playing the flute. Then suddenly another person joined in on the *hichiriki*. It made my hair stand on end!"

From historical readings it would seem that people seldom took a moderate view of the *hichiriki*; it was either an abomination or an instrument of great spiritual and musical power. However, even the stories extolling it can be interpreted in two ways. For example, there is a famous episode in the thirteenth-century *Kokon chomonshū* (Biblio. ref. 1·10, II, 990) about a robber who broke into the house of a man named Hiromasa. While Hiromasa hid quaking under the house, the robber proceeded to strip the rooms of everything in sight. When he had left, Hiromasa came out to survey the damage. The house was bare except for one item, a *hichiriki*. The story makes no comment as to why the robber chose not to take the *hichiriki* but goes on to relate that the forlorn Hiromasa picked up his only remaining worldly possession and began to play. Not long afterward the robber reappeared and returned all the stolen goods, saying that he had heard the sound of Hiromasa's *hichiriki* and was so moved by it that he was constrained to give back all he had taken. The story ends with a comment that robbers in the good old days were more sensitive creatures than they are now. We can only wonder what the *hichiriki* players must have been like.

One final tale credits the *hichiriki* with supernatural powers. In the same chronicle there is a story about Enri, a skilled *hichiriki* player, who accompanied his father on a trip to a distant province, where he had been assigned as governor. The people in that area were in dire straits due to a prolonged drought. All their prayers for help had been to no avail, so they pressed the new governor to see what he could do. On hearing this, his son immediately went to the main temple and performed for the gods on his *hichiriki*. Very soon afterward, the sky clouded over and rain began to fall. The *hichiriki* engendered so much rain, however, that there was a severe flood. This heavenly reaction, too, seems open to various interpretations.

By now the reader must have gathered that the tone of the *hichiriki* is rather distinctive. It has the nasality of an oboe but is much broader in sound, due to the thicker reed and the embouchure with which it is played (see Plate 33). This rather loose embouchure is necessary in order to produce the many microtonal variations (*embai*) on the fundamental melody that are characteristic of its music.

The *hichiriki* was probably of Central Asian origin, though it came to Japan from Chinese models and in various sizes. The contemporary *gagaku* instrument is one of the smallest variety, measuring some eighteen centimeters in length and having nine holes, two on the underside and seven on top. The tube is made of specially prepared bamboo and is wrapped with bands of cherry or wisteria bark. The fingering is directly related to the notation (see Appendix I). Through use of the embouchure and special fingering, a chromatic scale can be produced though it is never used as such. Divisions smaller than a half step are characteristic of its playing. In order to appreciate the subtlety of the *hichiriki* melody as seen in the third line of the score in Figure 10, it should be followed in combination with CD track 5.

One interesting aspect of the *hichiriki* and all *gagaku* instruments has to do with the classic way of learning the instrument. Under this system, the student learns the entire repertoire by a mnemonic method (*shōga*) before he ever picks up the instrument. It was noted earlier how this method eventually led to the creation of a new genre of vocal music that substituted poems for the solfège (see *imayō*).

The *hichiriki*, with its strong tone, is the center of the *gagaku* orchestra and is found in all types of *gagaku* music. Over the centuries, its strident tone has preserved the "Gothic" quality of Japanese imperial music and has provided a topic of conversation for delicate-eared court commentators of every period.

*Ryūteki*                        *Komabue*

The other main melodic instrument of *gagaku* is the flute. Three different types are used (Plate 35). The first is the *kagurabue*, already described in Chapter Two. This is used when *gagaku* music is performed with *kagura* or Shinto ceremonies. The second type of flute is the *ryūteki* or *yokobue*. This seven-holed instrument is of Chinese origin and is used for *tōgaku* music. It is the largest of the *gagaku* flutes and closely resembles the *noh* flute, which will be discussed later. The third kind is the *komabue*, a six-holed flute of Korean origin used in *komagaku*, and the smallest of the *gagaku* flutes. One interesting distinction between them all is the color of the piece of brocade that covers the closed end: green for the *komabue* and red for the *ryūteki* and *kagurabue*, as these are the proper colors for their respective dances. It is interesting to note that even in the West today red is still associated with things Chinese.

The notation and technique of the flutes are based on the same principle as that of the *hichiriki* (see Figures 43 and 44 in Appendix I). The flute's musical function is to follow the same basic melody as the *hichiriki* but to vary it slightly as it is played (compare the second and third lines of the score in Figure 10). This simultaneous variation on the same melody by several instruments is known as heterophony.

The last of the wind instruments is the most exotic: the *shō*, a lovely set of seventeen reed pipes that are placed in a cup-shaped wind chest (Plate 33). By blowing into this wind chest through a mouthpiece and closing certain holes in the pipes, a series of ethereal chords can be produced (see top line of the score in Figure 10). The Chinese predecessor of the *shō*, the *sheng*, is said to be the oldest known pipe organ. Tradition claims that it is meant to imitate the cry of the phoenix. The shape of the *shō* is also said to be modeled after that graceful mythical bird.

*Shō*

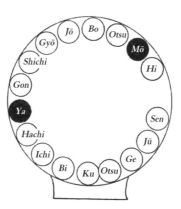

FIGURE 11. The pipes of the *shō*

Figure 11 shows the arrangement of the seventeen pipes of the *shō* in the wind chest and also gives the name of each pipe. Notice that two of the pipes are silent. Research[4] has indicated that they were used in ancient times but are now retained merely to keep the aesthetic balance of the instrument. The *shō* is an interesting compromise of beauty and practicality. Because of the peculiarity of the fingering problem, the pipes could not be arranged like piano keys, in a scalewise order. At the same time, if the pipes assigned to each finger were of the proper length to produce the correct pitch, the shape of the instrument would be very uneven. The compromise consists of two sets of pipes, symmetrically arranged in opposing pairs. On the inner side of the pipes, however, a slit is cut so that the actual acoustical length of the pipes can be varied. The same technique is used in the design of the Western reed organ which, historically, may also have been developed from the Chinese *sheng*. The harmonica and accordion are definite descendants.

The lower end of each pipe contains a thin metal rectangle in which a reed has been cut much in the manner of a harmonica reed. It is a so-called "free" reed. Each of these reeds is tuned by means of a small drop of wax. They are also coated with a special mixture to prevent the collection of moisture. This is the major problem of the *shō* player, as a pipe will not sound if the reed becomes too wet. In order to dissipate any dampness resulting from playing, it is necessary to heat the *shō* over a small charcoal fire. This fire (or now an electric heater) is kept in a white pottery bowl (*hibachi*) which can be seen at every *gagaku* performance. Whenever they have a spare moment, the *shō* players will be seen busily rotating the wind chests of their instruments over the heat.

Although the *shō* does play melodies in certain vocal forms and in *komagaku*, its primary function is harmonic. The eleven chords available on the *shō* can be seen in Figure 45 of Appendix I. The change from one chord to another is accomplished in the middle of the bar (see Figure 10). Each chord is begun quietly and brought to a crescendo just before it is time to change to the next chord (listen to CD track 5). To keep the sound continuous, both inhaled and exhaled air is used. When learning these chord changes, the student sings a simplified version of the *hichiriki* melody, using the names of the chords (derived from the name of the lowest note) as text.

---

4. See Kishibe Shigeo and Leo Traynor, "On the Four Unknown Pipes of the Shō," *Tōyō ongaku kenkyū*, No. 9 (March 1951). This article actually concerns four silent pipes because two different pipes could be used in the position of each one of the now silent tubes. The choice of which to insert depended on the mode of the piece.

Which chords are used is determined by the mode of the composition. Usually they are founded on the basic notes of the melody. However, the use of these chords is different from the Western concept of harmony. In the West chords tend to color a melody and drive it on by setting it in situations of tension which require release: in musical terms, by setting up chord progressions. The chords of the *shō*, however, do not serve this function; rather they "freeze" the melody. They are like a vein of amber in which a butterfly has been preserved. We see the beauty of the creature within but at the same time are aware of a transparent solid between us and the object, a solid of such a texture that the object inside is set off in a very special way. It is the solidifying effect of the *shō* that to a great extent gives *gagaku* its rather transcendental quality. The voice of the phoenix continues to intrigue the ear of man.

The sounds of the *shō* have enchanted Western listeners for decades. They are a source of justifiable pride for Japanese music scholars, who feel that little has changed over the centuries in *gagaku* performance practice. Nevertheless, foreign researchers have been puzzled by the fact that all other mouth organs in Asia basically play melodies and that the exotic tone clusters of the *shō* are found nowhere outside Japan. As shown in Figures 43 and 45 (pp. 284 and 285), the notation for the *shō* part simply contains a name. Is it a melodic outline or a cue sheet for chords, like those used in the West for popular music keyboard accompaniments or the figured bass for the harpsichord in Baroque music? Has it been misread over the centuries? Whatever the eventual academic conclusion, the present state of *shō* music remains a sonic pleasure for the listener and an inspiration for many composers, East or West. As Buddha has said, "All life is change."

Now that the instruments have been explained singly it is time to see how they are combined. There are three basic instrumental combinations: for *tōgaku*, *komagaku*, and *bugaku*. Plate 32 shows a standard *tōgaku* orchestra with three *shō*, three *hichiriki*, three *ryūteki*, two *biwa*, two *gakusō*, and one each of the *kakko*, *shōko*, and *taiko*. The *komagaku* ensemble differs in the fact that the *komabue* is used instead of the *ryūteki* and the *san no tsuzumi* replaces the *kakko*. Nowadays, the strings are also deleted from most *komagaku* pieces, though there are indications that they were used centuries ago. The music for *bugaku* is drawn from both the *tōgaku* and *komagaku* repertoires and hence uses the special instruments of the style of music to which its accompaniment belongs. String instruments are not used to accompany these dances, but the *dadaiko*, as stated earlier, is sometimes employed. The reasoning behind this arrangement is that the function of concert music (*kangen*) is to display the subtleties of the melody, while the function of dance music (*bugaku*) is to accompany. Therefore, a simpler, more rhythmic music is required for the latter. Not only do the instruments change but the style of playing the same piece is different when it is used as *bugaku*. Basically, the difference lies in a more restricted use of the microtonal variations of the melody by the *hichiriki*.

The vocal forms such as *saibara*, *rōei*, and *imayō* use smaller ensembles without drums. Rhythm is kept by means of a *shakubyōshi* clapper in the hands of the lead singer. In such forms, the *shō* occasionally plays the melodic line.

More facts concerning the use of the instruments in the various forms will be discussed in the section on the music itself. Suffice it to say that the instrumentation of each music is rigidly prescribed and based upon a tradition that is, while centuries old, changing over time. Contemporary compositions have used many new combinations of *gagaku* instruments with other sounds, including the electronic. For those of a more romantic bent, one can still just listen to the traditional *gagaku* sounds and dream of what Japan might have been like in ancient times.


## 3. Theory and Practice

### TONE SYSTEMS

As was mentioned in the discussion of Buddhist music, the theoretical tonal basis of Japanese music is Chinese in origin. Figure 7 shows the two main scales of early Japanese music theory, *ryo* and *ritsu*. The Chinese theory[5] provided the same twelve-note, untempered, chromatic scale that is the theoretical, basic tonal material of Western music. With this material the Chinese, like the Western theorists, constructed scales of seven pitches each. These scales were permutated in turn into eighty-four modes. By the time all this theory had been "Japanized," there remained only the twelve

5. For details concerning the Chinese generation of the pitch system see William Malm's *Music Cultures of the Pacific, the Near East, and Asia* (Upper Saddle River, NJ: Prentice-Hall, 1996), 177–78.

basic tones, two basic scale structures, and six modes. The Japanese names of the twelve chromatic tones are shown in Figure 12, starting with the note D, since this is usually used as the basic pitch of the Japanese tonal system. These terms are still used in *koto* music and in writings about ancient music.

FIGURE 12. The twelve Japanese tones

The six modes are divided into three *ryo* and three *ritsu* modes. These are shown in Figure 13. Notice that the *ryo* mode beginning on E has a special name in order not to confuse it with the *ritsu* scale that begins on E.

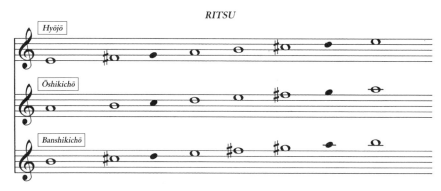

FIGURE 13. The six *gagaku* modes

The basic function of these six modes in *gagaku* is to provide the means of transposing compositions or of playing pieces at different pitch levels. In Western music, when we find that we cannot sing a tune at a certain pitch, we start on a different note and sing exactly the same tune at that new level. This is the usual Western concept of transposition, but the meaning of the term in *gagaku* is different. When a *gagaku* melody is rewritten at a different pitch level, the melody itself is changed. *Gagaku* theory calls these pieces *watashimono*, pieces that have "crossed over." Thus, when a piece is played in a new mode it actually becomes a new composition, a paraphrase of its parent melody.[6] A piece is never moved from a *ritsu* mode to a *ryo* mode but only within the three modes of each system. Pieces originally in the *taishikichō* (the *ryo* E mode) are never transposed. The explanation for all these restrictions is that the instruments of *gagaku* cannot easily play the necessary chromatic tones to make any further transpositions. This is slightly analogous to the limitation of keys in early Western instrumental music caused by untempered tuning.


RHYTHM

The rhythmic theory of *gagaku* allows for three basic rhythmic structures: units of eight, four, or two beats. The eight-beat structure (*nobebyōshi*) is used primarily for slow pieces, and the four-beat unit (*hayabyōshi*) for medium tempo. If a composition mixes units of two and four it is called *tadabyōshi*. When a fast *tadabyōshi* piece is used for dance it is sometimes changed into alternate measures of two and three beats. This beat is called *yatarabyōshi*.


THE JO-HA-KYŪ CONCEPT

So much for the basic theory. The next question is how are pieces actually constructed and held together? The essential aesthetic theory of *gagaku* and of much of the music thereafter is contained in the term *jo-ha-kyū*.

*Jo* means the introduction, *ha* is the breaking apart or exposition, and *kyū* is the rushing to the finish, or the denouement. The theory, as it pene-

6. A comparative score of "Etenraku" in *hyōjō* and *banshiki* modes is found in William Malm, *Music Cultures of the Pacific, the Near East, and Asia* (Upper Saddle River, NJ: Prentice-Hall, 1996), p. 228.

trated the various fields of Japanese music, came to be applied both to entire compositions and to individual phrases. It is analogous to the tenacity with which the binary theory of question and answer or arsis and thesis dominates Western music. In the chapters that follow we shall see more specifically how the ternary concept of *jo-ha-kyū* is applied to other Japanese music.

The pieces of the *gagaku* repertoire are classified as small, medium, and large. The distinction may have originated from the number of men required to perform the accompanying dances. Whatever the origin, it is worth noting that there seem to be differences in the scales and forms of pieces used within these three classifications. The large and medium pieces usually follow the tripartite *jo-ha-kyū* form, though there are indications that some pieces (for example, "Goshōraku") interpolated a fourth section, *ei*, between the *ha* and the *kyū*. The smaller pieces tend to have only a *ha* and *kyū* section. At the present time, it is common to combine various pieces in order to create a *jo-ha-kyū* form.


FORM

The formal structure can best be understood by looking at a full-blown *gagaku* piece and seeing what occurs during the three sections mentioned above. In a dance piece, the *jo* section occurs during the time when the dancer moves from backstage to center stage. In orchestral pieces, this is often the time for a *netori*, a short piece that is meant to set the tone of the mode in which the piece is written. First the *shō* enters with its particularly lovely phrase. This is followed, in turn, by the *hichiriki*, the flute, and finally the *kakko*. Then the *biwa* and the *gakusō* play their rather short melodies. The *netori* is actually a highly refined abstraction of the age-old custom of tuning up. It certainly surpasses the sound of a Western orchestra tootling before the first violinist or the conductor arrives on stage. The *gagaku netori* is a serene, subtle, and archaic flavor that reminds one of a seventeenth-century opera overture, in the style of Monteverdi. At the end of the introductions to certain *komagaku* pieces, the melodic line is taken up by the various winds in what amounts to a short stretto, each beginning at a slightly different time. The temporary chaos of free rhythmic canonic sound is strikingly contemporary.

After an introduction, the main body of the composition begins (CD track 5 starts here). A solo flute opens the main melody with the three percussion instruments (*taiko*, *shōko*, and *kakko*) usually in attendance. After the second main accent of the *taiko* (which normally occurs on the first beat of the seventh bar), the rest of the winds enter, the flutes and *hichiriki* playing the same basic melody, while the *shō* provides a tone cluster as a harmonic matrix. Usually on the last beat of the eighth bar, the first *biwa* arpeggio is played, its accent always coming on the first beat of the measure. On measure thirteen, the *gakusō* enters with its first standard phrase. From there on until the last eight bars or so of the composition, the ensemble plays tutti; there is no further attempt to change the sound. The color of the ensemble's tone is very rich but during the *ha* and *kyū* parts it remains essentially a monochromatic richness.

Though the dynamics and tone color of the orchestra do not change, there is usually a gradual increase in speed as the piece progresses. Finally, a special coda, called a *tomede*, occurs in which only the first-chair musicians perform.[7] The tempo becomes very free, the pace slackens, the chord of the *shō* thins out to two or three notes until ultimately only the *biwa* and *gakusō* are left. They play two or three very slow patterns emphasizing the dominant or tonic note of the mode. The *gakusō* ends the composition with a single plucking of the tonic.

There is one form, called *nokorigaku*, in which the cadences of various repeats of the music are played by different groups, the final cadence being given to the strings. This, however, does not alter the fact that once the basic instrumental sound is conceived, no attempt is made to orchestrate the piece in the Western sense of the term.

Such is the standard procedure for *gagaku* pieces, though the length of compositions varies and specific instrumental entrances do not always occur exactly as stated. The standard form of *gagaku* music is closed, that is, an A-B-A form.[8] In the process discussed above, the *netori* would be an introduction before such an A-B-A and the *tomede* would act as a coda. When one of the vocal forms is performed, like *saibara*, the process is somewhat different. The voice takes the first-phrase solo, marking time with a *shakubyōshi*. The chorus and instruments enter on the second phrase and proceed in the same tutti fashion until the verses are completed. In such

7. A useful but unfortunate Western term since *gagaku* musicians are often sitting on the floor.
8. In "Etenraku" A has two repeated periods (aabb) and B repeats one (cc).

cases there is no final coda. If *rōei* is sung, the first phrase of each stanza is performed by the soloist; during the rest of the time the chorus and instruments (if any) are used.

Much of the pleasure of *gagaku* is in its rare archaic flavor. To those who are accustomed to the dynamic drive of Western symphonic music, the static beauty of *gagaku* may seem very strange. In the West, music has been defined in terms of aural form in motion, but in *gagaku* both the formal and progressive elements have been minimized, leaving only the beauty of sound, the exotic creature in a slightly clouded drop of amber.

Listening to *gagaku* is a history lesson in sound and a transmigration back into the soul of the Heian courtier. As it stands, it is a shadow of its former self and yet it is still one of the clearest adumbrations left of the grandeur and artistic taste of the court of ancient Japan.

# CHAPTER FOUR

# NŌGAKU, THE MUSIC
# OF *NOH* DRAMA

## 1. Introduction

Members of the chorus place their fans before them and the flute rings out
with an ancient melody. The tune floats across the fine-grained expanse of
wood that is the stage, passes briefly the surrounding moat of pebbles, and
informs the audience on the other side that soon the five-colored curtain
over the stage entrance will sweep inward and up to allow the first character to begin his journey along the covered passageway that is said to divide
the spirit world from the real world. A *noh* play has begun.

Such a scene is available to anyone in Japan who can forget the curse of
the clock and pass with the actor over this bridge into another world.
Beyond the aesthetic and literary enjoyment so often extolled by devotees
of the *noh*, in modern times there is also the rare pleasure of a chance to
escape the temporal. That pleasure is never known by the people at concerts
in the West who always rush out during the last movement of a symphony
in order to catch the 5:53 train or to be first in line at the checkroom.

*Noh* is a study in literature, theater, aesthetics, and a type of *gesamt-
kunstwerk*, but for the moment let us examine it simply as music. It must
be understood that *noh*, more than Western opera, is a gestalt of equally
contributing arts, none of which can honestly be said to be more important than the others. Thus, when the bonds that hold them together are
severed temporarily for the sake of discussion, the individual art forms
may seem to be something less valuable than the whole. Few genres of
music are so delicately refined, yet some find listening to it dull or a trifle
undernourishing. Like one dish in a fine Japanese dinner, the flavor of

*nōgaku* can be lost when taken out of its original context. With this in mind, let us turn first to the historical background of *noh* and then its music.

## 2. The History of *Noh* Drama

The prototypes of *noh* were a good deal more raucous than it is in its present form. Its ancestors are not to be found among the stately court dances, as might be expected, but rather in the popular entertainments that offered an alternative to the pomp of Heian ceremonies.

Three types of entertainment are said to form the historical basis of *noh*: *sarugaku*, *sangaku*, and *dengaku*. *Sarugaku*, "monkey music," is believed to have originated as a shrine pantomime ritual-play which was later turned into a comic, popular theatrical. As the theatrical aspect of *sarugaku* grew, Chinese acrobats were included in the program. This genre was called *sangaku*. The *sangaku* acrobats were a part of Heian city life in much the same way that jugglers were an integral part of the market square scene in medieval Europe. The third influence, *dengaku*, or "field music," originated in rice-planting dances performed by the peasants. These were later brought into the court as a relief from the formality of ceremonial choreography (Plate 12).

As *sarugaku* and *dengaku* developed, they became more organized and also more difficult to distinguish. By the Kamakura period, the words *sarugaku-no-noh* and *dengaku-no-noh*, used to denote the two prototype forms, had become almost synonymous. For our purposes, the only differentiation that need be made between these early forms is that *sarugaku* originated as a temple ritual, *sangaku* as acrobatics, and *dengaku* as a folk-dance form.

The popularity of *sarugaku* and *dengaku* was immense among both common people and noblemen. Indeed, there were a host of different theatrical events that vied for the public interest, both inside the temple and shrine compounds and without. Like the medieval morality plays of Europe, various theatrical events appeared in conjunction with religious ceremonies for the enjoyment of the populace and the priests. The most famous remnant of this old tradition is *mibu kyōgen* (Plate 39).[1] These pan-

1. Plate 39 shows the finale of the comic play "Hōrokuwari," which opens every performance. The plates that are being knocked off the edge of the stage are covered with names. By breaking these plates, all sin and bad luck is destroyed. Any plates

tomimes are performed in the compound of the Mibu temple in Kyoto. Their mixture of the comic, religious, and historical is a very good example of the spirit that probably existed in the early days of *noh*.

Among the many theatricals of ancient times, one of the best known was *jushi*, a type of light entertainment performed after the Buddhist New Year ceremonies. This became so popular that it was performed all the year around, and performers were even invited to the various aristocratic estates to give *hirujushi*, "afternoon *jushi*." There was also a form called *ennen*, a type of priestly entertainment that eventually became secular. In the late Heian period, some temples were apparently as busy perfecting their *ennen* repertoire as they were working on their religious chanting. And, finally, mention should be made of *fūryū*, a very ambiguous term that meant a variety of things, from Heian foppery to religious processions similar to the Mardi Gras. At one time the government issued prohibitions against *fūryū*,[2] by which it meant not only street dances and entertainments but also the habit of dressing up in one's very brightest clothes for visiting the shrines on official holidays just to compete for moments of sartorial glory. The Western Easter parade, it seems, is not unique. *Fūryū* is noted in the history of *noh* because one often finds the words *ennen-no-fūryū* or *sarugaku-no-fūryū* in the study of *noh* music. The lively dances and music of *fūryū*, however, should be treated separately as components of a form of folk theater.

*Jushi, ennen, fūryū,* and other such early entertainments all had their influence on the most important precursors of *noh*: *sarugaku* and *dengaku*. The popularity of *dengaku* with the common man is noted in a tale from the *Taiheiki* chronicle, dated ca. 1349 (Biblio. ref. 1·10, I, 712). At that time a competition was held between two leading troupes of *dengaku* players. Stands were set up on a riverbank and a huge crowd assembled to view the show. Partisan feeling must have equaled that of a Western soccer game, for at one point the enthusiasm of the spectators ran so high that the bleachers collapsed. Panic ensued, thieves and soldiers moved in, and the day ended in bloodshed.[3] This did not seem to dampen the popularity of

that survive the fall are destroyed by the hordes of little boys who are always waiting below.

2. For the political aspects of this see Mary E. Berry, *The Culture of Civil War in Kyoto* (Berkeley: University of California Press, 1994).

3. The full tale is translated in P. G. O'Neill, *Early No Drama* (London: Lund Humphries, 1958), 75–77.

*dengaku* or *sarugaku*. In fact, these two forms continued in the public favor even after the founding of *noh* and did not completely decline until the advent of *kabuki* in the sixteenth century.

Another chapter of the *Taiheiki* (Biblio. ref. 1·10, I, 704) tells of the popularity of *dengaku* among the nobility. It relates how the shogun, Hōjō Takatoki (1303–33), invited the two *dengaku* actor clans, the Shinza and the Honza, to his palace in order to see a performance himself. He became so captivated that he neglected his official duties and spent his days enjoying *dengaku*. When these troupes performed, jewels were thrown at the actors' feet until there was a regular mound of precious stones on the stage. One night when the court was having a drinking party, Takatoki, in a drunken state, got up to dance *dengaku* in his elderly and clumsy way. He soon stopped, however, for a group of about fifteen players whom no one recognized appeared at the door. They danced beautifully, and the sound of their lovely voices attracted a lady-in-waiting outside the room. She slid open the door to peek at the actors and to her surprise saw that they were all in the shape of grotesque animals. So she quickly sent for the warrior Tokiaki, who came rushing to the banquet hall with his sword unsheathed, but the players heard him approaching and stole away. When Tokiaki entered the room he found the shogun drunk and asleep, while the light of his lamp revealed the footprints of animals all around the room. On awaking, the shogun remembered nothing of the occasion and feigned indifference to this ghostly occurrence, but the records report that soon afterward he gave up *dengaku* and took to staging dog hunts.[4]

As *sarugaku* and *dengaku* prospered, *sangaku* lost favor, and the acrobats were eventually replaced by comic plays called *kyōgen*, "mad words." The greatest change in these forms, though, occurred in the Muromachi period, when Kan'ami Kiyotsugu (1333–84) and his son Zeami Motokiyo (1363–1444) attempted to instill a more serious manner into *sarugaku-no-noh*. Originally minor functionaries at a shrine in Nara, these men were brought by the shogun Yoshimitsu to Kyoto, where they developed their special form of *sarugaku-no-noh*, later known simply as *noh*. In seeking a proper musical medium for their new form, they borrowed quite heavily from Buddhist chanting (*shōmyō*). This was natural not only because of the

---

4. In 1884 Ichikawa Danjurō based his new *kabuki* play, *Takatoki*, on another version of this legend.

chant's great dignity and solemnity, but also because the stories of the *noh* dramas were very Buddhist in spirit. The original *sarugaku* used an orchestra of three drums and a flute. These were retained in the newly developed *noh*. Thus a one-time Shinto priest, under the patronage of a secular leader (who apparently admired him as much for his looks as for his acting), combined sacred chanting with popular theatrical conventions and sections from well-known verses to produce one of Japan's most unique art forms, the *noh* drama. One might call it the greatest pastiche in the theatrical arts, for though none of the individual elements really originated with either Kan'ami or his son, their combining of these elements into a dramatic mold was an act of true genius.

In the Edo period (1600–1868), *noh* drama was supported not only by the aristocrat and the warrior but also by the rising city merchant class (*chōnin*) and affluent villagers. Public performances became popular and private lessons in the music were taken by members of every class.[5] As we will see, this egalitarian interest in *noh* still survives.

Though the texts for *noh* were based on popular Buddhist ideas, the originators of *noh* were primarily under the influence of the spirit of the esoteric Zen sect. Hence one finds in Zeami's major writings a repeated emphasis on the Zen-derived concepts of restraint and allusion as basic to *noh*. These tenets were followed by the first school of *noh*, the Kanze, and, while there is always change in a living art, they have been retained in the Kanze theater as well as in the major schools of *noh* still active today, the Hōshō, Komparu, Kita, and Kongō.

## 3. The Structure of a *Noh* Play

From behind the curtained stage entrance come the hoarse, wooden tones of the flute playing "Shirabe," the traditional warming-up exercise of every *noh* performance (Plate 41). As the last notes drift away, the curtain swoops upward and the musicians enter in a slow, stately procession. Their order is always the same: first the flute, then the shoulder drum, next the side drum,

5. For a study of Edo *noh* see Chap. 9 in Gerald Groemer's translation of Nishiyama Matsunosuke's *Edo Culture* (Honolulu: University of Hawaii Press, 1997).

and last the floor drum. Two drummers carry *shōgi*, simple, black camp chairs, which they set up in front of the pine and bamboo painting that forms the traditional backdrop of every *noh* stage. As these musicians approach from the left, the chorus (*ji*) enters through a small door at the far right-hand corner of the stage. The drummers and the flutist, collectively called the *hayashi*, sit in a row facing the front of the stage with the shoulder and side drums in the middle, the floor drum to the left, and the flute to the right, as shown in Plate 38. The latter two are seated on the beautiful but hard cypress-wood floor which has been specially polished to reflect the gorgeous costumes of the performers who are soon to appear. The chorus arranges itself on the right-hand side of the stage. Thus, with great serenity and dignity the musicians and singers take their places, and the play can begin.

Thick books have been written about the *noh* plays, their structure, and their philosophy. For our purposes, it is necessary only to understand the basic outline of the plays and how the music fits into this outline. A standard day of *noh* usually consists of five *noh* plays and three *kyōgen* comedies. There are, in addition, separate performances of sections from *noh* plays and "arrangements" of text excerpts. These are found most often in student recitals and derive their musical structures from the basic principles of *noh* itself, as will be explained presently.

*Kyōgen* comedies do not, as a rule, involve music. They are performed in a special type of heightened speech often set within poetic rhythmic units. Certain plays, however, do contain *noh*-style singing or popular songs of the Muromachi period filtered through the *noh* tradition. Since *kyōgen* is comic, these may include parodies of famous *noh* pieces, as well as other short songs (*kouta*) or short dances (*komai*) accompanied by singing. If drums and flute are used during *kyōgen*, they play simplified versions of *noh* music. There are, of course, special differences to be found in the music of *kyōgen*, but for the purpose of this survey, it can be considered essentially as modified *noh* music.

By the seventeenth century the tradition was established that a program of *noh* should include one play from each of five kinds: (1) *kami noh* or *waki noh*, congratulatory plays featuring a god or goddess; (2) *shura noh*, a tale about an ancient warrior; (3) *kazura noh*, literally a "female wig" play in which the main character is a woman; (4) *zatsu noh*, on miscellaneous subjects such as madness (*kyōranmono*), obsession (*shūshinmono*), and "present-day things" (*genzaimono*); and (5) *kiri noh*, closing pieces that include a supernatural figure. Today the number of plays in a performance varies greatly. The musical structure of each play depends on the character portrayed in much the same way that the form of Western operas varies with their plots. By discussing a typical play one can understand these particular variations.

The formal elements of *noh* plays are centered on the actions and emotions of one character performed by the *shite*, or principal actor. The second main actor, the *waki*, serves primarily as a foil for the exposition of the *shite*'s character. There may also be additional actors, *waki zure*.

The aesthetic of the *noh* form is the *jo-ha-kyū* concept (introduction-exposition-denouement) mentioned in our discussion of *gagaku* music. In *noh*, it was traditionally organized into five main units, or *dan*. These were placed in a two-act framework, with usually four sections in the first act and one in the second. It can be outlined as follows:

ACT I

| | | |
|---|---|---|
| *Jo* | 1st *dan* | *Waki* enters |
| *Ha* | 2nd *dan* | *Shite* enters |
| | 3rd *dan* | *Shite* and *waki* talk |
| | 4th *dan* | High point of the act; *shite* may dance and then exit |
| | Interlude | *Kyōgen* |

ACT II

| | | |
|---|---|---|
| *Kyū* | 5th *dan* | A complete act including a dance |

Twentieth-century scholars have placed the five *dan* and tripartite divisions for each act in the following manner:[6]

ACT I

| | | |
|---|---|---|
| *Jo* | 1st *dan* | *Waki* enters |
| *Ha* | 2nd *dan* | *Shite* enters |
| | 3rd *dan* | *Shite* and *waki* talk |
| *Kyū* | 4th *dan* | *Shite* brings plot to high point and dances |
| | 5th *dan* | *Shite* exits |
| | Interlude | *Kyōgen* |

6. Particularly Yokomichi Mario and Omote Akira, *Yōkyokushū* (Tokyo: Iwanami Shoten, 1960, 1963). Yokomichi's new approaches appear in translation in Frank Hoff and Willi Flindt, "The Life Structure of *Noh*," *Concerned Theatre Japan*, Vol. 2, No. 34, 1973.

Act II

| | | |
|---|---|---|
| *Jo* | 1st *dan* | *Waki* waits |
| *Ha* | 2nd *dan* | *Shite* returns, often as a new character |
| | 3rd *dan* | *Shite* and *waki* talk |
| *Kyū* | 4th *dan* | High point of the act, usually ending in dance by *shite* |
| | 5th *dan* | Concluding chorus |

In either form, these *dan* are further subdivided into more specific dramatic, textural or musical units. Some plays are only one act long, and there is great variety in the use and placement of *dan*, as the *noh* repertoire is large and long-lived. It is analogous to the problem one faces when analyzing Bach fugues on the basis of textbook fugue form or trying to fit all of Beethoven's sonatas into one formula. In addition, it is more often scholars than performers who are concerned with such problems. Rather than using one of the theoretical divisions of a play shown above, we will observe the musical conventions in the context of the most usual stage actions.

## 4. Musical Conventions of a *Noh* Play

1) The *waki* entrance. The secondary actor (and colleagues if necessary) enters along the covered passageway (*hashigakari*) that connects the mirror room to the stage. The flute accompaniment (with or without drums) is a *shidai* or *nanoribue*. A *shidai* song might also occur. The *waki* stops near the pillar that connects the stage to the walkway. This is called the *shite bashira* because it is the area where the principal actor often stands, the *waki bashira* pillar being diagonally across the stage where he eventually will be located. The *waki* then gives an introductory recitation (*nanori*) in which he identifies who he is and where he is going. He next crosses the stage toward his pillar area to the sound of a traveling song (*michiyuki*), usually begun by him and carried on by the chorus.

2) The *shite* entrance. The principal actor now travels along the passageway. His (or theatrically her) *shidai* music enhances a visual mood created by a slow-moving mass of ancient costumes and an evocative mask. Stop-

ping at the third small pine along the passageway, the *shite* usually starts the first song (*issei*). This is often followed by a recitation (*sashi*) which is a type of heightened speech like an operatic recitative, serving as a bridge between more lyrical sections. The major types of song (*uta*) in the play are the *sageuta*, which is in the middle and lower ranges, and the *ageuta*, which uses a higher range.

3) The *shite* and *waki* talk. The dialogues are usually marked as a *mondō* (unaccompanied stylized speech) or a *rongi* (more melodic interchange sometimes with drum accompaniment). They are often mixed with lyrical songs in the styles mentioned above. Another particularly poignant type is the lament (*kudoki*); this term is found in much of the *biwa* and *shamisen* lyrical music of later centuries.

4) The plot comes to a high point. The *shite* may dance and then exit. Dialogues, recitations, and songs lead to dance (*kuse*) accompanied by the *hayashi* ensemble, with or without singing, and ending with the chorus.

5) If there is a second act, a *kyōgen* is usually staged by special *kyōgen* actors. It may or may not be related to the central plot of the *noh* play. During this time the main actor is busy backstage changing into the costume and mask of the new role he will play in the second act. Instead of a *kyōgen*, one may hear a *hayashi* interlude in which long moments of silence are broken by the soulful cries of the drummers and by the sparse, resonant drum tones. Sometimes the flute joins in, its lone melody likewise seemingly devoid of rhythm or tempo. The overall effect is literally out of this world.

6) The second act may begin with passages of stylized speech (*kotoba*) and perhaps a waiting song (*machiutai*) before the *shite*'s return (*deha*) as a different person. Another mixture of dialogue, recitation, and song leads to a climactic *kuri* song and a dance (*kuse*). The *kuri* is significant musically because it has the highest note in the composition. The pitch itself is also called *kuri*. During this section the basic emotional tension of the plot is revealed. It is one of the most difficult sections to sing.

7) The highlight of the second act, like the first, is a dance, in which the spirit of the principal character is fully revealed. The general term for *noh*

dance is *mai*. Its music is dependent on the character of the dancer. The accompaniment may be *hayashi* alone. The *shite* and/or the chorus will sing before and after the dance. The dance is known as *shimai* if the chorus sings poetry throughout it. This is often followed by a short poem (*waka*) and finale (*kiri*) sung by the chorus.

# 5. Aesthetics

In the long history of *noh* there have been many rearrangements and distortions of the order outlined above, but it has remained the basic point of departure. There is much satisfaction to be derived from *noh* as good theater, but if one compares it with Western drama, it often seems to be lacking any real plot line. Nothing seems to have happened by the end of the play, and the two acts frequently have little connection. This could be explained by comparing the play with the tea ceremony, which developed concurrently with *noh*. The purpose of both the play and the ceremony lies not in the form but in the objects presented and the atmosphere created. In either case, one should not seek only an intellectual understanding but rather savor the highly specialized aesthetic experience. It must be remembered that the influence of Zen Buddhism, with its love of allusions and its emphasis on non-logical procedures, was strong when *noh* was developed.

In *noh*, everything is restrained in an attempt to produce as pure an aesthetic atmosphere as possible. One cannot approach a *noh* play looking for the Western concepts of extensive plot development or strong character delineations and interrelations. Historical research implies that the slowness of the action was not part of the original productions, but today it offers the audience time to absorb the mood and meaning of the text. The real action may be in one's own heart and mind rather than on the stage. In our modern rushed and action-filled life, perhaps this is the most precious gift *noh* drama has to offer.

# 6. Vocal Music

## SINGING STYLES

The singing of *noh* (*yōkyoku* or *utai*) developed its style from Buddhist chanting. Along with such temple chanting, it has retained through the ages the solemnity and introspection that are associated with religious music. Its spare melodic style has carried the masterpieces of medieval Japanese playwrights over the centuries into the present time. It evolved under the aegis of aristocratic patrons, though we noted earlier how public performances were provided for a growing urban society. The singing tradition still finds support on many social levels. It has remained fashionable as an edifying amateur accomplishment. One of my most pleasant incidental memories of Japan in 1956 was an impromptu concert of *yōkyoku* performed in my little home by a carpenter during his tea break. Decades later another surprise occurred at a University of Michigan reception for a visiting Japanese socio-psychologist. When he learned that I was a musician, he pulled out of his suit coat pocket a small *yōkyoku* songbook that he had carried with him for practice during the plane flight to America. The sensitive Japanese male is fortunate in that there are several such artistic yet "manly" arts in which he may find an outlet. For example, *yōkyoku* (along with karaoke and golf) remains popular with some businessmen. Thus, *noh* singing has found a place in modern society as a social grace as well as an integral part of the theater.

On the stage, *yōkyoku* is sung by both the actors and the chorus. The chorus leader (*jigashira*) is said to control the tempo of the chant by prolonging the sounds; he may even change the melody slightly and the chorus will follow him. In fact, there is a complex process of adjustment constantly going on between the chorus, *hayashi*, and the actors. This elasticity is a prime factor in the fluid movement that lies barely visible beneath the placid surface of the *noh* play.

The special voice quality of *noh* singing originates in the abdomen. Graces and vibratos are added to the tone to give it variety. The pronunciation of the words is an abstraction of ancient styles and further removes the plays from the everyday world. To appreciate *noh* as sound or as literature, it is necessary to steep oneself in a different language much in the way one approaches Chaucer or Shakespeare in the original. In both cases, what is lost in the immediacy of comprehension is gained in the transcendental euphony of words as sound.

*Noh* plays are set in two basic styles. One is called *kotoba*, or "words." This is the heightened speech style mentioned earlier and is used as recitative. The other style is called *fushi*, "melody," which is analogous to the aria sections of an opera. In *noh* there are two basic ways in which these more melodic sections can be performed: *yowagin*, the "soft" style used in lyric scenes, which seems to be the earlier style; and *tsuyogin*, the "strong" style used in masculine and warlike scenes.

## TONE SYSTEMS

Figure 14 shows the two tonal systems, in their theoretical forms, with Western pitches attached for the convenience of readers. The actual pitch of a performance, like much unaccompanied vocal music, is set by the performers. Speaking in general terms, the three pitch centers (*jō, chū, ge*) in the soft style tend to be set a fourth apart (G, D, and A in Figure 14). In the strong style, *jō* and *chū* are considered to be the same (A in Figure 14) and are generally a minor third above *ge* (F-sharp).

As seen in Figure 14, there are raised (*uki*) or lowered (*osae*) versions of the pitch centers. These usually move back to the central tones, particularly in the lyrical style. In Western music, it is analogous to the tendency of the seventh note of the major scale (*ti*) to resolve up (to *do*). This use of upper as well as lower "leading tones" to create melodic tension will be seen to be characteristic of most Japanese music.

Another possible analogy is that *noh* vocal music, like Western counterpoint, has conventional rules for the proper

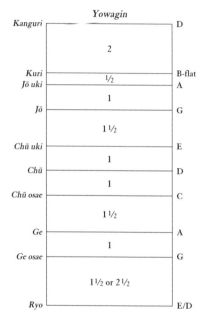
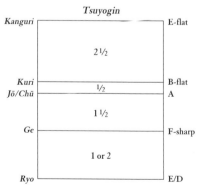

FIGURE 14. The *yōkyoku* tone systems

ways to approach or leave a central tone. Both traditions combine a variety of musical styles and rules to create equally affective melodies, though the sounds are very different.

## RHYTHM

The rhythmic structure of *noh* singing is based on an eight-beat phrase system (*yatsubyōshi*), though it may be treated very freely. The regulations determining the number of syllables sung within these beats are known as *nori*, literally, the way the text "rides" the rhythm. *Nori* can be applied to the general style of an entire composition or to the execution of a single phrase. While the basic text of *noh* tends to use the traditional poetic structure of seven- and five-syllable lines, there are, as in all world literature, many variations. Sung lines generally use one of the basic *nori*. In *chūnori* style ("medium rhythm") there are usually two syllables per beat, and in *ōnori* ("large rhythm") one syllable per beat. However, the most idiomatic style is *hiranori* ("plain rhythm"), in which the twelve syllables of seven-five syllabic lines are placed within eight beats. As these rules are applied to each phrase, they are modified to fit the particular situation.

The rules of *noh* rhythm, like those of Western harmony, fall under two categories: theory and practice. *Jibyōshi* ("basic rhythm") is the term used for theoretical demonstrations of *noh* rhythm. Like the chord progression found in a Western harmony textbook, *jibyōshi* examples are very useful in understanding a music theory, but they seldom look or sound like actual compositions. Examples A and B in Figure 15 demonstrate *jibyōshi* theory and C the practice of the method. Example A sets a line of text from *Matsukaze* in the *jibyōshi* form using the *mitsuji* ("three points") style of rhythm. B shows the same text set in what is called the *tsuzuke* ("continuing") style. C is a transcription of the same passage as heard on CD track 6 (just after the *hayashi* interlude). Listening to the performance, the syllables seem evenly spaced with some retards, but it should be noted that the counts in the mind of the singer are not even, and there may be more than eight beats to a passage. The rhythm of the drum music shown will be discussed later.

Given a music of such elastic rhythm and restricted melodic movement, it is not surprising to find that *noh* notation is not very specific in a Western sense of precise pitches and rhythms. Figure 42 in Appendix I is the notation for the passage transcribed in Figure 15C. It uses neumes plus indications of rhythmic or vocal styles. In practice, there is much that must be learned beforehand in order to sing this notation correctly.

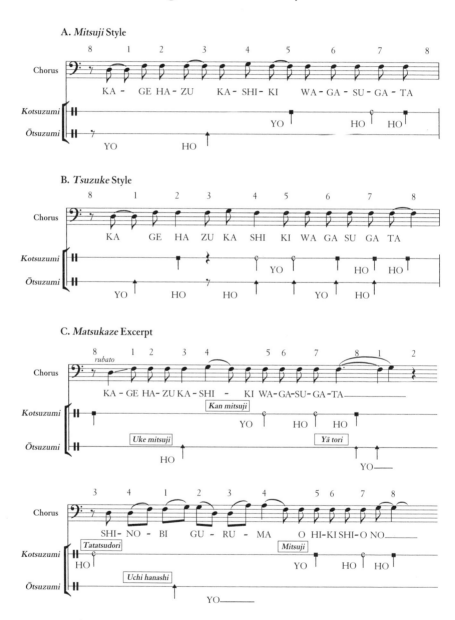

FIGURE 15. Theory and practice in drum-accompanied *noh* vocal music

# 7. Instruments of the *Hayashi*

## THE *NŌKAN*

*Nōkan*

The *noh* flute, called the *nōkan*, is a relative of the *ryūteki*, discussed earlier (Plate 35). Originally some of these flutes were made in an unusual way. A well-dried bamboo tube was split lengthwise into eight or sixteen strips and turned inside out so that the bark was on the inside. This reversed tube was then bound together with another, very thin bark, usually cherry. Only the holes were left unbound. The inside was lacquered red, and the outside wrappings black. Since the inner lacquering made the complicated process of turning the tube inside out largely unnecessary, this method is seldom used today.

The length of the *nōkan* is around thirty-four centimeters, but the internal pipe is only twenty-nine centimeters long, as the flute is solid from the mouth hole to the closed end. Gold relief is often inserted at the end just to emphasize the instrument's beauty and value. Like the *gagaku* flutes, the *noh* flute is fingered in an interesting manner (see Plate 40): the holes are covered by the middle joints of the fingers, not the tips as in most Western flutes. This helps to produce the indistinct, half-holed effects so characteristic of *noh*-flute music. In addition, there are times when the pitch is not changed but the tone quality altered by partly raising one of the fingers.

The performance styles of the three guilds of *noh* flutists—Morita, Issō, and Fujita—are different. Most players produce tones with very strong air pressure. This forceful attack produces a great deal of wind noise that requires a bit of getting used to on the part of the Western listener. The opening sound is often quite piercing and definitely not recommended for small rooms. On the open stage, however, it is quite effective. It must be remembered that originally these dramas were given on an outdoor stage in a palace or temple compound.

The *nōkan* has no definite tuning pitch, as it is the only melodic instrument in the ensemble, but the basic fingerings of the seven holes produce pitches near D, E, G, A, A-sharp, B, and C-sharp. In actual playing, there are a tremendous number of other tonal gradations used. One of the unique features of the *noh* flute is its variation in overblown notes. When one blows strongly on a normal flute it will produce a pitch an octave higher, but overblowing the various fingerings of a *noh* flute produces a variety of intervals from an octave to a minor seventh (like C to B-flat above). The reason for this phenomenon is that a thin tube (*nodo*, literally "throat") has been inserted into the flute between the lip hole and the first finger hole. This tube upsets the normal acoustical arrangement expected from a flute and is one of the most unusual features of Japanese instrumental construction. The origin of this device is not clearly known. One unsubstantiated story is that originally the *ryūteki* was used in *noh* ensembles until one day a flute was dropped and broken, and was bound back together with this small shank inserted to hold it steady. The resulting change of color and tonality became the accepted sound for the *noh* flute. One might wonder if there is any relation between the flute's ability to overblow a seventh and the fact that the upper and lower basic tones of the *noh* tone system are also a seventh apart. Whatever its origin, the fluid, ambiguous lines of the flute are uniquely those of *noh*.

Since there is no consistency either in the tuning of the *nōkan* or in the overblown pitches that each flute produces, there can be no deliberate relation between the pitches of the instrument and those of the vocal line. Western musicians, being used to highly specific scales and a vertical orientation toward harmony, often observe pitch relations between the various components of *noh*, but these actually seem to be arbitrary. Perhaps the best way to appreciate all *noh* music, though, is to listen to it in a Buddhist manner: i.e., given the evanescence of life and the impermanence of things, listen to a musical moment for what it is, appreciating its consistencies and not worrying about its differences. This is in contrast with the Judeo-Christian approach, in which an E-flat symphony must be in E-flat, and a first theme very specific and obvious. It does not mean that *noh* music is improvised or aleatory. It is as controlled as a Mozart string quartet, but in a Buddhist world there are many bodhisattvas, and each is part of the truth. Every performance of *noh* is "correct" in essential ways. To demonstrate this let us return to the flute music.

The functions of the *nōkan* are (1) the signaling or highlighting of structural moments such as beginnings and endings; (2) adding a timbre that creates a special atmosphere in either instrumental music or lyrical passages in the vocal line; and (3) providing melody for *hayashi*-accompanied entrances or dances. The most obvious structural signal for the flute is the piercing highest-pitch sound heard at the beginning and ending of most plays or certain sections within a drama. The atmospheric passages are often based on named patterns but performed in an improvisational, free rhythmic *ashirai* style in order not to interfere with the text or drum patterns.

The characteristics of *noh* flute music are best understood in dance accompaniments, so we will look at the music in conjunction with dance in more detail. The flute part in *hayashi*-accompanied dance consists of a specific arrangement of conventional patterns, usually of eight-beat length (*yatsubyōshi*). There are special patterns for several dances,[7] and others that identify each section of a dance. Most *noh* flute dance music depends heavily on four basic patterns: *ryo, ryo no chū* (or just *chū*), *kan,* and *kan no chū*. These are transcribed in Figure 16, although the generally narrow range and fluid style of the *nōkan* cannot be shown effectively in Western notation. In addition, there are many different versions of these four patterns, depending on the tempo and mood of the dance and the guild of the flutist. Figure 17 is a guide to the fast, Fujita-guild version of "Kami mai" heard on CD track 7. In slower pieces, the four melodies are more ornamented.

**FIGURE 16.** The four basic *noh* flute melodies

7. Examples are *gaku, kagura,* and *kakko.*

The patterns are learned by singing *shōga* (memory aids imitating the sounds of the flute). These mnemonic syllables are also used for the notation of the flute part (see Figure 47 in Appendix I). Figure 17 shows the order of patterns for the flute part used in the same "Kami mai" performance mentioned above. It contains an introduction (*kakari*) and three sections (*dan*). Without even hearing the music, it is obvious that the four basic patterns dominate the music, but note that there are different *dan no fu* patterns used to open each *dan*, and that the first and second *dan* have special fourth and fifth patterns (*oroshi* and *tori*) which help identify them as different sections. The third *dan* has a new pattern (*saishūdan*) as well as a final cadence (*tome no fu*).[8]

| INTRODUCTION | FIRST *DAN* | SECOND *DAN* | THIRD *DAN* |
|---|---|---|---|
| *kakari* | *dan no fu* | *dan no fu* | *dan no fu* |
| *ryo no chū* | *ryo no chū* | *ryo no chū* | *saishūdan no fu* |
| *ryo* | *ryo* | *ryo* | *ryo no chū* |
| *ryo no chū* | *oroshi* | *oroshi* | *ryo* |
| *kan* | *shodan oroshi* | *nidan oroshi* | *ryo no chū* |
| *kan no chū* | *tori no fu 1* | *tori no fu 2* | *kan* |
| *ryo* | *ryo* | *ryo* | *kan no chū* |
| *ryo no chū* | *ryo no chū* | *ryo no chū* | *ryo* |
| *kan* | *kan* | *kan* | *ryo no chū* |
| *kan no chū* | *kan no chū* | *kan no chū* | *kan* |
| *ryo* | *ryo* | *ryo* | *kan no chū* |
| | *ryo no chū* | *ryo no chū* | *ryo* |
| | *kan* | *kan* | *tome no fu* |
| | *kan no chū* | *kan no chū* | |
| | *ryo* | *ryo* | |
| | | *ryo no chū* | |
| | | *kan* | |
| | | *kan no chū* | |
| | | *ryo* | |
| | | *ryo no chū* | |
| | | *kan* | |
| | | *kan no chū* | |
| | | *ryo* | |

FIGURE 17. Flute patterns for "Kami mai"

8. This is not true for the Kanze school performances.

This example illustrates how *noh* dance music moves forward through conventional signals and section markers until a unique final cadence appears. Western music also moves through time with conventional signals and cadences, but seldom in such a deliberately restricted manner. Perhaps the only feature *noh* dance music might share with Western music is found if Figure 17 is turned onto its right side. The music is seen to come to its longest climactic section three-fourths of the way through the piece (the second *dan*) and then has a shorter section with a special closing pattern. This is the way traditional composition is taught in the West.

The indefinite quality of the *noh* flute's tone and its music are eminently suited to supporting the drama without interfering with the declaiming of poetry, providing an excellent solution to the problem of the use of music within a drama. The drums provide yet another dimension.

## THE *KOTSUZUMI*

There are three types of drums used in *noh*: the *kotsuzumi*, *ōtsuzumi*, and *taiko*. The *kotsuzumi*, though the smallest of the group, is the most important drum in *noh* and is one of the unique Japanese contributions to the world of music. It is related to the *san no tsuzumi* in the court orchestra, which in turn has Korean relations. Its final form and manner of playing, however, seem to be something unknown in either court music or the music of Korea and China.

| *Kotsuzumi* | *Ōtsuzumi* | *Taiko* |

All the *noh* drums consist of five basic parts: a wooden body (*dō*), two skins (*kawa*), and two sets of ropes (*shirabe*) that hold the skins to the body (Plates 43 and 44). The body of the *kotsuzumi* is made of cherry or zelkova (*keyaki*) wood. Like a good violin, this wood must come from just the right tree growing in just the right place.[9] The inside of a good drum is carved

---

9. For details see William Malm, *Six Hidden Views of Japanese Music* (Berkeley: University of California, 1986), Chap. 1.

by hand with special patterns called *kanname*, which are deemed very important for the tone of the drum. The lacquer outside may make a drum a work of art, but it is the carving inside that makes it a good or poor musical instrument. The skins of the *kotsuzumi* are made of horsehide. These are stretched over iron rings and then stitched with hemp thread, which is covered by the inner black lacquer circle one sees on the face of the drum (Plate 44). The back of the skins is built up with clay so that the body will fit snugly onto the center of the skins. The only major difference between the back skin and the playing skin is that a small patch of deerskin is placed in the inside center of the back skin. This controls the reverberation of the skin and hence the tone. Control is also exerted by small patches of paper that are applied to the outside of the rear skin immediately opposite this inner patch. Called *chōshigami*, this paper is newly applied at each performance and has an amazingly significant effect on the tone of the drum. The number of patches applied depends on the weather, the tension of the ropes, and the sonic preferences of the player. The wetting and application of this paper is a puzzle to many a newcomer to a *noh* or *kabuki* performance; it has the look of a private conversation between the musician and his drum.

One set of the *kotsuzumi* ropes holds the two heads against the body while the other is looped loosely around the drum. By squeezing this encircling rope, tension is created on the skins, which raises the pitch. The manner of holding these ropes varies with the school of drumming, as does the exact method of tying the ropes. Plate 43 shows one of the common styles. Notice that the little finger is anchored by means of an extra loop of string, called a *kojime*.

The five basic sounds of the *kotsuzumi* are onomatopoeically named *pon*, *pu*, *ta*, *chi*, and *tsu*. *Pon* (notated as *po*) is produced by striking the center of the head. Two to four fingers of the right hand are used, depending on the school of drumming followed. The ropes are held loosely until the moment of impact when they are squeezed quickly to produce a lovely liquid waver to the tone. The coordination and perfection of this technique is the pièce de résistance of Japanese drumming.[10] *Pu* is similar to *pon* but lighter and played with only one finger. *Ta* has a wonderful crack to it and

---

10. The timing of the squeeze also differs between schools of drumming.

is produced by hitting at the edge of the head with two fingers while exerting maximum tension on the ropes. *Chi* is a lighter version of *ta* played with the ring finger. *Tsu* (also called *pe*) is executed by leaving the hand on the front head and allowing the rear one to produce the tone; it is traditionally limited to use in the ritual dance "Sambasō."

When the drum is not in use, it is often tied up by a separate rope known as a *shimeo*. The tying and untying of this rope is ideally done with careful ceremony, and it takes one or two lessons simply to perfect the correct technique. Stage manners are equally as important as playing technique in the study of *noh* drumming. As in the tea ceremony, it is not just what you do but how you do it.


## THE ŌTSUZUMI

The *ōtsuzumi* is similar to the *kotsuzumi* except for its larger size and the addition of rings carved on the outside of the drum. Cherry or Chinese quince is considered the best wood, and the inner carving is simpler. The skins, usually cowhide, are constructed like those of the *kotsuzumi* except that they are bigger and not lacquered. There is no need to build up the back of the heads with clay, as the thickness of the doubled-over hide is sufficient to hold the heads on the body. The front head is slightly thicker than the rear, and no control patches or control papers are used.

One reason why the *ōtsuzumi* heads are not lacquered is that they must be heated for at least an hour before a performance. This shortens the life of the skins. In professional circles, a set of skins is not used after ten performances. During *noh* performances, a freshly heated drum is often brought on stage halfway through the play. Held on the left hip (Plate 38), the *ōtsuzumi* is struck with one to three fingers of the right hand. Sometimes these fingers are covered with hard papier-mâché thimbles known as *yubikawa*; these enhance the sharp dryness of the drum's characteristic tone. Deerskin thimbles may also be used to produce a softer tone. The palm of the hand may be covered by another layer of deerskin (an *ategawa*), which is tied to the hand with thin threads. The traditional fan carried by all musicians serves as an emergency device for the *ōtsuzumi* player: if the head should split during a performance, he can beat out the rhythm with his fan instead. The fan is also said to be used when a lighter accompaniment is desired, though this is seldom seen in performances.[11]

The rope system of the *ōtsuzumi* begins with one set that holds the heads very tightly against the body. The second rope (in this case, the *kojime*) is looped through five strands of this binding rope and pulled together in order to make the body even tighter against the skins. There is an extra rope (the *dōnawa*) which serves only a decorative function, and is draped from the drum onto the floor in front and behind the player. Since the functional ropes are quite tight, they do not offer any margin for further control of the tone.

Tone control for the *ōtsuzumi* comes from the proper movements of the entire arm. The basic sounds are *chon*, which is the strongest; *tsu*, the weakest; and *don*. The latter is produced by leaving the hand on the drum after the impact and letting the rear head produce the sound as in the *tsu* beat of the *kotsuzumi*.

## THE *TAIKO*

The last member of the *noh* drum family is the *taiko*. Instead of the *tsuzumi* hourglass shape, it has a barrel form. The body averages twenty-six centimeters in diameter and fifteen centimeters in height. Zelkova wood is considered the best for the body, and the skins are made of either horse or cow. Carving inside the body is relatively unimportant. The construction of the skins is basically the same as that of the *tsuzumi* except that they are larger. The top skin is thicker than the lower, and a patch of deerskin, to which all the blows are directed, is attached in the center. There is a thinner patch immediately below this one for the purposes of tone. The rear head has no additional patches.

The *taiko* rope system is similar to that of the *ōtsuzumi* in that it is very tight and requires a great deal of strength to secure properly. One set of ropes holds the skins to the body and the other encircles the drum. The drum is set on a special stand that grips the encircling ropes and holds the

---

11. In drum lessons the teacher sits opposite the pupil and beats out the rhythm of all the parts with two leather-covered fans (*hariōgi*) on a special box called a *hyōshiban*. It is quite a feat of coordination, as various kinds of beats are indicated by different strokes with the fans. Throughout this the teacher is singing the words and correcting the student (see Plate 42).

drum off the floor so that it can resonate freely. The *taiko* is played with two thick but lightweight sticks (*bachi*) with beveled ends. Their length averages thirty centimeters.

There are four basic sounds produced: small, medium, large, and muffled (*shō*, *chū*, *dai*, and *osameru*). The muffled tone is created when the stick is left on the skin, often with a slight roll beforehand. This stopped sound is characteristic of the *taiko*. Special arm movements are used to perform the cadential pattern called *kashira* (see Figure 18), which consist in the left arm carrying the stick to the right shoulder while the right stick is lifted high (Plate 45). It is a striking effect when the left stick suddenly shoots forward instead of the expected right. The calls (*kakegoe*) that accompany this movement add to its excitement. The *kashira* pattern illustrates two recurring themes in this book: the aim of getting the maximum effect from limited material (in this case only two strokes on the drum), and the underlying notion that it is not just what you do but how you do it. More information about the various strokes of the *taiko* will be found in the discussion of *taiko* notation in Appendix I.

One final note should be added concerning the playing technique of the *taiko*. Unlike the loose wrist common in Western drumming, the *taiko* calls for a straight arm from the elbow to the fingers. The sticks are held loosely, but there is no drum rolling in the Western sense of the term. The technique abets the special restrained sound of this rather large drum, as does the deerskin patch that slightly muffles the tone. Much more sound could be made on the *taiko*, but the Japanese musician has chosen to limit his technique and concentrate on the chosen tone spectrum along with the grace of movement involved in producing a tone. This preoccupation with the style of tone production as well as the tone itself adds greatly to the finesse of a good *noh* performance.

## 8. Drum Music

Except for most dialogue sections, the sounds of the *hayashi* are heard throughout a *noh* play. Since the flute parts have already been discussed, we will turn to the music of the drums—the *tsuzumi*, used to accompany singing as well as dance, and the *taiko*, used in some entrance music and in most dance sections.[12]

*Kotsuzumi* and *ōtsuzumi* music uses named patterns often of eight-beat lengths.[13] They do not always play the same pattern at the same time, though their rhythms are intimately connected. Figure 15A contains the most common pattern, *mitsuji*. The term means "three points" (note that beats of the "lucky" numbers 3, 5, and 7 are emphasized). Variants of *mitsuji* are seen in Figure 15C, each having a different but related name (*uke mitsuji*, *kan mitsuji*) as they both belong to the same group (or *tegumi*). A Western analogy would be the C-major and C-minor chords. They share two pitches (C and G) but differ in one (E or E-flat). They can be recognized by ear and their names evoke the specific sounds to an informed listener or performer. The same is true for drum patterns.

The next most common *tsuzumi* pattern is *tsuzuke* ("continuing"), seen in Figure 15B. Note the clear marking of the third beat by the *ōtsuzumi*. In performance, it is possible for the *ōtsuzumi* player to change the pattern, as its sound is heard first, but the order in which drum patterns occur is generally conventional. It was noted earlier that the leader of the chorus may also make such "onstage" changes in the music.

The overall beat of the vocal and drum lines can either be matched (*hyōshi au*) or unmatched (*hyōshi awazu*). In the unmatched beat, the rhythm of the drums does not match that of the vocal or *nōkan* line, though it may have a steady beat (*noribyōshi*) or be purposely uneven (*sashibyōshi*). In Figure 15C one can see that, while the basic beats (3, 5, 7) tend to match, the lyrical unevenness of the tempo allows the singers and the drummers to think of their space between beats in a different manner. The space between the two lines of text illustrates that not all *noh* music is eight beats long. A four-beat *tori* ("take out") passage is accompanied by the appropriate drum patterns, but the attenuated calls of the drummers turn this short unit into an elongation of time that seems to suspend the listener in limbo.

Perhaps the greatest surprises when hearing *noh* for the first time are these shouts (*kakegoe*) made by the drummers, which serve to mark the time between beats and help to make each pattern sonically unique and

---

12. It is said that the *taiko*'s use in dances is limited to plays that involve deities or demons but not ghosts. Like any broad rule, there are exceptions.
13. See William Malm, "The Rhythmic Orientation of Two Drums in the Japanese *Noh* Drama," *Ethnomusicology*, Vol. 2, No. 2 (September 1958), 89–95.

recognizable. They may have originated as practice devices that were later taken into the performance itself and, becoming further abstracted, eventually formed an integral part of the overall sound image of *noh*, serving both practical and aesthetic functions.

A pattern is not correctly played unless both the drum sounds and calls are performed in the proper order. It also has to be the order authorized by the guild of the performer. For example, the drummers' calls in the *kotsuzumi* pattern *mitsuji* could be "*yo, ho, ho*" or "*ho, yo, ho*," depending on the guild. Pity the student who performs it wrong.

*Taiko* music also consists of a series of named patterns arranged in a prescribed order.[14] This can be clearly seen in Figure 18, which is from a *taiko* reference book.[15] The terms along the top line are the names of the basic dances of *noh*. The vertical columns list the names of the patterns to be used and the order in which they are performed in this opening section (*kakari*) of the dances. Just by scanning horizontally across this chart, one can see that almost all drum music starts and ends with the same conventional sequence of patterns while, internally, there is more variation. One could create a similar kind of chart for the common practice music of the West in the eighteenth century, with the tonic chord dominating the list and a dominant/tonic unit found at major cadences. The bottom two horizontal lines of the chart in Figure 18 serve the same cadential purpose, not only for all the opening sections of the dances listed but also for most of the endings of each section (*dan*) that follows. These two patterns (*uchikiri* and *kashira*) are transcribed below the chart so that listeners can learn to recognize a *taiko* cadence in any recording or performance they hear.[16]

The major East-West difference in our analogy is that the Japanese chart consists of horizontal, rhythmic patterns and a Western chart would contain vertical, instantaneous sounds called chords. This is, in fact, one of the main differences between Western music and that of most of the rest of the world. The basic orientation of traditional Western music is harmony, and thus it uses a fairly simple scale structure so that sounds are "in

14. See William Malm, "An Introduction to *Taiko* Music in the Japanese Nō Drama" *Ethnomusicology*, Vol. 4, No. 2 (1960).
15. The chart is from the *Komparu ryū taiko zensho* (Tokyo: Hinoki Shoten, 1953) p. 254.
16. These, plus the patterns *tsukegashira* and *oroshi* seen in Figures 46 and 47, can be heard on CD track 7.

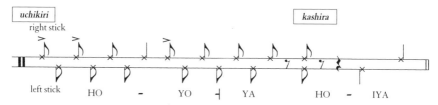

| 下端之舞 | 盤渉樂 | 樂 普通 | 樂 序無 | 物神樂 | 樂神 序無 | 樂神 序有 | 早舞 | 神舞 | 天女之舞 | 中之舞 | 盤渉序舞 | 序之舞 | 眞之序之舞 | カヽリ（融・海人・當麻・邯鄲のカヽリは少し異る。後に記す） |
|---|---|---|---|---|---|---|---|---|---|---|---|---|---|---|
| 込半打 | 出打頭中置一 | | | | 打込 | 打切 | 込 | | | 打 | 切 打 | 込 | 打 | |
| 頭スリ付 | ・打返頭付頭 | 打返頭 | | 頭一 | | 頭五 | | 頭二 | | | 頭五（略式皆三）| 雨月放生川頭六（略式皆四）老松白樂天頭七 | |
| 付 | シ ロ ヲ | | | 刻半・小拍子 | | | シ ロ ヲ | | | | 半子刻・小拍 | 半刻・合一コイ | |
| （寶替2 4） | 1 | | | 2 | | | 〃〃森下觀寶 021 | 〃〃噌寶下觀 031 | | 下觀寶 031 | 下觀寶 021 | 下觀寶 223 | 〃〃森下觀寶 223位 〃〃噌寶下觀 235位 | |
| | | | | | | 地　　短 | | | | | | | | |
| | 刻 | 半 | | | ケ カ 打 | | | | | 刻 | 半 | | | |
| （寶替6 4） | 森噌75 森噌76 森噌32 | 森4 噌5 | | | 〃〃森下觀寶 463 〃〃噌寶下觀 564 | | 下觀寶 564 | 下觀寶 463 | 下觀寶 554 | | 〃〃森下觀寶 554位 〃〃噌寶下觀 664位 | | | |
| | | | | 切 | | 打 | | | | | | | | |
| | | | | | 頭 | | | | | | | | | |

FIGURE 18. First page of a *taiko* dance music outline, with the two cadential patterns

tune" vertically. The rest of the world is concerned either with a more sophisticated scale or rhythmic system. Let us follow the rhythmic system of *noh* further by turning to the *tsuzumi* drum patterns.

Although the same names for various rhythmic patterns appear in the music of all three drums, this does not mean necessarily that they all use the same pattern at the same time. The notation for the drums shown in Appendix I is primarily a teaching device, and in a professional's music book one will usually see only the names of the patterns written alongside the text of the play or in "cue sheets," such as that shown in Figure 18. Since there are some two hundred of these patterns for each instrument, it takes several years before one can read this type of score easily. There is also the problem of the exact relation of these patterns to each specific situation.

This can be learned only by experience. It remains the guarded secret of teachers, who inculcate this esoteric knowledge by a slow rote method. An additional problem is that each instrumental guild may have its own particular version of a given pattern.[17]

The *hayashi* was defined as consisting of three types of drum and a flute. One of each instrument is used in *noh* with the exception of the dance "Okina" where the ensemble consists of one flute, one *ōtsuzumi*, and three *kotsuzumi*. In special performances of *noh* selections, one may hear an *issei itchō*. This is a section of a *noh* drama performed by one singer and one drummer, where the drummer must synthesize the complete *hayashi* part on his one instrument. For this reason, livelier sections are usually chosen. The problem is rather like the one faced when reducing a symphony at the piano. Sometimes such drum parts may become improvisatory, though only within definite limits. There is also a form called *itchō ikkan* that uses one drum and one flute, with or without a singer, and on rare occasions one may hear an *itchō* for solo drum, usually the *kotsuzumi*. These performances offer an excellent opportunity to appreciate fully the tonal variations possible on that instrument.

The *hayashi* of the *noh* is one of Japan's unique contributions to music. As used in *noh* and further developed in *kabuki*, it is perhaps the most original concept in all Japanese music. Its sound, musical structure, and relation to the drama are all quite special. This may be understood more clearly after a study of the vocal music of *noh*, though the best way to appreciate it is to hear for oneself the power and uniqueness of the *hayashi*.

## 9. Performance Practices

The term "correct" performance is complicated by the fact that *noh* music is interpreted by different guilds. Figure 19 lists the major guilds for each of the musical specialists in *noh*. Vertically, any guild from any group can be combined for a performance, because the basic conventions of each play

17. In Figure 18 the sets of arabic numbers in some dances indicate how many times the *taiko* repeats the pattern *kizami*. It is based on the guild to which the flute player belongs, identified by the Japanese characters above the arabic numbers.

remain the same, though the form and text may vary. Thus, with only one brief rehearsal (*mōshi awase*), an excellent performance can be created. Horizontally, however, one cannot combine all the guilds. A Kanze *shite* and a Hōshō chorus cannot work together, nor could a Kanze and Ōkura *kotsuzumi* combine. Of course, since there is seldom more than one instrument of each type in a performance, the problem does not usually arise. Nevertheless, the principle of guild difference in music interpretation is an important one.

| | |
|---|---|
| *shite* and *ji* | Kanze, Kita, Kongō, Komparu, Hōshō, |
| *waki* | Shimogakari-Hōshō, Takayasu, Fukuō |
| *kyōgen* | Izumi, Ōkura |
| *nōkan* | Morita, Issō, Fujita |
| *ōtsuzumi* | Takayasu, Kadono, Ōkura, Ishii, Hōshō |
| *kotsuzumi* | Kō, Ōkura, Kōsei, Kanze |
| *taiko* | Komparu, Kanze |

FIGURE 19. Guilds of *noh* performers

## 10. Summary

The *noh* drama has been presented in bits and pieces. It is now time to view it as an artistic entirety. Growing out of a host of early theatricals, *noh* theater found a means of combining the arts of music, dance, drama, and decor in such a way as to retain the best elements of its predecessors while deleting their mutual inconsistencies. This effect was achieved by building each play on a central evocative theme, by creating poetry that was in keeping with this mood, and by maintaining and developing this central idea through all the other dramatic arts. Likewise, each art was held in check so as to keep the reality of the theme from being destroyed by the intrusion of the reality of the component arts. In *noh*, the balance between highly refined abstraction and the dramatic necessity of human emotions is one of the most delicate and perhaps most successful attempts in world drama.

Musically, the singing and the rhythm of the *hayashi* have been shown to be subject to intense systematization. The singing is centered on the poetry, to whose rhythmic and emotional changes the *hayashi* remains alert as it does to the movement of the actors. The flute, as the only melodic instrument, provides a necessary contrast to the mauve tone colors of the singing and the percussion of the drums. The calls of the drummers have been cultivated until they have become not only rhythmic signals but also important elements in the general emotional mood of the plays.

The structure of a *noh* play has often been likened to a mosaic. Each dramatic or musical unit is a microcosm, answering the logical requirements of its own little universe. These pieces of various emotional tints are put together in such a way that each reinforces the overall mood of the frame in which they are set. This frame is not necessarily a plot in the Western sense, but rather the quality inherent in the "idea" behind the implied plot.

For the musician, the main interest may be in the "horizontal" conception of music. Western music can usually be analyzed "horizontally" or "vertically," that is, one can follow the composer's ideas as they progress in time or take one particular instant and discover what the relation of the various lines is to each other. In simplest terms, it is like studying both melody and harmony. In *noh* music, a vertical cross section of the music will often reveal apparent chaos. The chorus and the flute are involved in two completely separate melodic lines while the drums may be playing rhythmic patterns of dissimilar lengths and names. If one views each passage in a horizontal manner, however, one can see each part working in concord with the basic requirements of the text. The text is the clue to the understanding of much of the music. It is the raison d'être for most of the rules that have grown up around the music. This intimate connection is one of the best examples of the literary orientation inherent in most Japanese music.

The music of *noh* is not the product of one mind. After the poem has been written, it is passed on to the various *hayashi* players and main actors, who compose their own parts. Such a system can only be successful with a music that is highly systematized. *Noh* theorists have seemed sometimes a bit precious in their aesthetic and dramatic writings, but when plays have been entrusted to the care of sensitive actors and musicians, the results have been something quite lovely and unique. A good *noh* play has a composite beauty, a beauty derived from many different minds and from all the theater arts.

*Noh* presents a fascinating paradox. As a dramatic form one would expect it to relate to time and place, yet often it evokes timelessness. There is much truth in the usual translation of the word *noh* as "an accomplishment," for in the field of the theater that is indeed what it is.

| CHAPTER FIVE | *BIWA* MUSIC |

# 1. Introduction

Beneath the ancient gates of Kyoto there has passed a multicolored pageant of disorderly events known as history. The slaty eyes of the gargoyles and dragons that festoon their eaves have viewed imperial grandeur, religious pomp, and periodic bloodshed resulting from constant struggles for power. If those fabulous creatures have a memory, perhaps they can recall also the regular temple fairs. The strident chaos of buying and selling still assaults their stony ears, but from the depths of their memories they may be able to conjure up the twang of a *biwa* and the tense voice of a blind storyteller who sat within the shadow of the gate. Though these men were as sightless as the gargoyles, they recreated with their music much of the same color and pathos that imbued the events to which those creatures bore witness. For a few pennies, the shopper could rest from his haggling and relive via the blind priest-musician the famous legends of mighty warriors and noble ladies in their moments of glory and defeat.

The blind *biwa* priests are no longer seen at temple fairs, but the spirit of their songs remains in the theater music of Edo and in the modern *biwa* concert schools. The glowering audience of temple-tile creatures has been replaced by pseudo-Baroque cherubs that cling to the prosceniums of modern theaters. However, the human listeners are basically the same. They still love a good story, and as long as there are *biwa* musicians with enough talent to re-create the old tales, there will be those willing to hear them. What the gargoyles may remember, mankind can still imagine with the help of the *biwa* and its music.

## 2. The History of *Biwa* Music

The *biwa*, like the Western lute, has come in many sizes and shapes and from many cultures. The *biwa* as used in Japan today has two main sources: India and China.[1] There is a legend that Buddha had a blind disciple to whom he taught the art of singing sutras to the accompaniment of the *biwa*. Another legend claims that the son of the famous Buddhist king Asoka of India became just such a blind *biwa* player himself. There is much disagreement concerning the real origins of this music, but it is fairly certain that it was transferred to China around the third century. There, this instrument, known as the *pipa*, evolved further, apparently under Central Asian influences. It is this Chinese-style lute that seems to have come to Japan sometime in the Nara period.

*Pipa*

In Chapter Three, we mentioned the handsome Chinese lutes that survived in the Shōsōin storehouse of the period (p. 106). The *gakubiwa*, used in the imperial *gagaku* music, was also discussed. In addition to its use in the orchestral ensemble, the instrument seems to have had an extensive solo repertory as well. Playing the *biwa* was an important social grace for the courtier of the late Nara and Heian periods. The great literary monument to that age, *The Tale of Genji*, is replete with scenes in which the *biwa* plays an important role. Likewise, the *biwa* appears in genre paintings (Plate 46) as often as the lute is found in pictures of the European Renaissance. Unfortunately, only a few remnants of ancient *biwa* notation have survived. If the performance style was at all similar to that of the orchestral *biwa*, it must have been very simple and meant to be primarily a vocal accompaniment.

While the nobility were busy with their music and their amours, a very different kind of *biwa* music developed in the south of Kyushu. Here, blind priests using a smaller *biwa*, more like the Indian models, appeared singing sutras. There are many legends concerning the arrival of this music in Japan. Some place it as early as the seventh century, but it was not until after the tenth century that such priests really appeared in significant numbers.

1. Historically speaking, there are three different-shaped lutes that are known to have entered Japan. Only two of them, however, are in use today. For a detailed study of their origin see Biblio. ref. 5.5.

They were called *biwahōshi* (*biwa* priests) or *mōsō-biwa* (blind *biwa* players).[2] The best-known story of the founding of this tradition concerns the Enrya-ku temple in Kyoto. The story relates that when the temple was built the grounds were found to be infested with poisonous snakes. In order to drive them away, eight blind *biwa*-playing priests were brought from Kyushu to perform their sutras. Ap-parently they were successful, as four *biwa* priests

Mōsōbiwa

were retained permanently in Kyoto. One of the priests who returned to Kyushu was particularly famous for his talent and was recalled to the capital whenever any plague or other natural calamity made it necessary to exorcise the spirits. This man was Jōjuin, the traditional founder of the Chikuzen school of blind *biwa* players. The other main school, the Sa-tsuma, was said to have been founded by one of the priests who stayed behind in Kyoto, named Manshōin. The supposed relation between these two men varies considerably according to the allegiance of the authors of the various histories of blind-priest *biwa* music. The important thing, though, is that the difference between Chikuzen and Satsuma styles existed even in the early blind-priest traditions. (The term "blind priest" is used here in order to differentiate between these early styles and the music known by the same names that appeared later.)

Singing priests led a wandering life. Traveling from village to village, they sang their magic sutras wherever a local god had shown signs of being obstreperous or displeased (Plate 47, CD track 8). Their clientele came more and more from the peasantry and less from the big temples and noblemen. Eventually their music became known as *kōjinbiwa*, named after Kōjin, a household kitchen god in the Tendai sect of Buddhism. By the Kamakura period, many of these men were reduced to begging. They ceased to travel and spent their days hanging about temple gates and seeking alms with a few stanzas of their once magic sutras. It is pos-sible that some of these men may have begun to improvise stories in order to attract more attention and hence more alms. In any event, these

2. In the twentieth century non-blind amateur enthusiasts in Kumamoto city adopted the term *higobiwa*, named after Higo, the title of the former feudal domain. The term was applied later by researchers to the entire tradition but not by the performers themselves.

itinerant sutra singers laid a foundation for much of the great theater music that was to follow.

In the decline of the blind-priest *biwa*, the Chikuzen school suffered more than the Satsuma, for the latter continued to enjoy respectability under the patronage of the Shimazu clan, in the Satsuma district of Kyushu. The headquarters of the school moved from Kyoto to Satsuma at about the time of the great shogun Yoritomo (1147–99). This school continued to flourish until the general deterioration of the clan system in the Edo period. One must not think, however, that the Shimazu clan was a twelfth-century house of Esterhazy. These men were warriors and as such were more alert to warfare than to art. They discovered in the association of blind musicians a ready-made spy ring, for these priests had their own nationwide organization, rather like the old Society of Jesus in Europe. They were free to travel all over Japan in a manner that few other people could do. Under the Shimazu aegis, they soon developed a good ear for news as well as for music.

In the Kamakura period the most important development in *biwa* music was the founding of the great narrative tradition, *heikebiwa*. The stories of the battle between the Heike and Genji clans were already well known to the warriors of the new, bloody period. They served as an inspiration in battle and a consolation in defeat.

*Heikebiwa*

These stories had probably been told many times by a variety of storytellers, but it was not until the establishment of a *biwa* version that the *Tale of the Heike* (*Heike monogatari*) became an important literary and musical genre (CD track 9).

The origin of *heikebiwa* is open to debate. The best-known account of its creation claims that it was first written by a court official named Fujiwara no Yukinaga (ca. 1189). This man had always prided himself on being an excellent *gagaku* musician and dancer. One day he was asked to perform a dance of seven sections. He started off confidently but forgot two sections before he finished. The jokes made at his expense must have been bitter indeed, for tradition relates that he finally left the court and retired in shame to the mountain monastery of Hieizan. There, under the encouragement of a Buddhist priest named Jichin, he proceeded to write the story of the Heike clan and their decline. This story was then taught to a blind *biwa* priest named Shōbutsu, who, in turn, went about the country singing the tale in a new style of music.

Exactly how much truth there is in this story will probably never be known, but it does point out nicely the three main streams of music from which *heikebiwa* evolved: *gagaku*, Buddhist *shōmyō*, and blind-priest *biwa* music. More will be said of this in the latter part of this chapter.

The popularity of *heikebiwa* was immense. Both the court and the warrior camp found this music novel as well as germane to their own times and problems. Loyalty and bravery in battle, beauty and fidelity at home, a Buddhist acceptance of the evanescence of life: all these moods are found within the *Tale of the Heike*. It was an apt artistic medium for a strife-torn period; it also provided a new source of livelihood for the tottering profession of blind *biwa* players.

The strains of *heikebiwa* music drifted among the polished rafters of the rich man's mansion as well as the weather-beaten tiles of the temple gate. Each social class enjoyed the stories in its own particular style, and many schools developed to meet the tastes of these varied audiences.

In the fourteenth century, all professions for blind people, both medical (massage, acupuncture, burning moxa application) and musical (*biwa*, *koto*, and later *shamisen* and *kokyū*), were organized into an association called the Tōdōza. It was much like a modern union. In fact, in the musical field, one could not perform without a license from the association headquarters. Within this political framework, however, there was a continual proliferation of differing musical styles. The two main schools of the Kamakura and Muromachi periods were the Ichikata and Yasaka. The Yasaka group claimed to use the original text, while the Ichikata music was based on a special edition that was supposed to have been given to one of their virtuosi by the emperor himself.

With the appearance of the *shamisen* and the many new styles of theater music in the Edo period, *heikebiwa* began to lose favor. The style remained static, while the times changed rapidly. By the mid-twentieth century, it seemed that only a few old men in Nagoya could recount the *Tale of the Heike* as it was heard by the Kamakura warriors and the temple gargoyles. At the turn of the new century, at least one young blind musician (Imai Tsutomu, Plate 48) took on the awesome task of performing *heikebiwa* in the traditional style, while others musicians set about producing different versions of the legend in new *biwa* genres.

As *heikebiwa* declined and blind sutra singers almost disappeared, other more timely *biwa* styles developed. The most important of these evolved among the Satsuma musicians under the patronage of the Shimazu clan. These men had done valuable service for the clan during the turbulent Kamakura and Muromachi days, but by the sixteenth century their usefulness as spies was beginning to wane. They were therefore assigned a new task, that of

*Satsumabiwa*

"improving" the members of the clan with edifying music. In the previous chapter were listed many theatricals and other forms of popular entertainment that flooded the country in the Muromachi period. It was the intention of the ruling members of the Shimazu clan to protect their warriors from the deleterious effects of overexposure to this supposedly vulgar music. To this end, "popular" music was forbidden among members of the clan, and the cultivation of light classics was recommended. These consisted of three kinds of music: (1) music for a small type of vertical flute called a *tempuku*; (2) music for a special form of warrior dance called *samurai odori* or *heko odori*; and (3) new forms of narrative *satsumabiwa* music. Through these three artistic pursuits, they hoped to build up a clan of modest but sturdy soldiers.

The success of this interesting experiment in musical propaganda is open to debate, but the musical results are very definite. From the sixteenth century on, a new style of narrative music can be said to have come into being. At first, the pieces were carefully arranged as suitable for various ages and sexes, but eventually a repertoire evolved that consisted primarily of war stories. It differed from the *heikebiwa* style in that the music was more in keeping with contemporary fashions, and it continued to develop as styles changed. This music eventually was popular among the common people as well, its style becoming less pompous and more dramatic (CD track 10). By the Edo period, it had spread throughout the southern part of Japan and no doubt had some part in the styling of the music for the fast-growing arts of *kabuki* and the puppet plays.

One of the acts of the Meiji Restoration of 1868 was to abolish the exclusive privileges of the blind performers. This spelled death for most of what remained of the old *mōsōbiwa* and hastened the demise of *heikebiwa*. Fortunately, many of the men who played important roles in the early government of the Meiji period came from the provinces of Satsuma, and they brought to the capital more than just new ideas of statesmanship: they brought *satsumabiwa*. This music was now open to anyone, and many people took it up as a hobby. Emperor Meiji was a great fan of such music and is said to have taken up the practice himself by means of phonograph records.

In the late nineteenth century, the term *chikuzenbiwa* appeared once more, though the old sutra-singing Chikuzen music had died out long before.[3] This new style was created out of a mixture of narrative *biwa*, *satsumabiwa*, and *shamisen* music. It took the name partly because it began in the Chikuzen district of Kyushu and also because it used, at first, a small *biwa*

*Chikuzenbiwa*

like the old blind-priest *chikuzenbiwa*. The style, in its classic form, has a certain grandeur that the more melodramatic schools lack. Unfortunately, being less showy, it is less suitable for presentation on the stage. The beauties of *chikuzenbiwa* can best be heard in a small room, while the power of *satsumabiwa* is quite striking on stage (listen to CD tracks 10 and 11). In the age of the microphone, *satsumabiwa* seems to be faring better, but both forms, while comparatively young, continue to enjoy a modest growth.

In the twentieth century a number of new *biwa* schools have appeared, of which the Kinshin and Nishiki are the most famous. The latter was founded by a woman, Suitō Kinjō, and is highly influenced by *shamisen* music. Most use *satsuma*-style instruments. Non-Japanese performers can also be heard in *biwa* concerts. Contemporary attempts to infuse Western techniques (such as *biwa* "orchestras") have been rather disastrous, but there have been certain very effective dramatic works in which *koto* and flutes have been added as mood music. Takemitsu Tōru's "November Steps," for Western orchestra and *biwa*, stimulated international interest in the instrument and its music. The *biwa* has always been eminently suitable for the accompaniment of storytellers; as long as it does not lose sight of this dramatic orientation, it should have a future.

3. When I say a form has died out I mean that it has ceased to be of any musical or historical significance or influence today. It is characteristic of Japan that as soon as one says that a certain art form has disappeared, an old artist is discovered in some out-of-the-way village. Such persons are the hope of research scholars and the incubus of general survey writers.

# 3. The Instrument and Its Music

Over the centuries the *biwa* has been subject to many modifications in construction. Certain features, of course, have had to remain constant in order to retain the *biwa*'s characteristic tone. The most important of these is the relation of the frets to the strings. On a Western guitar, the strings are very close to the fingerboard so that when they are pressed against the frets a definite pitch is produced. It is impossible, however, to push down the strings of a modern *biwa* against the neck, as they are set very high above it and the frets themselves are quite high.[4] This method of construction makes two different playing techniques possible. First, one may simply press the strings down on top of each fret; this produces a definite pitch but the number of pitches available is limited to the number of frets. This is the system used on the *gakubiwa*. The second method is to push the string down between the frets. In this manner a variety of pitches can be produced depending on how hard one presses. This method stretches the string and is only possible with a string of some elasticity. Such a long, elastic string (made of gut or silk) has a very "twangy" sound, much like that of a rubber band. When this sound is amplified by the body of the instrument, it produces one of the most characteristic features of the *biwa*'s tone, its *sawari* or "rattle."[5]

The shape and size of the body of a *biwa* are also open to great variation. In general, it is made of two pieces. The back is a solid piece of wood that has been hollowed out to make a sound box (see Plate 51). A soundboard is then glued over this cavity, usually with two crescent-shaped sound holes. A special strip of wood, cloth, lacquer, or leather is sometimes placed across the body to protect it from the blows of the plectrum. The interesting aspect of this so-called *bachimen* is that only the older-style *biwa* are played in such a manner that the plectrum actually strikes this place. The present-day Satsuma and Chikuzen schools play above this spot. However, tradition has prevailed, and the cover remains below while the plectrum continues to scratch the wood some fifteen centimeters higher (see Plate 49).

---

4. The frets became progressively higher as the instrument evolved. The *gakubiwa* frets are just slightly higher than those of a standard Chinese *pipa*. Those of the *heikebiwa* are a bit higher still, and the *chikuzen* and *satsuma* frets even more so.
5. When the *shamisen* first appeared, many things were done to its neck in an attempt to capture this same sound.

One of the most important factors in the tone of a *biwa* is the placement of the tailpiece, that is, the piece of wood to which the strings are attached. Depending on the thickness of the sides of the *biwa*, the tailpiece may be attached either over solid wood or over the hollow section. The "correct" placement is entirely a matter of taste, and there is great variety within each school of *biwa* music. Other features, such as the number of strings and frets and the kind of plectrum used, also vary within each school as well as between local branches. These differences, therefore, will be mentioned as the specific music styles of these schools are discussed.

The *gakubiwa* and its music have already been studied (p. 106). It has four frets and four strings and is plucked with a small bone plectrum. Only the pitches produced by pressing directly on the frets are used. This is the instrument that is said to have been primarily a Chinese development.

The *heikebiwa* is somewhat smaller. It has four strings (usually tuned G, B, D, and G'), five frets, and uses a larger, wider plectrum. The instrument and its manner of playing seem to have been influenced by the blind-priest *biwa*. For one thing, the strings are played between the frets, unlike the *gakubiwa*. Perhaps its most interesting feature musically is the fact that the frets are not the same distance apart on all the instruments, which can make for considerable variation in the actual scales produced. Of course, since the tones are produced by stretching the strings behind the frets, one can compensate somewhat for this discrepancy; but the frets of the *heikebiwa* are much lower than those of later *biwa*. This is but another example of the fascinating ambiguity in tonal relations between parts that has been noted in Buddhist chanting and in the music of the *noh* flute. Experiments with this kind of flexibility were hardly known in the West until the twentieth century.

There is controversy among scholars as to how *heikyoku*,[6] the singing of the *Tale of the Heike*, was first performed. Some believe that at first only a fan was used to beat out a rhythmic accompaniment to the narration. Such fan rhythm (*ōgibyōshi*, Plate 19) was still used by street musicians in 1955. The truth is probably that both the *biwa* and the fan were used during the formative period. From the standpoint of music history, however, the development of the *biwa* accompaniment is more important.

6. The term *heikyoku* refers to all music dealing with the *Tale of the Heike*. However, in this book it refers only to *biwa* music, as the earlier forms are not discussed.

The common *biwa* version of the *Tale of the Heike* is organized into two hundred episodes (*ku*), which are in turn divided up into phrases, each of which is assigned a stereotyped manner of singing. Between the phrases, other standard melodies are played by the *biwa*. The choice of these melodies depends on the length of the phrase and on its mood. In the thirteenth century, there were thirteen of these patterns, but since then as many as twenty-three patterns have appeared. Recent research implies that all the basic *biwa* melodic conventions used in the entire performance today are found in a long instrumental "secret piece" (*hikyoku*) that precedes the narration.[7] As a

FIGURE 20. *Heikebiwa* and *satsumabiwa* versions of the same text from *Tale of the Heike*

7. My thanks to George Gish of Tokyo for bringing this theory to my attention. The last part of this prelude can be heard on CD track 9. For the concept that most *koto danmono* are based on one *gagaku* piece see Biblio. ref. 7·2.

rule, the voice patterns and the *biwa* patterns are not performed simultaneously. Though some of the same names are used to designate them, their melodies are quite different. The characteristic style of performance (CD track 9) is for the *biwa* to sound the beginning pitch, the voice to sing the phrase, and then the *biwa* to re-enter with either the pitch for the next phrase or some melodic pattern that reflects the mood of the text.[8]

The influence of Buddhist chanting is most noticeable in the vocal style and in some of the terminology. Both, in turn, are found in the music of the *noh* drama. Thus, terms like *ageuta*, *sageuta*, and *kudoki* are found in all three traditions. Later *shamisen* genres continued to use the terms, though often with new meanings. Figure 20 illustrates a typical *heikebiwa* vocal line, with long sections of narration set between notes a fourth or fifth apart plus a few seconds (D) below a pitch center (E). The music becomes more complex as the story evolves, but this phrase is reminiscent of the basic tone system discussed earlier in the Buddhist and *noh* drama.

*Heikebiwa* music is internally highly organized. The tonal movement, tempo, mode, and meaning of each musical phrase are strictly regulated. As these phrases are applied to specific texts, they are subject to modification, but the overall organization is ever present. To the modern ear, *heikebiwa* may sound rather dull, but to the ears of the audience for whom it was originally written it had great novelty and power. One often reads in the history of Western music of the tremendous reaction audiences had to the first violin tremolos in opera or the first orchestral crescendos at Mannheim. One need only take a similar historical perspective to realize what an important role *heikebiwa* played in the development of Japanese narrative music. Remember also that, like most narrative traditions in the world, the story is more important than the music.

The mendicant priests needed a portable instrument as they wandered to various villages and houses. Thus the *mōsōbiwa* is the smallest of the *biwa* family. The fingerboard and neck attached to its narrow body, as well as the frets, can sometimes be removed so that the entire instrument can be packed in a cloth and slung over one's shoulder. The blind musician was then led either by his wooden staff or by an assistant who held the other end of the staff as they walked on to the next place.

8. A convenient summary of tonal tendencies in the *heikebiwa* patterns and many vocal or *biwa* examples are found in the *Ongaku jiten*, IX, 217, and in Biblio. ref. 1·14.

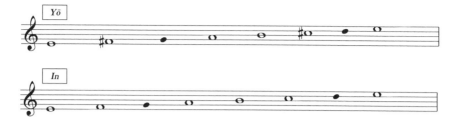

FIGURE 21. The *yō* and *in* scales

The peasant nature of both the performer and his audience is evident in the tonal system heard in the music as it is now played. It uses the *yō* and *in* scales, shown in Figure 21. On CD track 8, one hears a Kannon chant accompanied by a jaunty pentatonic tune in the *yō* scale, with only a short change to the half steps of the *in* at the end of the excerpt. Both have a pentatonic core with alternate pitches possible on the second or fifth notes. The core of the *yō* scale is basic to folk music all over the world, but the half notes in the *in* scale are particularly Japanese. These two scales dominate most Japanese music after the sixteenth century.

The *satsumabiwa* is narrower than the *heikebiwa* but has a much larger scroll. The ancient blind-priest *satsumabiwa* is said to have had three strings and six frets, but the most common version of this instrument has four strings and four frets. These frets are very high. One of the characteristics of *satsuma*-style frets is that there is a large gap between the first and second one. The most spectacular feature of the *satsumabiwa*, however, is the plectrum (*bachi*), which is a very wide, thin piece of wood (see Plate 50). This produces a resounding whack when struck against the body—a sound that characterizes the *satsuma* style. The string can also be given a twist by a backstroke with the plectrum, producing a very twangy sound without the usual precedent percussion. The finger technique of the left hand uses alternations of single fingers and two fingers together. The latter are used when several different pitches are produced from the same finger position by means of pressing down the string. A wide vibrato and a left-hand pizzicato are also common. The typical tunings for the *satsumabiwa* are shown in Figure 22, A and B. These differ according to the various branches of the school. Tuning C is used by the Nishiki branch for its five-stringed, five-fretted *biwa*.

Musically, the *satsumabiwa* style is related to its *heike* predecessor. Stan-

FIGURE 22. *Biwa* tunings

dard melodies for both the voice and the instrument are used. The "edify-ing" *satsuma* style created for the Shimazu clan (*samuraifū*) is said to have been quite stately, while the style that developed through the support of the townspeople (*machifū*) is more flashy. It is this latter style that prevails in the *satsumabiwa* of today. The second excerpt notated in Figure 20, giving the *satsuma* rendition of the same text, shows a related but more elaborate use of fourth or fifth jumps and seconds around pitch centers. However, the vocal melismatic performance heard on CD track 10 indicates that the influence of popular theatrical music is great. Although, historically, the modern *chikuzenbiwa* is given credit for incorporating *shamisen* techniques into *biwa* music, it can now be said that they belong equally to both schools.

An important difference between the modern *biwa* schools and the *heike-biwa* is that the voice and *biwa* parts are no longer always separated. While in present-day *biwa* music there are many sections of narration in which only the reciting tone is given with short *biwa* interludes as in the *heikebiwa* style, there are also many parts in which the voice and *biwa* perform together. Because of this, one often sees performances in which there are separate singers and *biwa* players.

Since the voice part is restricted to given patterns, the major develop-ment in the vocal line centers around the embroidering of these lines with turns and melismas, as heard on CD tracks 10 and 11. Much like the old opera singers, these *satsuma* and *chikuzen* virtuosi delight in prolonging important phrases with special unwritten vocal peregrinations. Again, as in opera, the passages where such opportunities exist are known by the fans, and well-executed melismas are greeted by shouts of approval from the audience. One of the charms of *biwa* music when I heard it in the 1950s was to observe the way in which the audience and the performer worked on each other's enthusiasm. More recent performances seem to be gener-ally more sedate.

The *biwa* accompaniment is also arranged in specific patterns. These units, however, are often more melodic and extensive than those used in *heikebiwa*. The *satsumabiwa* music is the showiest in this respect, and some of the patterns can produce quite a dramatic effect. A typical *satsuma* example is *kuzure*, which is used during war scenes: a fast alternation between a low string and a very high note which is the *biwa* equivalent of the violin tremolo or the sudden diminished chord in old-time movie thrillers. For a *chikuzen* version, listen to the *biwa* at the end of CD track 11.

The twentieth-century Kinshin branch of *satsumabiwa* has been the boldest in experimenting with new forms. On the whole, when straight *shamisen* styles have been imitated, the results have not been very impressive, but some effective work has resulted from borrowing the dramatic styles of more popular *shamisen* narrative genres. The music may not be very profound, but it is undeniable that when little sister has been lost by the river during a typhoon, the *biwa* can whip up one of the most effective storms in all Japanese dramatic music.

Another musical specialty of the Kinshin school is the singing of *shigin*, Chinese poems done in Japanese style. These poems were first created in the late Edo period and have no direct connection with the old Heian-court *rōei* Chinese poems. The original *shigin* were sung unaccompanied or in concert with a *shakuhachi*. After the Meiji period, they were used to accompany a type of posturing sword dance called *kembu*, which is said to have made them more rhythmical. Later they began to appear in *biwa* concerts, and eventually the *biwa* was also used for accompaniment. *Shigin* were particularly popular during the days of the Russo-Japanese War.[9]

*Biwa* music in general is replete with heady melodrama, and contemporary *satsumabiwa* has made an honest attempt to capture the common audience without completely losing its more aristocratic origins. Since there are still performers alive who represent all the major styles of *satsumabiwa*, one has a choice. The addition of foreign performers from Europe and the Americas has lent color to that tradition.

The *chikuzenbiwa* in its classic form is the smaller of the modern *biwa* (Plate 49). It is said to be more directly related to the Indian form of lute. It also bears the closest resemblance to the old blind-priest *biwa* (compare it with Plate 47). Two types of *chikuzenbiwa* are common: one with four strings and five frets, and another with five strings and five frets. Since

---

9. Japan's first wide-screen movie was about Emperor Meiji and this war. Throughout the plot, the emperor's emotions were expressed through the singing of *shigin*.

modern *chikuzen* music developed more directly out of *shamisen* music, the *biwa* itself is held not in the upright position of a *satsuma* performance but sideways like a *shamisen*. Actually, the original *biwa* playing position was with the *biwa* held like a guitar while sitting cross-legged (see Plate 30). The upright position developed in the Meiji period. The *chikuzen* plectrum is unlike the usual *biwa bachi*, being thick and blunt like that used in the *gidayūbushi shamisen* genre. In classic *chikuzen* style, the percussive sound of the plectrum on the body of the *biwa* is not used as much as in *satsuma* music. One must keep adding the word "classic," because many contemporary *chikuzen* players borrow both the instruments and plectrums of various *satsuma* traditions. The fingering technique of the *chikuzenbiwa* is essentially the same as that already described. The standard *chikuzen* tuning is shown in Figure 22D. The tuning of the five-stringed *biwa* is the same as the five-stringed *satsuma* instrument.

The music of the *chikuzenbiwa* incorporates features of the other *biwa* styles plus those of narrative *shamisen* music, with the influence of the music of puppet plays (*gidayūbushi*) being particularly strong. The *chikuzenbiwa* is most effective in lyrical sections, its intimate tone lending itself more naturally to such music. While some of the most typical *satsuma* music occurs during the *biwa* interludes, a more representative *chikuzen* music is *nagashi*, in which the *biwa* and voice perform together. This can be heard on CD track 11 at the second paragraph, "His heartfelt prayer" (*makoto yori*).

The individual melodies of *chikuzenbiwa* are given picturesque names. Some are named after seasons, though their use in compositions does not always relate to the season in question. Other sets of melodies are simply numbered; for example, there are some fourteen *ban* (*ichiban, niban, sanban,* etc.), fifteen *gō*, and twenty-five *chō*. In the notation they are marked only by number. Certain patterns are named after birds and animals. Much the same naming process is found in *satsumabiwa* and in *gidayūbushi* as well, though the specific names and their meanings may be different. The frets of the *biwa*, moreover, are sometimes named after the elements (wood, fire, earth, metal, water), which perhaps reflects the instrument's Chinese origin.

The old ballad singer of the West belongs to the same tradition as Japan's *biwa* musicians. The *Iliad* and the *Odyssey* were preserved for centuries on the lips and lyres of Greek musicians. From the Nordic *Kalevala* to the tales of Barbara Allen, it has been the singers who have kept the old tales alive and fresh. Such a tradition is fast dying under an irresistible barrage of celluloid dream worlds and electronic chips. This fate may be the inevitable price of scientific progress. Fortunately, in Japan the narrative tradition has risen far enough above the folk level to be able to take advantage of the advances of modern technology without being destroyed by them. *Biwa* music, though subject to new and very strong competition, is still an element in the overall picture of Japan's musical life. Much of its storytelling function has been usurped by radio, television, and films, but it still retains that rare combination of music and drama which only narrative singing can offer. The setting and society may have changed, but the *biwa* bards of Japan continue to capture the imagination with tales of love and adventure.

Japan's drama-loving audience is large enough to support many different narrative forms. The temple fairs still exist in competition with the convenience store and discount sales campaigns, and *biwa* music can be heard over the radio or bought on CD. Perhaps few other countries have Japan's talent for knitting the old and the new into one multicolored tapestry.

# CHAPTER SIX

# THE *SHAKUHACHI*

## 1. The History of the *Shakuhachi*

One of the easiest ways to approach the music of another culture is through its flute literature. There seems to be something in the tone of the flute that has a universal appeal. This catholic quality is amply illustrated by the example of the *shakuhachi*. Foreigners of the most diverse nationalities consistently point to *shakuhachi* music as one of the first forms of Japanese music for which they developed a liking. The plaintive tone of this simple vertical stalk of bamboo is one of the many romantic elements of a tourist's evening in Kyoto. Thus, the *shakuhachi* deserves a separate chapter by virtue of its popularity as well as its rather interesting history.

There are many end-blown flutes in the world, particularly in pastoral societies. In Japan there are four kinds: the small *tempuku*, which was discussed in Chapter Five (p. 154), the *gagaku shakuhachi*, the *hitoyogiri*, and the modern *shakuhachi*. The *gagaku shakuhachi* is believed to have been introduced in the Nara period along with all the other *gagaku* instruments. There are several examples found in the eighth-century Shōsōin warehouse including ones made of stone, ivory, and jade![1] *Shakuhachi* teachers are mentioned among the court musicians and, though no longer used today, the instrument is seen in some earlier ensembles (look at the "foreign" *rinyūgaku* musicians in Plate 27).

The original Chinese instrument may have evolved from pitch pipes. In ancient China, the proper tuning of the imperial music was of great importance to the maintenance of earthly and celestial unanimity, and every

---

1. See Biblio. ref. 3.7.

new emperor required a new measurement of the pipes used to tune the court orchestra. A band of such pipes, called a *paixiao*, became part of the orchestra itself. In Plate 27, one musician can be seen busily blowing on a Japanese version of this instrument. This type of panpipe was eventually disassembled, and each pipe was fitted with five holes so that melodies could be played on it. Called a *dungxiao* (in Japanese, *dōshō*), this is said to be the origin of the Japanese *shakuhachi*. The term *shakuhachi* is believed to be a corruption of the Chinese measurement for one such instrument, the Japanese pronunciation of which is *isshakuhassun* ("one *shaku* and eight *sun*," approximately fifty-six centimeters). The length of these early *shakuhachi*, however, varied considerably.

The major difference between the tubes of the panpipe, as used together

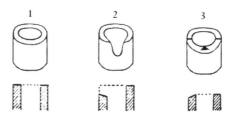

FIGURE 23. The evolution of the *shakuhachi* mouthpiece

or separately, and the structure of the early *shakuhachi* can be seen in Figure 23. The original pipe was merely blown across the top just as children do on a hollow reed or a bottle. When the pipes were used separately, a niche was cut in the edge and the end was either covered by the lower lip of the player or closed by a node in the bamboo. This type of mouthpiece can still be seen in modern Chinese vertical flutes, though they are longer and thinner than the ancient forms. The *shakuhachi*, however, is unique in the way in which its mouthpiece is constructed. It is cut obliquely outward, the exact opposite of the Chinese manner. This is believed to be a Japanese innovation. Much later, a small piece of ivory or bone was inserted so that the playing edge became finer and less susceptible to wear.[2] This insertion is called a *tsuno* or *hasami guchi*. Its shape varies. Figure 23 (3) shows its most common form.

The *gagaku shakuhachi* was still fashioned after the Chinese model and

2. For a detailed account of how this is done see Biblio. ref. 6-6.

produced the Chinese pentatonic scale (see Figure 2). It flourished during most of the Heian period and is mentioned often in the literature of the time. But in due course it died out, and since then has never been revived with particular success.

One reason for its demise was the appearance in the Muromachi period (1333–1568) of the second main type of Japanese *shakuhachi*, the *hitoyogiri* (Plate 53). It is this instrument in which the new type of blowing edge is seen (without the insert), and the arrangement of the finger holes is similar to the modern *shakuhachi*: four on the top and one behind. The scales it was able to produce were Japanese folk scales, but being shorter than the modern *shakuhachi*, it sounded higher.

There are legends that would suggest the *hitoyogiri* also may have come from China or even Southwest Asia. All that is known for certain is that, during the Muromachi period, beggar priests appeared playing this instrument. Part of the meager baggage that these men carried on their wanderings was a straw mat, which served as their bed, and for this reason they became known as rice-straw priests (*komosō*). These are the predecessors of the more famous *komusō* to whom we shall come presently. The sweet, high tone of the *hitoyogiri* was pleasant but transitory. A majority of its music disappeared with the decline of the beggar-priest tradition, though it was used in the pleasure-houses of the early Edo period and as a cultural hobby (Plate 53). By the nineteenth century, the music was all but forgotten. The narrowness of the instrument made its tone rather thin, and it could not compete with the more full-bodied sound of the modern *shakuhachi*. Though it was used occasionally as an addition to lighter *shamisen* music such as *kouta*, twentieth-century attempts to revive it have been isolated, and it seems unlikely that the *hitoyogiri* will ever come into general use again.

The modern *shakuhachi* is basically the product of the Edo period. It is difficult to form an accurate picture of how its music evolved, as faking historical documents was a favorite pastime of Edo writers. One thing is certain: the main figure in the growth of this music was the *komusō*, a new kind of wandering priest (Plate 54). These basket-hatted men can still occasionally be seen on the streets of modern Japan. From behind their wicker visors, they have viewed the flow of Japanese life from the seventeenth century to the present, yet their interest in the daily affairs of the towns-

*Shakuhachi*

people was not always a passive one. Although it is believed that their name is a corruption of the word *komosō*, mentioned earlier, their function in society was very different.

The ranks of the Edo-period *komusō* were not drawn primarily from the seekers of Buddha's paradise; rather, they were filled with *rōnin*, masterless samurai who had lost their original rank and privileges during the violent clan struggles that marked the late sixteenth century. These men sought satisfaction more in earthly revenge than in heavenly rewards. It was from their ranks that many of the early Christians were drawn. When the Christian movement was halted by the slaughter of Shimabara in 1638, many of these *rōnin* felt their entire class was going to fall victim to the paranoid vengeance of the shogun's government.

It is believed that one group of these desperate men formed a *komusō* group in Kyoto called the Fukeshū.[3] In secret, they acquired a building associated with one of the larger Buddhist temples in the hope that the shogun would not view their activities as part of a Christian revival. This, their headquarters, they named the Myōan (or Meian) temple. Despite this precaution, they were subjected to suspicion from other ancillary temples: in addition to their dislike of the *rōnin*'s unsavory background, these other temples were probably afraid of guilt by association.

In order to secure their position, the Fukeshū faked a number of papers claiming their historical origins as coming from China; they also produced a copy of a license from the first Edo shogun, Ieyasu, giving them the exclusive right to solicit alms by means of *shakuhachi* playing.[4] Armed with these documents, they finally notified the authorities of their existence and asked for official recognition of their temple and their rights. When the government bureaucrats received this request, they immediately demanded the original Ieyasu document. The Fukeshū claimed that it had been burned years earlier. It seemed certain that this group was destined to be short-lived until one of the shogun's wiser advisers suggested that their request be granted. His reasoning was that destruction of the group would only scatter and further embitter already vengeful men. It would be safer to grant them their much coveted security and preferment, on condition that they

3. The following account is based on the incomplete research of the late Nakatsuka Chikuzen. A résumé of his work can be found in Biblio. ref. 1·21, 244–48. See also Biblio. ref. 6·9.
4. An excerpt from this document can be read in Biblio. ref. 1·10, II, 1027.

act as spies for the government and keep track of the goings-on of all the other *rōnin*. Such a proposition was made and accepted.

To facilitate the exchange of information as well as control of the organization, the *komusō* headquarters was moved to Edo, the seat of the shogun's government. Their "religious" center was established in the Ichigatsuji and Reihōji temples outside the city, while their "business" center was located in Asakusa, in the heart of the entertainment district. From there, they could fan out along the avenues and back alleys of this famous pleasure district, playing a few soft melodies and overhearing equally intimate conversations. Eventually, with the Meiji Restoration, the organization was abolished, but the tradition of the "stool pigeon" lived on at least in fiction if not in fact.

With the discussion of the so-called *fukeshū shakuhachi*, we enter for the first time into the colorful life of old Edo (Tokyo). While *shakuhachi* music was not one of the great influential forms of music during the Edo period, the *komusō* who played it were common figures in the genre painting and novels of the times. We find in the tales of the *komusō* one of the myriad reflections of Edo life by which we can vicariously savor the spice and danger of the period. For example, take the instrument itself. The *hitoyogiri* was a small, narrow bamboo tube. The *shakuhachi*, by contrast, is longer, much thicker, and uses the bulk of the root end for the bell of the instrument. The reason for this extreme change in design is found in the violence of the age. When these ex-samurai became wandering priests, they were denied the protection of their double swords. They therefore redesigned the *shakuhachi* so as to make it a formidable club as well as a musical instrument. This is perhaps the only instance in music history in which the practical necessity of self-defense was a major factor in instrument construction. A dramatic example of this can be seen in the *kabuki* play *Sukeroku*, about an *otokodate*, a "chivalrous commoner," identified by the outlandish color combination of his costume and the *shakuhachi* stuck in the back of his belt for use both in making romantic music and defending the weak or destroying the bad.

The seventeenth and eighteenth centuries in Edo have a ribald quality that often reminds one of Boccaccio and fourteenth-century Europe. For instance, there is a tale in an Edo-period jokebook (see Biblio. ref. 1·10, II, 1026) concerning a gentleman-about-town by the name of Ōtori Ichibei. This man seems to have had no profession whatsoever, and his only talent was an alacrity for telling "strange things to young people." He also had a flair for adventure and dangerous enterprises. On one occasion he got into an argument with a *komusō* while enjoying the hospitality of a local wineshop. In the heat of the debate, Ichibei grabbed the *komusō*'s *shakuhachi* and, his mouth being full of wine, played it with his most insulting orifice! In one of the greatest understatements in Japanese literature, the episode concludes with the comment that this is the first known instance of anyone of his class playing this instrument.

Obviously, the *shakuhachi* music of this period was not very Buddhist. Popular theater tunes and folk songs were more appropriate, and the pieces from that period reflect the more soulful forms of such music. Although, legally, no one was allowed to play the *shakuhachi* without a license from the *komusō* headquarters, it gradually began to appear in the provinces and within the geisha quarters. The *komusō* costume, with its basket hat, also became a favorite device for anyone wishing to travel incognito. A variation of this hat is seen frequently in *kabuki* dramas, especially when the police inspector calls.

The original Kyoto *komusō* group became known as the Myōan school of *shakuhachi*, now more commonly called the Meian. The teachers of the Tokyo center called their school the Kinko. In the early Meiji period, a third main school appeared, devoted to teaching the general populace: this was the Tozan school. As the two priest-run schools lost their preferment in the Meiji reforms, they also turned to teaching pupils of all classes.

In the late Edo period, the *shakuhachi* had begun to be used as a secular solo instrument as well as in *koto* ensemble music (see *jiuta*). This precedent saved *shakuhachi* music from a sudden demise during those dark days of the early Meiji period when most Japanese music was considered uncivilized and even worthless. As the mood of the times became more temperate, the schools of secular *shakuhachi* flourished. Even the Western-oriented university students found that playing the *shakuhachi* added an old-world charm to their terribly serious personalities. The use of the *shakuhachi* as accompaniment for *shigin* poetry was mentioned in Chapter Five.

As one of Japan's more Western-sounding instruments, the *shakuhachi* was also used extensively in the experiments of the new Japanese music movement in the 1920s and 1930s. Perhaps the most famous and successful composition of this movement is the late Miyagi Michio's *koto-shakuhachi* duet, "Haru no umi" (The Spring Sea). This piece has been heard in every combination, from violin and piano to the Philadelphia Symphony. For all its arrangements, it still sounds best in the original, as Miyagi made excellent use of the characteristic melodic style of the *shakuhachi*. Unfortunately, many composers are still obstinately trying to match the sound of the symphony by forming massed Japanese bands. The theory that ten *shakuhachi* sound ten times better than one is typical of the kind of traps into which much of modern "traditional" Japanese music has fallen. To equate volume with quality is the worst kind of misconception of both Japanese and Western music. Luckily, there is still a large segment of modern *shakuhachi* music that is devoted to solo or chamber-music literature. In addition, in the late twentieth century there has been a significant growth in the number of non-Japanese performers and even instrument makers. It is they who have increased the interest and repertory internationally. There is even *shakuhachi* jazz. An occasional *komusō* can still be heard, but the aesthetic center of *shakuhachi* music seems to remain in personal, private performances and the intimate concert salon.

## 2. The Instrument and Its Music

As outlined in the history section, the characteristic properties of the *shakuhachi* are (1) the oblique blowing edge with its bone or ivory insertion in the center, (2) four holes on the top and one on the back, and (3) the bowed line of the instrument and slight tapering away from the bamboo root, which forms the bell. The latter quality is not always found in natural bamboo, so *shakuhachi* makers must often improve on nature and bend the wood until it has taken on the accepted, aesthetically pleasing shape. The forte of many Japanese artists, in fact, has been their ability to subject nature to man-made laws of form without making the results seem artificial.

Although the outside thickness of the instrument varies, the inside diameter is very carefully regulated by judicious cutting with special rasps and files. In the Myōan-school *shakuhachi*, one often finds that the ridge of the node in the bamboo is retained on the inside.[5] In most *shakuhachi*, however, it is removed. Looking down the barrel of a *shakuhachi*, one sees a skillfully rounded, lacquered tube with a deceptively simple line.

The length of the *shakuhachi* varies. The standard length is 54.5 centime-

5. It is the Myōan *shakuhachi* that also has a differently shaped ivory insert.

ters. There are also seven- and nine-holed instruments. There were two twentieth-century experiments that tried to combine the qualities of a flute with those of a *shakuhachi*. The first consisted of a horizontal *shakuhachi*, which really amounted to a bamboo bass flute, as the fingering and embouchure were, of necessity, different from that of a traditional *shakuhachi*. The other experiment retained the all-important mouthpiece but added a flute-like key system to the body so that Western chromatic scales could be played. This so-called Ōkura-aulos (it was invented by Ōkura Kishichirō) was unsuited for traditional music and a new literature especially written for it never appeared. Nevertheless, it is an excellent example of the experimental spirit of twentieth-century Japanese traditional musicians and their eagerness to make some compromise with Western music. Like most of the Western-style experimental pieces of the 1920s, these works have fallen by the wayside.

While the five holes of the standard *shakuhachi* produce the tones D, F, G, A, D, there are a host of other tones available by the process known as *merikari*. This is a system of combining half-holing (only partially covering the hole with the finger) with changes in embouchure in order to produce many different pitches from a single hole.

Theoretically, there are three levels of lowness (*meri*) and three of highness (*kari*) for each fingering. These differences, however, do not represent Western half-step gradations but more often very slight changes of a quarter tone or less. A comparable technique was noted in the discussion of the *noh* flute. In *shakuhachi* music, it is exploited to a much greater degree. It is one of the characteristic qualities of the *shakuhachi* playing technique.

Another important refinement in *shakuhachi* music is the execution of the ending of each breath phrase. In Figure 24 one can see that every such phrase has a final grace note. Listening to CD track 12[6] not only demonstrates the fluidity of the line but also the flexibility of the composition. A correct performance of the proper grace note for each melodic situation is considered the mark of a true professional, but the "correct" composition is a matter of who is performing and what school is represented. Stylistically, this use of ending graces is another typical feature of *shakuhachi* music that differentiates it from Western traditions, in which final notes of phrases tend to just stop "cleanly." The *shakuhachi* phrase often leaves one hanging in musical

6. The CD is played by the late national treasure, Yamaguchi Gorō (1933–99).

space with the brief flick on a pitch below that of the melodic "final" tone. One floats on a thin, beautiful stream of bamboo sound.

Other techniques to be noted in Figure 24 are the constant use of dynamic swells and the free rhythmic structure of the section. One of the main purposes of these swells is to allow the performer to display the different tone qualities available on the *shakuhachi*. From a whispering, reedy piano, the sound grows to a ringing metallic forte only to sink back into a cotton-wrapped softness, ending with an almost inaudible grace note, seemingly an afterthought.[7] It is a combination of all these musical idioms that produces feelings of mystery and melancholy in the minds of many a listener.

One must not be misled, however, into believing that the form of the music is as vague as the mood it evokes. While *shakuhachi* music is one of

In Scale

FIGURE 24. Opening of "Hifumi hachigaeshi"

the freest in Japan, it still has discernible formal principles at work in every composition. The main distinction is that these principles have not been formalized into a written theory such as was seen in most of the Japanese music studied so far. In pure *shakuhachi* music, there is no explicit concept of *dan* sections or the application of the *jo-ha-kyū* theory, though a detailed analysis of many such pieces might reveal the existence of both. Such an exhaustive analysis has not yet been done. The comments concerning *shakuhachi* form that follow are based on the study of only a fraction of the repertoire. Hence, they should be considered as general observations and not as definitive statements on the structure of *shakuhachi* music.

The music for the *shakuhachi* is divided into three main categories: (1) *honkyoku*, the original pieces; (2) *gaikyoku*, borrowed pieces; and (3)

7. This is basically a description of the Kinko-school *shakuhachi* style. The Myōan-school phrases are shorter and more "breathy." However, the account given above is indicative of what is considered to be the typical playing style.

*shinkyoku*, new pieces. In the first category are found the basic pieces said to have been composed by the school founders and other early masters. Of course, these vary with each school, but there are three compositions, "Kyorei," "Mukaiji," and "Kokūreibo," that are considered to be the classic foundations of all *shakuhachi* music. Legend claims that these pieces were brought from China with the first teachers and were passed down through the *komusō* tradition. The melodic style and scale structure of the present-day versions, however, date from the Edo period.

The characteristic scale used in old *shakuhachi* pieces can be seen in Figure 24. This is known as the *in* scale. The *in* and the *yō* scales (see Figure 21), together with their permutations, form the basis of most of Japanese art and folk music of the Edo period. The musician will notice in Figure 24 that one characteristic of the *in* scale is the emphasis on a half-step upper neighbor (E-flat) and a whole-step lower neighbor tone (C).

*Shakuhachi* pieces vary in length from a few minutes to half an hour. In general, the music tends to follow a rondo-like form, that is, there is an alternation of one basic melodic idea with sections of new music. For instance, Figure 24 is the first section of the piece "Hifumi hachigaeshi." If we call this section A, the form of the entire composition could be represented by the scheme A-B-A-C-A. The returns of the main theme are not exact, the melody being subjected to constant variations of a highly subtle nature.

In addition to the rondo form, there is a tendency for *shakuhachi* pieces to begin in a low or medium register, build to a high climax, and then drop back to quieter music. These climaxes appear most often in the new music sections of rondo-like pieces. It is in such sections that one finds the more angular melodic lines with many skips. These sections also tend to be longer than the returns to the main theme. The final statement of section A is usually quite brief. One factor that adds to both the appearance of thematic germs and to the sense of wandering is the limited range of *shakuhachi* melodic styling. The various melodic germs do not have definite names as they do in *biwa* music and some of the other forms studied; nevertheless, one becomes aware of very specific melodic types. Depending on how they are used and how familiar one is with the style, these tend to create a feeling of unity in the music. They also enhance the more common reaction to such music, the false impression of aimless wandering. Perhaps the *shakuhachi* composers have done in music what the artisans have done in constructing the instrument: managing to give the illusion of a sound as natural as the wind blowing in the pines while covertly subjugating this sound to the artificial laws of musical form.

The second category of *shakuhachi* music, *gaikyoku*, represents all music either borrowed from or played in concert with the *shamisen* or the *koto*. In the middle of the nineteenth century, many *shakuhachi* solos were based on famous *shamisen* pieces. It reminds one of the way in which early Western keyboard music often was derived from existing choral works. In both cases, a new form sought its base in an already established idiom and then gradually developed an independent style quite different from the original. In the case of the *shakuhachi*, the form of such pieces remained basically that of the original, and the only significant difference was in the instrumental styling.

The most common combination of the *shakuhachi* with the *shamisen* occurs in *jiuta*. This form, when it developed as a *shamisen* genre, usually involved a *shamisen*, a *koto*, and one other instrument. Sometimes it was the bowed *kokyū* (Plate 58), at other times it was the *shakuhachi*, but by the late nineteenth century the *shakuhachi* had become the most common addition (Plate 56). Its function in such music is to play a melismatic version of the basic *shamisen* line (Chapter Seven will discuss this further). Neither of these *gaikyoku* styles can be considered to be a truly independent *shakuhachi* form, since the *shakuhachi* is subservient to the style of the original piece in music borrowed from the *shamisen* repertoire and acts only as a reinforcement of the main melody in *koto* music.

The *shinkyoku* category covers all the pieces written since the "old days." When this period ends is a matter of school and clan. The form and style of these new pieces cover a wide range, including a great many Western-style experiments. Perhaps the most unfortunate of these are the massed *shakuhachi* bands mentioned earlier. It is really quite sad to hear the subtle beauties of the *shakuhachi* disappear in a gust of sound emanating from twenty or thirty instruments of varying intonations. However, in the last decades of the twentieth century, the growth of international interest in the *shakuhachi* has increased the number of successful solo or small ensemble compositions. The intriguing tonal variations found in electronic music seem already available on the *shakuhachi*, just waiting for composers to adapt to new idioms.

There are a few old pieces that use *shakuhachi* ensembles. In some Buddhist temples, a small group of *shakuhachi* may be used to accompany the service. There are also *shakuhachi* pieces that are meant to be used as aids for Buddhist meditation. Edifying texts are printed along with the music notation. But classical duets are the best-known forms of *shakuhachi* ensemble music. Among them is "Shika no tōne" (The Distant Sound of the Deer), which represents the mating calls between a buck and his doe. The two *shakuhachi* play divergent melodies that gradually become more alike until they are one. The symbolism may be rather obvious, but the music is lovely. The titles of *shakuhachi* pieces in general are replete with such picturesque images that bespeak of romantic ideas and old customs. For instance, the title of the piece transcribed in Figure 24, "Hifumi hachi-gaeshi," means "One, two, three, return the bowl," referring to the journey of the beggar's bowl from his hands to the house owner's and back to the beggar priest. For the largess contained therein, such music was performed by the ancient *komosō* and *komusō shakuhachi* players.

*Shakuhachi* music today rests primarily in the hands of professional teachers and their secular pupils. It is still used by some as a means of meditation, but most of the great works in the *shakuhachi* literature were created in a basically secular context. As long as there are competent teachers and a sufficient number of amateurs to support them through lessons, these finer products will continue to survive. European and American *shakuhachi* musicians and instrument makers exist in Japan as well as abroad, and foreign societies and newsletters add to its contemporary vitality.

The *shakuhachi* and its music are designed for introspection. With a modicum of materials, the player can reap a harvest of quiet pleasures. In a crowded and busy world, such simple means of refined musical recreation and relaxation are to be coveted by any culture. Perhaps this is one of the most important intrinsic appeals of the *shakuhachi* today.

A full *noh* ensemble is seen in this 1956 performance of the play *Takasago*.

The *mibu kyōgen* pantomime plays in Kyoto resemble ancient Euro-
an morality plays and retain the style of the early folk theatricals that
pired the creators of *noh*.

40. The *nōkan* is the only melodic instrument in the *noh* ensemble. Note that the holes are covered by the middle joints of the fingers, producing the half-holed effects characteristic of its music.

41. Before every *noh* performance, the musicians play the warm-up piece "Shirabe," while the lead actor absorbs his role in a mirror.

42. Traditional Japanese music is taught piece by piece through rote methods. Here the teacher beats out the pattern of the *tsuzumi* drum with two leather-covered fans on a "rhythm box" (*hyōshiban*) while singing the vocal or the flute melody.

43. The *kotsuzumi* hand position allows the player to squeeze the ropes and hence change the tone.

44. The *kotsuzumi* is reassembled at every performance so that the rope tensions will be correct for weather and stage conditions.

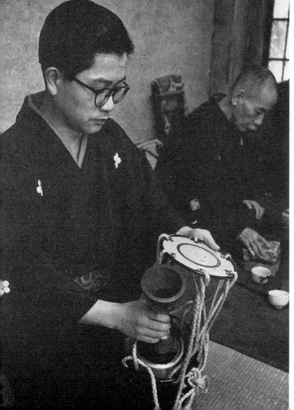

**45.** The *taiko* drummer is executing the *kashira* pattern in the play *Hagoromo*. The white costume and mixed genders suggest an amateur recital.

Heian-period gentry often courted their ladies by playing the *gakubiwa*, as seen in this famous scroll of *The Tale of Genji*.

47. A *mōsōbiwa* performer chant prayers or stories.

48. Imai Tsutomu carries on the blind *heikebiwa* tradition of reciting the *Tale of the Heike*.

49. Hirata Kyokushū (1905–64) taught *chikuzenbiwa* only to those who first prayed all night beneath the waterspout at the Kiyomizu temple in Kyoto.

**50.** This *satsumabiwa* performer looks like a traditional blind priest narrator, but his eyes are closed only to better envision the dramatic scene he is describing.

**51.** *Biwa* makers still use traditional tools to carve the body out of one piece of wood. Potential *biwa* soundboards are seen stacked on the shelf behind him.

52. The *shakuhachi* is best heard in solo performances.

53. A priest and two gentlemen enjoying sweet *hitoyogiri* melodies in this drawing from the early nineteenth-century *Shichiku kokinshū*.

4. *Komusō* musicians used to collect temple funds in the box hanging around their neck and information with their eyes and ears inside a basket hat (*tengai*).

55. An idealized picture of a 1950s Japanese family enjoying Japanese culture.

56. A *sankyoku* performance, 1977 (*koto*, Fujii Chiyoga; *shamisen*, Ambiru Hiroka; *shakuhachi*, Aoki Reibo).

57. The *koto* hand position for th Yamada school. Note the place ment of the picks.

The *kokyū*, Japan's only bowed instrument, being played by
yagi Michio.

59. The Ryukyu *sanshin* is the predecessor of the Japanese *shamisen*.

60. Female *gidayū* performers have been popular in little theaters for over a century.

61. Male *gidayū* performers are best heard in the *bunraku* theater.

73. The intense concentration and dramatic expressions of the *tayū* narrator are clearly seen in this sequence of photographs of the late Takemoto Tsudayū performing in a 1956 puppet theater.

74. A *nagauta* ensemble is the major lyrical music of the *kabuki* but here is performing in concert.

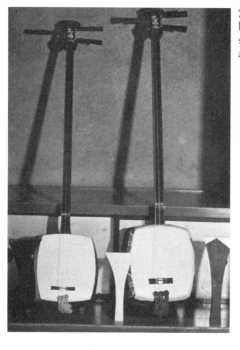

75. The *gidayū shamisen* is much more heavily built than the *nagauta* one. The three plectra shown are (left to right) used for *jiuta*, *nagauta* and *gidayū*.

. The *hanamichi* ramp from the back of the eater to the stage is the major entranceway r actors. The *geza* musicians see them through its in the scenery wall where the ramp meets e stage.

. Onstage music is called *debayashi*. In this scene from *Kan-chō* the musicians are in their usual position, though scenery ay change matters.

78. Behind the bamboo blind the offstage *geza* musicians provide all kinds of special music and sound effects. Here the play requires the sound of a *noh hayashi*.

79. In this scene from *Momijigari* the *tokiwazu* musicians are placed on a dais at the foot of the *hanamichi*, the *nagauta* are stage left, and the *gidayū* are barely visible above the stage left entrance. Such mixtures of music are called *kakeai*.

192

# KOTO MUSIC

## 1. Introduction

While much of the repertoire of the *biwa* and *shakuhachi* is a product of the Edo period, it is the music of the *koto* and the *shamisen* that best represents this very musical era. The *shamisen* belongs to the world of the theater and all the turbulent excitement that the entertainment districts of Edo represent. The *koto*, by contrast, developed out of a court tradition and gradually entered the home as an accomplishment for the daughters of the rising commercial class as well as those of the nobility.

The *koto*'s harp-like tone added a gentler hue to the generally gaudy picture of Japan from the seventeenth through the nineteenth centuries. This quality helped *koto* music survive during Japan's Westernization. It met the approval of Victorian taste and did not suffer from the unsavory past or un-Western sound of the *shamisen*. As seen in Plate 55—a 1950s photo—the *koto* became a symbol of middle- and upper-class traditional music in the home; but it now competes with the Western piano and the Suzuki violin in the battle of homespun art against ready-made entertainment. In both East and West, the best one can hope for in this struggle is some kind of truce. At present, however, our concern is not with the battle but with the description of Japan's main defending champion, the *koto*.

## 2. The History of the *Koto*

Originally, the word *koto* was used generically for all kinds of stringed instruments. Even the *biwa* was known as a type of *koto*. The practical use of the word in Japan, however, refers to any one of the various horizontal, plucked chordophones. In China, this type of instrument came in two basic forms, those with bridges and those without. The best-known bridge-less zither in China was the seven-stringed *qin*. It was often called the favorite instrument of Confucius, though scholars feel he preferred the *se*. Still, literature and paintings depict the *qin* as the proper instrument for a wise man to play. A beautiful example is to be found in the eighth-century Shōsōin warehouse, and it is mentioned in many early Japanese books. The forlorn heroine of the tenth-century *Ochikubo monogatari* lamented that she had never learned to play the *qin* though she was skilled at the *koto*.[1] The *qin* was used sporadically in Japan by Sinophile courtiers, scholars, or well-to-do merchants.[2]

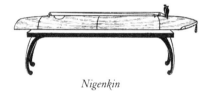

*Nigenkin*

Japanese developments in bridgeless zithers include the one- and two-stringed *koto* (*ichigenkin* and *nigenkin* or *yakumogoto*), which flourished in the late nineteenth century. Around 1920 in Nagoya, Morita Gorō created a new version of the two-stringed *koto*, on which one pushes down buttons above its metal strings like a Western autoharp. It was named the *taishōgoto* after the Taishō era (1912–26), when it was invented, and became a popular amateur pastime in the provinces. It was even used on radio to accompany dramas.[3]

Bridged zithers are the most common in Japan. They developed out of the Chinese *se* tradition. Two members of the *koto* family have already been mentioned, the *wagon* and the *gakusō*, the former having six strings that were tuned by means of six high bridges made of twig forks, and the latter more closely modeled after the Chinese forms, with twelve or thirteen

1. *The Tale of the Lady Ochikubo*, trans. by Wilfred Whitehouse and Eizo Yanagi-sawa (London: Peter Owen, 1970), p. 2.
2. See Appendix IV of Robert van Gulik's *The Lore of the Chinese Lute* (Tokyo: Sophia University, 1969).
3. The author heard groups performing on it in Argentina and in Hawaii. The *yakumogoto* is taught in Guam.

strings and firmer bridges of ivory or wood. The full-bodied tone of the court *koto* made it more suited for solo use.

Though both Chinese and Japanese zithers are found in the Shōsōin storehouse, imaginative writings have often spoken louder than facts in tracing the origins of the *koto* in Japan. In the late tenth-century novel, *The Tale of the Hollow Tree* (*Utsubo monogatari*), one finds the hero, Kiyohara no Toshikage, cast on the shores of China, where his adventures include lessons on the *qin*, and when he eventually returns to Japan he brings with him instruments called "seven-stringed *koto*." This fictional account has confused historians, as the Chinese characters for *qin* and *koto* are intermixed. An addition to the problem is that there is, in fact, one seven-string zither preserved in the Shōsōin with a *qin*-size body, *koto*-style string holes, and tuning pegs like those of a *biwa*! Scholars wisely call it simply a seven-stringed instrument. Perhaps it is the result of the inventive mind of some Japanese musician seeking to improve on all the Chinese instruments that dominated Nara-period court music.

Another traditional claim for the introduction of the *koto* into Japan is that the *gagaku* musician Fujiwara no Sadatoshi first brought the solo *koto* music tradition of China to Japan in the ninth century; but there is little chance of proving this musically, as all the solo *koto* literature of the Nara and Heian periods seems to have been passed on in the form of aural learning or as "secret" pieces, i.e. compositions that were taught only to selected students. (The "hiding" of specific compositions by the teacher or guild that "owned" them was common in many *hōgaku* genres and has remained so to this day, although recordings have now invalidated the tradition.) In the turbulent Kamakura days that followed, the music was lost in the chaos of crumbling imperial power.

While we cannot view this music firsthand, we can get a vivid if vicarious impression of its beauty via the literature of the period. In *The Tale of Genji* alone, there are no less than fifteen different occasions when either the *koto* or the *wagon* are an important part of the story. For example, when Prince Genji is in exile in Akashi,[4] he consoles himself by playing his *koto*. He is joined by a retired courtier with whom he reminisces about the music and other pleasures of the court in Kyoto. True to the romantic theme of

4. See *The Tale of Genji*, trans. by Edward G. Seidensticker (New York: Knopf, 1978), Chap. 13ff, 266, 277, 325.

the book, the old man has a daughter who also plays the *koto*. However, it is not until Genji is about to return to the capital that he induces her to play for him. On parting, he leaves his own *koto* with her with the promise that he will be as constant as its middle string, for it is always tuned to the same pitch. The prince left more than just his *koto* behind. Eventually, the lady of Akashi and the baby are brought to the environs of the capital. When Genji first rides out to see her, he hears the strains of his own *koto* being played in the same tuning as the one in which it was set on his departure....

Finding beautiful ladies by means of their *koto* music seemed to be a favorite convention among many Japanese writers. In the *biwa* saga, the *Tale of the Heike*, a trusted vassal is sent to find the emperor's recently lost paramour.[5] Her hiding place is unknown but her *koto* playing is so beautiful that the man has only to ride through a likely district until he hears her play. The system works, and the girl, Kogō, is returned to the emperor. The story has a typical Heike-style ending. After a child is born of this union, the enemies of Kogō at court ambush her and commit the twenty-three-year-old beauty to a nunnery. Soon thereafter, the emperor dies.

Many a courtier and warrior met a more violent death in the struggles that marked the end of the Heike dominance. Musically, it is the survivors of these bloodbaths that are of the most interest. From the twelfth century on, a steady stream of court women fled to the relative security of Kyushu. Though refugees, they still traveled with a baggage train proper for a person of their standing. Thus, we read that the remnants of solo *koto* music could be found in northern Kyushu long after it had disappeared from the capital.

This was not the first *koto* music to appear in the provinces. There is some reason to believe that popular Chinese *koto* music and Confucian texts came directly to Kyushu much earlier. Unfortunately, only the legends concerning this importation have survived, and there is no music with which to test the hypothesis. The music brought by the refugees was believed to have been based on the style of *imayō*, *rōei*, and *saibara*, the three main vocal genres of court and temple music. Whatever may have been the basic source of this early Kyushu music, the present-day survivals stem from a sixteenth-century school known as Tsukushi, the name of a district

5. See *Tale of the Heike*, trans. by Helen Craig McCullough (Stanford: Stanford University Press, 1988), Chap. 6.

in Kyushu. This so-called *tsukushigoto* was founded by the priest Kenjun (1547?–1636). It is interesting to note that what is traditionally accepted as the first piece of this school, "Fuki," is based on *etenraku imayō*, one of the favorite court forms of music (see page 100). Kenjun is said to have composed ten pieces using a form known as *kumiuta*, consisting of a group of short poems, usually with no topical connection, which were set to music and sung in a given order. This was the start of *sōkyoku*, music for the *koto*.

The music of the Tsukushi school stands on the borderline between present-day popular *koto* music and the old court *koto* tradition. Unfortunately, this style never regained the protection of the court; it had to fare for itself among the priests and Confucians of Kyushu. The teachers kept an aristocratic aloofness from their environment, the rules of the guild specifying, for example, that *tsukushigoto* could not be taught to blind men, and even women were barred from playing this music for some time.[6] The latter prohibition seems strange since the distant origins of the music were brought to Kyushu by female minds and fingers. The irony of the edict, however, is that the only remaining performers of *tsukushigoto* in 1957 were two women and, by 1998, only one of their students, also female.

Out of the original repertoire of "secret" and "most secret" pieces, only a fraction has been retained. Today, this music is performed in a slow, languid style somewhat like that of the *imayō*, from which it may have developed. It is difficult to tell how much the style has changed over the past three hundred years. Fortunately for the music historian, recordings have saved this tradition from complete oblivion. A detailed analysis of this music and its history may give us a clue as to the style of those ancient *koto* pieces that drifted through the gardens of the Heian palaces. The court *koto* tradition escaped the ravages of war only to succumb to the inevitable death march of time. We can only be thankful that *tsukushigoto* managed to hold on so long. Perhaps the final irony of the situation is that one of the most efficient executioners of traditional music, mass communication, should also become the final repository of its remains.

History is usually written with a polemic slant. Music history is no exception. The explanation of how popular (in Japanese, *zoku*, or "vulgar")

6. From our study of *biwa* and *shakuhachi* music we know that most blind musicians were merely beggars. Much as in the West, the social status of musicians in general remained extremely low until the twentieth century.

*koto* music developed out of *tsukushigoto* is a good case in point. It is said that a student of Kenjun's named Hōsui went to Kyoto to perform. He played poorly and was not accepted at court, so he traveled on to Edo. There he met a blind *shamisen* player to whom he taught the basic songs of *tsukushigoto*. When the Kyushu headquarters learned that he had instructed a blind man, Hōsui was expelled from the school. However, the damage was done. This blind musician took the name Yatsuhashi Kengyō (1614–84) and went to Kyoto, where he set up the Yatsuhashi school of popular *koto* music.[7] Precisely what innovations he made remain uncertain, but we do know that he borrowed the original *kumiuta* of *tsukushigoto* and rearranged them to suit more popular tastes.[8]

His *shamisen* background may have been an influence. One interesting change can be observed in the case of the above-mentioned piece "Fuki." The tuning for the Tsukushi version is one of the old *gagaku* modes, while that used for the same piece in the Yatsuhashi school is in the folk *in* scale (see Figure 21). One of the early names for these blind *koto* players was *insei*, which can be translated as "singing in the *in* scale." Perhaps the same historian who claimed that Hōsui taught in Edo because he failed in Kyoto also chose the Chinese characters that appear in old texts for the word *insei*, which translate as "a lewd voice."

It may be that Yatsuhashi composed no original pieces himself. Until 1957, there was even serious doubt as to whether *yatsuhashigoto* had ever really existed as a separate school, but an old Yatsuhashi teacher was discovered that year in Nagano, complete with music and a genealogy chart.[9] The full significance of this discovery has not yet been ascertained. Nevertheless, the fact that the early seventeenth century saw the flourishing of popular *koto* music is undeniable.

One of our best sources for information on *koto, shakuhachi*, or *shamisen* music of the early Edo period is the *Shichiku shoshinshū*, by Nakamura Sōsan, printed in 1664. Among the pieces credited to the Yatsuhashi school in this book are such famous classics as "Rokudan," "Hachidan," and "Midare." Some scholars claim that at least the first composition may

7. The term *kengyō* is a title bestowed on blind artisans (including musicians) of great talent. It is somewhat analogous to the Western term "maestro."
8. Biblio. ref. 7-11 contains thirteen basic pieces in Japanese and Western notation.
9. Cf. Kishibe Shigeo, *Tsugaru sōkyoku ikutaryū no kenkyū* (Hirosaki: Tsugaru Shobō, 1976).

have been of ancient Chinese origin. This theory is based partially on the fact that the same piece exists in the *koto* music of the Ryukyu Islands, but in a Chinese tuning.[10] There are also Ryukyu pieces called "Ichidan" and "Nidan." Since *ichi* means "one," *ni* "two," and *roku* "six," there may have been a series of *dan* pieces before the creation of the surviving "Rokudan."

In addition to the flourishing of a new *koto* solo literature, the seventeenth century also saw the *koto* used as dance accompaniment and in special ensembles. It was not until the end of the century, however, that something truly new occurred in the field of *koto* music. At that time, a teacher named Ikuta Kengyō (1656–1715) founded a new style of *koto* music based on existing *shamisen* forms, particularly *jiuta*. This term originally meant the *shamisen* music of Kyoto in contrast to its Tokyo counterpart. It did not come to mean a special form until Ikuta used the term to designate his new-style *koto* music. His big innovation was to combine the *koto* with the *shamisen* and to develop a music that emphasized the instrumental part more than the vocal. Up until his time, the *koto* had been primarily a vocal accompanying instrument. The *jiuta* ensemble was called *sankyoku*, "music for three," because a third instrument was usually added (see Plate 56)—either the *kokyū* or the *shakuhachi*, with the latter taking precedence by the end of the Edo period. Further discussion of *jiuta* will appear later in this chapter. Suffice it to say here that the basic form of *jiuta* is an alternation of vocal sections with instrumental interludes.

At the end of the eighteenth century, another *koto* teacher turned to *shamisen* music for the raw materials of a new style. Yamada Kengyō (1757–1817) borrowed the styles of various Edo narrative *shamisen* forms (*itchūbushi*, *katōbushi*, etc.). Under the influence of such music, the Yamada school developed a style in which the voice line was more important. Indeed, the main distinction between the Ikuta and Yamada schools is still explained in terms of their respective instrumental and vocal orientations. At present, there is a basic repertoire of standard pieces that are considered their common heritage. The new compositions in both schools, though, tend to be more instrumental; it is primarily in the products of the nineteenth century that this vocal–instrumental distinction is most noticeable.

10. The Ryukyu Islands *koto* school is also called Yatsuhashi, but as yet no historical connection has been established between this school and the mainland group by the same name.

In the early nineteenth century the Ikuta musician Yaezaki Kengyō (d. 1848) of Kyoto further developed *jiuta sōkyoku* by the addition of a second *koto* line (*kaede*), which played more independently from that of the *shamisen* part. The Kyoto style became known as *kyōmono* and was characteristic of Ikuta music of the period. The *jiuta*-accompanied *kyōmai* dances such as "Yuki" (Snow) still maintain this stately Kyoto style.

In the twentieth century, *koto* music has been the most successful of all *hōgaku* forms in its attempts to create a new style of music based on Western ideas. The man most prominent in this field was Miyagi Michio (1894–1956). His untimely death (blind from early childhood, he fell from a speeding train) ended a truly brilliant career. Miyagi was one of the few creative artists able to provide compositional backing for the credos of the pamphleteers who clamored for a new Japanese music. From the mass of Japanese compositions created since the 1920s, only a few works by Miyagi and his Yamada-school counterpart, Nakanoshima Kinichi (1904–84), have survived. They prove that new *hōgaku* could sound as good as Debussy. Miyagi's death marks the end of that era. Composers like Mamiya Michio (b. 1929) have created works more clearly influenced by postwar Western idioms.

By the end of the twentieth century, *koto* music could be heard in almost all modern styles, but, as in Western music, the traditional repertory is still preferred in concerts.

## 3. Music Lessons

In Francis Piggott's 1893 book on Japanese music (Biblio ref. 1·15), he describes a typical *koto* lesson at the turn of the century. What he said concerning *koto* teaching methods probably applied to other instruments as well. A comparison of his description with the more recent one given in the following paragraphs may point out some of the constants and variables in the music-teaching tradition of Japan.

A teacher's home is usually his or her studio. Here, on certain days of the week and for a specified number of hours, the teacher is available for lessons. The problems of lesson scheduling do not bother the Japanese traditional teacher. In Japan, it is a matter of first come, first served. This has an advantage in that you are never late for a lesson. It also means that to complete your day's lesson it may take twenty minutes or three hours; it all depends on how many students are waiting ahead of you. The students may sit in the studio where they can follow the course of the piece being taught (see Plate 42 for a drum lesson) or wait in an adjoining room where they can talk quietly or listen to the music next door. In winter, a knot of pupils can usually be found huddled around a table that is warmed underneath by an electric heater.

The lesson itself consists of a twenty-minute playing of the particular composition under study that week. Usually the teacher plays simultaneously. There are some students who cannot readily read the notation and so learn the entire piece by imitating the teacher. To assist in this rote teaching method, the latter will sing a solfège as he or she plays, if there is no special vocal part in the piece. The order in which one learns the repertoire of a particular school is set; it is very difficult to learn a piece out of order and impossible (openly) to learn a composition belonging to another school. Before the extensive use of printed notation, one had to pay a special fee to learn certain pieces. Today, this system has changed, though certain compositions are still considered sacrosanct. There is something to be said for the refusal to let a student learn a certain piece before being qualified to play it.

In 1956, an average teacher received one thousand yen a month for giving two twenty-minute lessons a week. By the end of the century, the fee was from ten thousand to twenty thousand yen for three lessons a month. Inflation has also raised the price of an instrument from a few hundred dollars to well over a thousand. These are usually purchased from a maker approved by the teacher.

Another financial and artistic challenge related to learning a traditional instrument is the *natori*, the professional name that makes it possible for one to be an official member of a guild, to teach, and to perform in concerts. After learning a certain number of compositions, one is allowed to apply for a professional name. The difficulties involved vary with the school and the type of music being studied, but one factor is constant: it costs money. In the "headmaster system" (*iemoto seido*) of certain guilds, one must pay, pyramid-style, from one's teacher to the head (*iemoto*) of the entire school in order to acquire a professional name. In most schools, one must also be able to play, and rigid performance tests are administered before one is granted the privilege of buying a name. However, there are a few less reputable groups who specialize in bestowing "professional" names on less qualified students eager to have such diplomas for social or other reasons.

The choice of a professional name is also regulated. One takes the school name—for example, Yamada or Ikuta—and then creates a title that includes part of the teacher's name. The custom can make for much confusion when meeting a group of professionals from one school.[11]

Every teacher has a full-scale recital at least twice a year. These are endurance contests for both the audience and the teacher. It is not unusual for the teacher to appear in every number from the concert's beginning, at eleven in the morning, until the finale, around eight o'clock in the evening. The audience is not expected to show an equal degree of tenacity; one comes and goes freely, with ample time off to enjoy the presents received. Japan is one of the rare places in the world where the audience is sometimes given a gift for coming, though in the West an after-recital reception is common enough. Bean cakes and candy were the usual fare in Japan in the mid-fifties, with coin purses, key chains, and even saké not unknown. The secret to the finances of these programs is that every student pays to perform. In 1957, *koto* recitals may have cost each student approximately ten dollars a composition. Inflation and yen values have since increased the cost tenfold. In Japanese dance recitals, the bill in 1957 was more often fifty to eighty dollars, but by the 1990s it was in the thousands. For this reason, student recitals seldom have many solo numbers.

An important element in the Japanese teaching system is the formation of an ingroup. While the lessons may be mechanical and somewhat impersonal (though not unfriendly), the weekly waiting for lessons with a group of one's peers develops a sense of companionship between the students. The fact that one is not allowed to study with other teachers reinforces this sense of belonging. Student-teacher parties and outings are common. The fortunes and misfortunes of each individual are theoretically the concern of the entire group. The relations between the myriad branches of the

11. On one occasion, I met a number of drummers who were named respectively, Tanaka Sadenji, Tanaka Sakiji, Tanaka Sataji, Tanaka Sashichirō, and Tanaka Satojūrō. When some of them formed a new guild they all became Semba plus a new set of personal names! They also had their family names, most of which I never did know.

same school are tenuous, but within the closed group there is an interrelationship not unlike that found in a good church social club in the West. Like church youth groups, there are parties and games for the children. The adult students, however, usually enjoy a more robust evening than would be tolerated by most churches.

As a social unit, the *hōgaku* teacher and his or her students form a strong link with the customs of the feudal past. As a teaching method, *hōgaku* instruction might seem to the time-oriented Westerner unnecessarily slow. The rote method, as used in Japan, is constantly in danger of producing musical automatons.[12] It is only the most inspired teacher who can surmount the endemic difficulties presented by traditional teaching techniques. This system originated in a period when notation was less common and many of the students were apprentices who had committed their lives to the learning of the repertoire. Today, such pupils are rare. Young would-be professionals attend the *hōgaku* department of the Tokyo National University of Fine Arts and Music, and there are scholarships for lessons at the National Theater. Modern teachers must depend on amateur students who only have a limited amount of time to spend on committing long traditional pieces to memory.[13] Notation was developed to meet this new situation along with recordings and videotapes. Even with that, one is constantly amazed at the Japanese amateur's ability to retain a vast number of pieces under these conditions.

The teaching methods of both the East and the West have influenced each other. The rote method of the Suzuki violin system illustrates such a combination, as does its industrial distribution structure. The *hōgaku* world has adopted similar developments, primarily inside Japan, though there are some international *koto* and *shakuhachi* conferences, clubs, and publications, reflecting a foreign desire to participate in the special experience of being a part of that world. Although limited in numbers, there are also

12. In lessons in the *noh* flute, my teacher would illustrate the fingering of each note of the melody on the edge of his closed fan. When all the notes had been learned in order, the rhythm was added. The entire melody was never played beforehand so that one had no idea of the overall sound of the piece. This is an extreme but not untypical case of Japanese rote-teaching methods. Of course a Japanese student already knows the tunes. I was literally new in the country.
13. Music lessons were part of upper-class education for centuries, but the rise of the middle class in the Edo period broadened the base of amateur lessons and increased the need for teaching aids like notation.

foreign musicians with Japanese professional names who teach and perform in both Japan and the West. Just as Yamaha pianos are common in the West, Western-made *shakuhachi*, too, are now sold in Japan. While music is not an international language, the desire to search for beauty and pleasure in sound is universal. As the global village shrinks, we are learning to appreciate our neighbor's garden.

## 4. Instruments of the *Koto* Ensemble

There is a legend that the shape of the *koto* originated from that of a crouching dragon. If true, the dragon must have been a very sweet-natured specimen to inspire the creation of such a lovely-sounding and physically attractive instrument. The modern *koto* has thirteen twisted silk or nylon strings and a body made from two pieces of paulownia wood. One piece of

*Koto*

this wood is hollowed out to form a sound box. The other piece is used as a plank to cover the bottom. There are two sound holes in the ends of this plank, which also make it possible to restring the instrument easily. The average Yamada *koto* is 180.5 centimeters in length. The Ikuta *koto* is longer and narrower. Short practice *koto* and playable miniature souvenirs also exist. The larger seventeen-string bass *koto* (*jūshichigen*), invented by Miyagi Michio in 1922, continues to be used in modern music.

Two factors are important in the construction of a good *koto*. One is the manner in which the wood is cut from the tree. An excellent instrument will always show sharp parabolic designs on the surface created by the rings of the tree. The other factor is less evident: on the inside of the *koto*, special patterns called *ayasugi* are carved in order to improve the tone.

One distinctive feature of the Japanese *koto* is its use of moveable bridges (*ji*), which, in addition to wood and ivory, are sometimes made of plastic. By adjusting these bridges, any thirteen-note scale can be produced. In practice, the number is limited. The *gagaku koto* (*gakusō*) uses six tunings. The *tsukushigoto* borrowed one tuning from *gagaku* and, in the Edo period, added another based on folk scales. The popular *koto* schools developed a host of different tunings, some of which became standard while others were used only for certain compositions.[14] The two most common tunings, *hirajōshi* and *kumoijōshi*, are shown in Figure 25. Notice that they are in the *yō-in* scale system. The court *koto* and the early *tsukushigoto* kept to the *ryo-ritsu* scale tradition of *gagaku*.

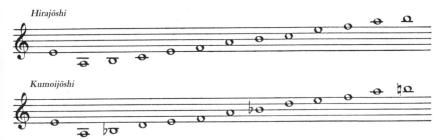

FIGURE 25. *Koto* tunings

Besides the notes available through the adjustment of the bridges, there are also pitches that can be produced by pushing down on the strings with the left hand (*oshide*). This movement stretches the strings so as to produce whole or half steps as needed. The technique is typical of popular *koto* styling. Normally the strings are plucked with ivory picks (*tsume*) attached to three fingers of the right hand (Plate 57). The shape of these picks varies: the Ikuta picks are square and the Yamada picks are parabolic. Because of this, the Ikuta performer sits at an oblique angle to the instrument, while the Yamada player sits at a right angle.

There are many performance techniques available, such as upstrokes, glissandos, and tremolos which greatly extend the tonal range of the *koto*.[15] In addition, the strings may be played with the bare fingers of the left hand. In modern works, harmonics are used much as they are in Western harp music. A more unique playing method is the twisting of the string with the left hand; this produces an extremely subtle change in the pitch and tone of the string. Another interesting method of playing is a sweep along the length of one string with two fingers, which produces a strange swishing sound. In recent years, many other techniques have been added to the

14. *Koto* tuning lists are found in Biblio. refs. 7·1 and 7·9.
15. See Biblio. ref. 7·9.

playing of the *koto*, but the devices mentioned above are considered the basic *koto* techniques.

Before passing on to the music itself, we should take a look at the other instruments used in *koto* ensembles. The *kokyū* (Plate 58) deserves mention by virtue of the fact that it is Japan's only bowed instrument. Varying in size, the average length of the *kokyū* is sixty-nine centimeters. It has been used with two, three, and four strings. In the case of the four-string *kokyū*, the top two strings are in unison. The normal tuning for the *kokyū* is in two fourths (*sansagari*), though there are rare pieces using a tuning of a fifth and a fourth (*niagari*). The common *shamisen honchōshi* (a fourth and a fifth) is not used. The origin of the three-string *kokyū* has usually been credited to Chinese fiddles like the *huqin*, but an equally strong case can be made for the influence of the Portuguese rebec, which came to Japan in the late seventeenth century and is said to have appeared in Edo around 1720.[16] The creation of the four-string *kokyū* is attributed to Fujiue Kengyō, later in the eighteenth century. He is also said to have made the bow longer. There are two guilds of *kokyū* players: the Udesaki in the Kansai (Kyoto/Osaka) area, and the Fujiue in Kanto (mostly Tokyo).

*Kokyū*                    *Huqin*

Besides its use in the *koto* trios, the *kokyū* was popular as a dance-accompanying instrument. In prints of the Edo period, one can see an ensemble of several *shamisen* and one *kokyū* accompanying a veritable chorus line of dancing girls who perform for the delectation of a group of affluent customers. In addition to its use in these Edo-style nightclubs, the *kokyū* found a place among the offstage instruments of the theater. It is still in common use in the puppet plays (*bunraku*), especially during sad scenes. Finally, the *kokyū* should be mentioned as another instrumental accouterment of the wandering street musicians.

16. See David Waterhouse, "An Early Illustration of the Four-Stringed Kokyū with a Disquisition on the History of Japan's Only Bowed Musical Instrument," *Oriental Art*, Vol. 16, No. 1 (1970), 162–68.

When well played, the *kokyū* sounds similar to the violin, though it has a smaller dynamic range. As can be seen in Plate 58, the bow is quite loose. In performance, the hairs are pulled tight by grasping them with the ring finger and little finger of the right hand. The bow is held in the manner of a chopstick. Another interesting aspect of the *kokyū* is its very high, arched bridge (*koma*). Because of this arch, one must turn the instrument in order to play on different strings. To facilitate this, the *kokyū* is set on a peg that is placed between the knees. It is fascinating to watch an expert player spin his instrument back and forth as he performs.

The *kokyū* is played with a wide vibrato. This type of string tone is found all over the Orient and represents one of the distinctive tonal elements by which we identify Oriental bowed instruments. With the introduction of the Western violin, the *kokyū* lost its popularity, and today its solo literature is all but forgotten, its use in *koto* ensembles rare. Outside the theater sound-effects room, there seems to be no place in modern Japanese life where the *kokyū* can find patronage. Perhaps it will fall victim to the same fate allotted to many old Japanese *biwa* and become an unplayed wall decoration in modish Western homes.

In *koto* ensemble music, the *shamisen* is called the *sangen*. The Yamada school *sangen* relates to the *nagauta shamisen* in size, while the Ikuta school uses a larger instrument, derived from Edo *jōruri*. The plectrum also is quite different, having a very thin edge, often made of tortoiseshell. When this is combined with a heavier bridge, the tone produced is much softer than that of the normal *shamisen*. This tone is felt to blend more easily with that of the *koto*. In theory, it should be simple to distinguish between the Yamada and Ikuta *sankyoku* performances because of this difference in *shamisen*. In modern practice, there is often much borrowing of plectrums, bridges, and instruments so that such distinctions are less categorical.[17]

## 5. *Koto* Music

Now that all the instruments have been discussed, it is possible to investigate the music itself. As noted, the generic term for *koto* music is *sōkyoku*.

17. When a Yamada ensemble is playing an Ikuta instrumental interlude, the *shamisen* will often use a specially wide bridge called a *daibiro*, which is meant to produce a sound similar to that of the Ikuta *shamisen*.

This music can be divided into two types, that with singing and that with none. The oldest type of vocal *koto* music, *kumiuta*, has already been mentioned. In the early *tsukushigoto kumiuta*, each set consisted of several poems, the singing of each poem being considered a *dan*, or "step." This term is the keystone to any discussion of *koto* music form. The *tsukushigoto dan* were sixty-four beats long. The Yatsuhashi *kumiuta* used a similar form except that each *dan* was one hundred and twenty beats long. It is interesting to note that each poem was sung in four phrases, a method common with the performance of court *imayō*. *Kumiuta* composed after the middle of the eighteenth century tend to have shorter *dan*.

The main type of instrumental *koto* music is *shirabemono*. All the strictly instrumental compositions fall under this term. The piece "Rokudan" is a classic example of this form.[18] A basic theme is presented and, with each successive *dan*, it is subjected to variation while new material is interpolated between the phrases of the original theme. The "sameness" in *koto* music relates to a compositional method common in all Japanese traditional arts. The talent of an artist is not so much in originality as it is in the skilled handling of conventions, be they plants in a painting or gestures in a dance. An example in *koto* music is Figure 26. These few notes and rhythm pattern can be found throughout *koto* music, particularly in *danmono*. Like the conventional cadence patterns of eighteenth-century Western music, the familiarity of this *koto* pattern gives the listener the security to relax and enjoy both standard and new pieces in a known sonic environment. Indeed, late twentieth-century research has suggested that the entire *shirabemono* repertory is based on variations of the tune "Etenraku," as sung in the *imayō* tradition.[19]

**FIGURE 26.** A melodic convention in *koto* music

An important form of *koto* composition is the *jiuta*. This music is sometimes called *tegotomono,* because its notable contribution to *koto* music is

18. Piggott published the first transcription and analysis of "Rokudan" in Biblio. ref. 1·10. Later studies are found in Adriaansz and Wade, 7·2 and 7·9.
19. See Adriaansz, Biblio. ref. 7·2.

the use of *tegoto,* instrumental interludes. The innovation is in the addition and extension of the instrumental transitions occurring between the songs in the pieces. In its simplest form, it consists of three parts: a fore song (*maeuta*), an instrumental interlude (*tegoto*), and an after song (*atouta*). (An opening song and first interlude can be heard on CD track 13.) As this form evolved, it became longer. Thus, one can find pieces that consist of an instrumental introduction, a song, an interlude, a song, and an instrumental close. Obviously, one could go on indefinitely splitting songs and interludes into further songs and interludes. Normally, though, such music does not extend beyond a six-part form: introduction-song-*tegoto*-song-*tegoto*-song. As a rule, there is no thematic connection between the various interludes.

The usual contemporary *jiuta* ensemble consists of a *shamisen*, *koto*, and *shakuhachi* (Plate 56 and CD track 13). Both the *koto* player and the *shamisen* player usually sing. In such an ensemble, the *shamisen* plays the main melody, while the *shakuhachi* follows the general contour of this melody, and the *koto* adds ornamentation as they go along. The *shakuhachi* is the most melismatic of the group, but even its simultaneous variations (heterophony) are rather simple. The Japanese say that the *shamisen* is the bone, the *koto* the flesh, and the *shakuhachi* the skin of a *jiuta* composition. The analogy is picturesque but not quite appropriate, as the affinity of the instrumental parts is closer than that of the anatomical ones.

The basic ensemble can be expanded. If a second *koto* is added, it may be used to further embellish the melody, especially during the instrumental interludes (listen to CD track 13). During the song sections, the accompaniment is more subservient to the vocal line. The most unique technique, involving two *koto*, occurs in the instrumental interludes when *uchiawase* and *dan'awase* are used. *Uchiawase* refers to the compositional process in which the basic *koto* (the *honte*) plays the original melody while the second *koto* (the *kaede*) plays a completely independent melody. Obviously, this is possible only with songs in the same tuning. Sometimes the superimposed song must be altered in order to fit. Nevertheless, in the technique of *uchiawase* we hear once more the common Japanese tendency to use the same melodic material in more than one composition.

Although borrowing melodies is common in Western music also, one seldom finds the simultaneous use of unrelated tunes, except for the Renaissance quodlibets and early polyphony. The real difference between the

Eastern and the Western techniques is not so much the frequency of use as the manner in which it is applied. The rules of Western counterpoint tie the disparate melodies together into a single polyphonic unit. The use of *uchiawase* in *koto* music, by contrast, produces more the effect of an obbligato. This is due, in part, to the fact that chordal sounds resulting from the use of two *koto* lines are reminiscent of the effects realized by the French impressionists. So, when two *koto* are playing different melodies within such an unchanging tuning system, the effect to the Western ear is that of two arpeggios being played on one chord.

The *dan'awase* technique listed above differs from *uchiawase* in that material from the original melody is superimposed upon itself. This is possible because of the sectional (*dan*) organization of *koto* music. One may take the second *dan* of an instrumental part and perform it simultaneously with the exposition of the first *dan*. To a certain degree, this is "paper music," for it is impossible to recognize a variation on a theme before you have heard the theme. *Dan'awase* represents one of the most Western-like forms of Japanese traditional composition.

In contemporary performances, any one of the above-mentioned techniques may be heard. For example, although the famous *koto* piece "Chidori" is set in a four-part *jiuta* form (introduction-song-interlude-song), it can be done as a solo piece, a *koto* duet, or with one of the other ensembles mentioned above. The music of the *koto* is always open to rearrangement. "Rokudan," though officially a *shirabemono*, can be heard with a *jiuta* ensemble. Actually, the term *jiuta* represents today more a manner of performance than a group of specific compositions.

It is almost impossible not to play a melody on the *koto*. By merely improvising on the strings in some rhythmic frame, one can produce something that would pass for a tune, albeit a wandering one. Perhaps this is one reason why the *koto* was particularly successful during the early years of experimentation with Westernized Japanese music. It had a ready-made harmonic frame that was familiar to the West and thus, a priori, was able to produce melodies pleasing to Western tastes. In the early days, this was a godsend, but later it proved to be a stumbling block.

There were attempts in the nineteenth century to use new scale structures in *koto* music. The Western major scale became *orandajōshi*, in honor of the merchants from Holland (*oranda*) who introduced it. The pentatonic scale (see Figure 1) was called *kankanjōshi*, after the name of a piece played by devotees of Chinese Ming and Qing dynasty music (*minshin-gaku*). The concept of changing tunings within a composition appeared by the twentieth century, but modern *koto* composers were averse to extreme modulations until the late twentieth century. Moving bridges in the midst of a composition had been used earlier. The newer technique involved placing a set of differently tuned *koto* around the performer for use in one piece. By this method, atonal compositions were possible. Other experimental compositions used faster rhythms and unusual effects, such as knocking on the wooden body or hitting the strings with a drumstick. As with similar music in the West, the audiences for such novelties remained limited. Mamiya Michio is one of the more successful of the experimental composers.

Miyagi Michio was mentioned earlier as one of the pioneers in twentieth-century *koto* music. His invention of the seventeen-string bass *koto* widened the range of sounds for his "new Japanese music" (*shin nihon ongaku* or *shin hōgaku*). Additional efforts at modernizing the music include *koto* concertos with Western or Japanese orchestral accompaniment, large *koto* bands (often with dozens of *shakuhachi*), and special mixed ensembles of Japanese instruments.

The spirit behind contemporary *koto* composition is sincere, but its discussion is outside the topic of this book and the knowledge of its author. One would need to write a very technical and specialized book to do justice to the accomplishments of these pioneers in new Japanese sounds which, after World War II, were called *gendai hōgaku*, "contemporary traditional music." Suffice it to say that they continue to seek new sonic directions for their lovely instrument.

<table>
<tr><td style="width:170px; background:#bbb; padding:20px;">CHAPTER<br>EIGHT</td><td></td></tr>
</table>

# THE *SHAMISEN* AND ITS MUSIC

## 1. The Instrument and Its Background

Of all the traditional instruments of Japan, the *shamisen* undoubtedly has the greatest variety of uses. It is the backbone of *kabuki* music, a vital ingredient in geisha parties, a social grace in private homes, and the vehicle for a host of folk musics. The *shamisen* repertoire of art music is one of the great cultural legacies of the Edo period. At the same time, the *shamisen*'s sharp but slightly wistful tone still pervades the atmosphere of modern Japanese life.

Mid-seventeenth- and eighteenth-century sources claim that the *samisen*, or *shamisen*, was first introduced into Japan around 1562 at the port of Sakai near Osaka, but the earliest document to actually mention it in Japan is a 1574 diary entry by Uwai Kakken noting that a mission from the king of the Ryukyu Islands included a *"shahisen"* player. The particular instrument

*Sanshin*

*Sanxian*

that appeared at that time was the Ryukyu *sanshin* (Plate 59) which, like its Chinese ancestor the *sanxian*, had three strings, a small wooden bridge, a snakeskin covering, and was strummed with a pick. Other late sixteenth-century diaries affirm that the new instrument became popular in Japan. The Japanese version of the instrument changed in shape, building materials, and playing styles. Again seventeenth- and eighteenth-century sources provide undocumented tales about *biwa* players who created the new model and were the major performers of its music. There is logical if not historical support for this idea since, before this time, the *biwa* was Japan's only plucked lute and the *biwa* priest a major source of narrative music. Likewise, the shapes of early *shamisen* plectrums seem similar to those of older *biwa*. The change of the skin on the instrument from snake to dog or cat may be more environmental than musical (big snakes are rare in Japan), but the design change of the body from a single, oval piece of wood to four separate pieces seems to be a Japanese innovation. The resulting sound and music are yet another example of a creative and aesthetically pleasing "Japanization" of Asian continental and island traditions.

Plate 75 shows the most common forms of *shamisen* used today, that is, the instrument used for *nagauta* music and that featured in puppet-theater accompaniment. Just as there are many different styles of *shamisen* music, there are also many variations in *shamisen* construction. These individual variations will be mentioned as specific types of music are discussed. Certain features, however, are basic to all *shamisen*.

*Shamisen*

The body (*dō*) of the instrument is made of four pieces of wood, preferably red sandalwood, mulberry, or Chinese quince. Concert models are carved inside with a herringbone pattern known as *ayasugi*, which is said to improve the tone greatly. The body is covered on the top and bottom with catskin or, in cheaper models, dogskin or plastic. To protect the top skin from the blows of the plectrum, a small half-moon of skin (*bachigawa*) is added at the top and center. The long neck (*sao*) of the *shamisen* is made of three pieces of wood that can be disjointed for convenience in carrying.

The thickness of this neck varies with the type of music performed as does the gauge of the three twisted-silk strings. Nylon strings are also being used now. The strings are attached to a rope tailpiece (*neo*) at the lower end and to three large pegs (*itomaki*) above; these pegs are made of ivory, wood, or plastic.

Because of the sensitivity of the skin, the shape, weight, material, and placement of the bridge (*koma*) are very important to the tone of the *shamisen*. The most common bridge is made of ivory, though plastic and wood are also used. The plectrum (*bachi*) also varies in size and shape (Plate 75 shows three of them). The concert plectrum is made of ivory, while the practice models are made of wood or plastic. The wooden plectrums are ingeniously constructed of three different kinds of wood so that the rear and center portions have greater weight for balance, while the striking edge has resiliency for tone.

The tone is the most unique aspect of the instrument. In addition to its sweet-sour resonance, it has a drum-like snap and, in the lower register, a twangy hum somewhat like that of a jew's-harp. The drum effect is caused by the snap of the plectrum as it hits both the string and the tight catskin at the same time. The reverberation (*sawari*) is created by a small cavity and an extra metal bridge at the top of the neck. The lower string does not rest upon this bridge, whereas the other two strings do. This causes the lower string to vibrate against the cavity, while the other strings, being raised, pass over it. The sound created by this novel device may actually have been an attempt to imitate the much stronger reverberation of the *biwa* strings, though its historical origins are unknown. Some modern *shamisen* have a special screw in the neck that helps to adjust the strength of the *sawari* sound.

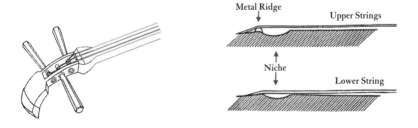

FIGURE 27. The *shamisen* upper bridge design

There are a dozen little accessories for the *shamisen*, but the only one that need be mentioned here is the *yubikake* ("finger hanger"). This is a small knit or stretch-nylon device that is put between the thumb and first finger of the left hand in order to make it easier to slide the hand up and down the back of the neck. Modern civilization has infringed upon this traditional piece of equipment, and *yubikake* may now be bought in various shades to match milady's kimono. There are also a variety of colors for the pads of rubber that can be placed under the *shamisen*, or between the wrist and the *shamisen*, so that the instrument or arm does not slide out of position.

As shown in Figure 28, there are three basic tunings for the *shamisen*. The first is *honchōshi*, or "original tuning," which consists of a perfect fourth and a perfect fifth. The second is *niagari*, or "raise the second," which is a fifth and a fourth, and the last is *sansagari*, or "lower the third," which is two fourths. Other tunings, particularly in modern pieces, are also used. In addition, when a second obbligato *shamisen* (*uwajōshi shamisen*) is involved, a cappo (*kase*) may be attached to its neck to tune it higher, usually with its two lower strings matching the top two of the basic (*honte*) *shamisen*.

FIGURE 28. *Shamisen* tunings

Since *shamisen* music is primarily vocal there is no fixed basic pitch to which the instrument is tuned. It varies from G to D, B being used most commonly in transcriptions. It must be remembered, therefore, that the pitch of any transcription of *shamisen* music is arbitrary or, at the most, represents only the tonality of the one particular performance from which the transcription was made. Thus, there is no set pitch for a composition such as a song in B-flat major or a symphony in D minor. There is, however, a concept of "happy" and "sad" tunings as is found in the Western major/minor concept. Specifically, *honchōshi* is said to be best for solemn music, *niagari* for gay, and *sansagari* for melancholic or serene music. The practical application of this theory is nebulous, yet the concept must be mentioned, as it forms part of the psychological outlook of the more traditional-minded musicians.

# 2. The History and Form of *Shamisen* Music

We have noted in our religious and *biwa* chapters how itinerant storytellers were part of street life throughout Japanese history and survived in rural Japan well into the twentieth century until the spread of mass communication. In the sixteenth century, the most important development within the *biwa* narrative tradition was the form called *jōruri*. The word *jōruri* is an abbreviation of the title of a story called *Jōrurihime monogatari*, which translates picturesquely as "The Story of Princess Lapis Lazuli." Actually, it is the tale of the early years of the great military hero, Yoshitsune, who figures so strongly in the *Tale of the Heike* mentioned earlier.

In the Edo period when the Buddhist *sekkyō* scripture narrators (see p. 75) and street singers began to use *shamisen* as accompaniment, the term *sekkyō jōruri* appears. Some of the early *shamisen* narrators may have been former *biwa* performers, and the word *jōruri* soon came to mean any one of a dozen different types of narrative *shamisen* music dealing with any subject matter from ancient to modern times. Such music also goes under the general term *katarimono*, meaning songs primarily concerned with narration, as distinguished from *utamono* (or *utaimono*),[1] songs primarily concerned with melody. The main distinction between the words *jōruri* and *katarimono* is that *jōruri* is a historical term while *katarimono* is a word imposed on narrative music by later scholars for the sake of contrast with *utamono*. The difference between *katarimono* and *utamono* is much like the distinction that is often made between French opera, with its orientation toward the lyrics, and Italian opera, which emphasizes the voice and melody. In practice, the distinction is often not clear in either the Japanese or European case. Nevertheless, such categories do serve as convenient devices for dividing up the study of a many-faceted style of music. We shall start with the narrative traditions.

## KATARIMONO—NARRATIVE SHAMISEN MUSIC

Figure 29 gives some sense of the richness of the *shamisen*'s history. Rather than treating all the lines and unfamiliar words as just a genealogy of genres, one should try to think of them in terms of the lives and works of creative

---

1. While both words mean "sung thing," some scholars prefer to reserve the word *utaimono* for vocal music of the *noh* drama or for court vocal music.

*shamisen* musicians who struggled through a complicated world of inter-relations and influences. Their music became famous though, as in all world music histories, much of it faded over time. Yet, as we have noted before, one of the more impressive characteristics of the Japanese music world is its ability to keep at least one living example of almost every genre alive. When looking at the historical chart, think of the living traditions and people who enriched Japanese life for centuries.

We have discussed the ancient origins of *sekkyō* and *jōruri*. *Naniwabushi* comes next in our musical journey because, though a product of the late nineteenth century, it grew out of *saimon* and blind-priest (*mōsōbiwa*) traditions. These stories accompanied by *shamisen* were first found in Kyushu and called *rōkyoku*, but the tradition soon moved to the mainland, where the genre was named *naniwabushi*, "songs of the Osaka region." It was the heir of the dramatic *utazaimon* storytelling tradition mentioned in Chapter Two. The *utazaimon* artist spun his tales of love before a crowd of common folk, gathered in the shrine compound. *Naniwabushi* has kept this contact with the general public. In this sense it is comparable in appeal to country and western music in America, though the topics dealt with and the style of delivery are more highly developed.

Contemporary *naniwabushi*, though commercialized, still retains the basic quality of what is believed to be the original narrative style. Its formal elements are the common denominators of storytellers all over the world: (1) a short instrumental overture, (2) a scene-setting song, (3) straight dialogue set in a light background of mood music, (4) occasional songs at crucial points in the plot, often commenting on the emotions or fates of the characters, (5) instrumental interludes, particularly at points of action or scene changes, and (6) a final song summing up the story, often with some moralizing thought to end it. Within this framework one can set storytellers from time immemorial, whether they be European, African, or Oriental. The differences lie in the moral outlook of the society by which they are influenced and in the particular musical idiom employed.

Contemporary performances involve a *shamisen* player, hidden behind a screen at the back of stage left, and a narrator, standing in bright costume before a lectern on a table covered with an elaborate cloth. The narrator's head moves back and forth as a dialogue between different characters in the story is carried on. The music is explosive, a thick-necked *shamisen* being played with a blunt plectrum to produce sudden, sharp sounds inter-

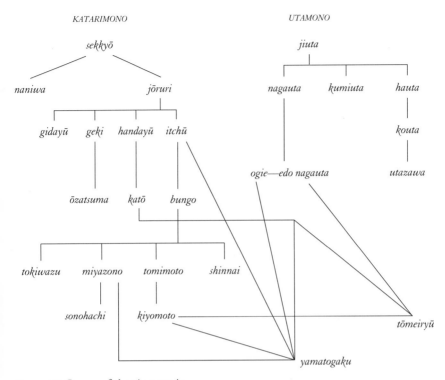

sekkyō                                    jiuta

naniwa          jōruri        nagauta   kumiuta    hauta

gidayū  geki  handayū  itchū                        kouta

ōzatsuma  katō  bungo          ogie—edo nagauta    utazawa

tokiwazu  miyazono  tomimoto  shinnai

sonohachi      kiyomoto                              tōmeiryū

yamatogaku

**FIGURE 29.** Genres of *shamisen* music

spersed between much lighter passages played on the highest string. This
gives the extremely rough-toned, cold-steel vocal line a rhythmic drive
which it could not have alone. Before the advent of the *shamisen*, storytellers used to beat out an accompaniment on their left hand with a closed
fan or with various percussion instruments (see Plates 19 and 20). This early
accompaniment might help to explain the sudden spurts of sound that are
so typical of *naniwabushi*. One must also mention as part of the style the
equally piercing calls of the *shamisen* player. These cries fill many rests in
the music. Though originally signals to the narrator and perhaps teaching
devices, they have now become an important dramatic element in the
music, much like the *noh* drummer's calls mentioned in Chapter Four.

Though the term *rōkyoku* is found in Japanese music reference books, it
is seldom a topic of academic research. Perhaps the explanation for this
intellectual boycott is found in the following story. In 1911, a famous *naniwabushi* singer named Tōchūken Kumoemon made a recording and,
soon afterward, recorded the same piece for another firm. A civil lawsuit

charging violation of the copyright laws followed. When the case came to court, the defense brought up the question of whether *naniwabushi* was really music. If it weren't, then his client could not have violated any music copyright. In order to settle this problem, a group of music experts was brought in and, after due deliberation, the decision of the court was handed down: *naniwabushi* was not music—case dismissed. Ever since that time, few Japanese scholars have deigned to write on this subject since it was, by official decree, "not music." One must add that there had always been a strong feeling in scholarly circles that it was too low-class for serious study.

This musical segregation is probably due to its commercial popularity, for it is one of the few kinds of traditional music that managed to keep abreast of the times, at least until the mid-twentieth century. Radio broadcasts of *naniwabushi* came complete with sound effects, soap-opera theme songs, and guitar or Western orchestral backgrounds mixed in with *shamisen* mood music. Between long sections of straight dialogue, one could hear a completely traditional singing voice declaiming, "She takes the bus and gets off at Nihombashi." Thus, singers continued to entertain, blissfully ignoring the fact that, legally, they didn't exist. In more recent years, this form of entertainment has suffered a decline in popularity but, as we noted before, traditions seldom die out entirely in Japan.[2]

Figure 29 shows only some of the many genres that developed under the category of *jōruri*. In general, one can say that a new music was formed whenever a pupil deviated enough from his teacher's style to be in contrast or conflict. This applied as well to guilds of performers within a single genre. Genealogical charts of performers[3] often show not only who studied with whom but also who separated from whom. If one wanted to change the way of doing things, the only recourse was to leave the guild and found a new one. When new styles and repertoires were created, the music became a separate genre. As seen in Figure 29, the names of these genres were usually from the family or personal name of their founder.[4] For example, *katōbushi* was founded by Masumi Katō (1684–1725), and *bungobushi* was

---

2. Recordings and videotapes are still available. In 1999 I could still enjoy *naniwabushi* concerts on the ground floor of the Mokubakan theater in Asakusa, Tokyo.
3. Many are found in the *Gendai hōgaku meikan* book series (Tokyo: Hōgaku to Buyō, 1966– ).
4. An exception is *gekibushi* (fl. 1648–59). It was started by Fujiwara no Naomasa, whose courtly rank was *geki* in the Satsuma district, and the genre's founder is usually listed as Satsuma Geki.

founded by Miyakoji Bungonojō (1660?–1740). The figure shows the geneal-ogy of only a few of the better-known *shamisen* musics.

Each genre of *shamisen* music tends to have a specially built instrument as well as a different bridge weight, string gauge, and plectrum design. The playing style also has characteristic conventions, and the voice quality is unique to each genre. All these distinctions may be lost on first hearing, but the connoisseur can spot them easily. Since the twentieth century, groups of devotees have kept alive many of the genres seen above through *koten ongaku* ("classical") concerts. In these groups, the surviving head (*iemoto*) of the tradition passes on its repertory primarily to amateur stu-dents. With the advent of recordings, we now have several generations of such classical music preserved, if not maintained.

Sometimes the distinction between genres lies in the type of text chosen. Many, such as *katōbushi*, for example, make a specialty of domestic tragedies. In these stories the brother-in-law is often the villain, and the hero is beset with the age-old mother-in-law problem. One can well understand why such forms would find popular support and sympathy regardless of their musical qualities. *Bungobushi* (now almost extinct) is another example of a *bushi* with a special style of story. Bungo (as he is usually known) created such vivid descriptions of love affairs, usually ending in double suicides, that the government apparently issued a ban on his music in order to stem the alarming rise in double suicides by musically inspired lovers. But dou-ble suicides have been rather a national pastime for centuries, and another less romantic explanation gives the real reason for the demise of *bungobushi*. It seems that Bungo's music was in direct competition with *katōbushi*, which happened to be a favorite among certain members of the Japanese army. When *bungobushi* showed signs of winning the struggle, the *katō* musicians did some lobbying, and *bungobushi* was banned. Such cases as this show that a study of Japanese music is not without its social and politi-cal ramifications. The proliferation of *bushi* is often based on non-musical conflict. Genre terms like *miyazono*, *sonohachi*, and *tomimoto* are derived from the names of musicians whose music entered the fray in the eigh-teenth century only to fade away to an occasional performance at the *koten* concerts mentioned earlier.

Styles of singing or playing were cited as distinctive features of a genre. Anyone who has heard the fantastic flights of a *shinnaibushi* singer can never confuse these vocal peregrinations with any other style. This music, developed by Tsuruga Shinnai (d. 1810), earned the rather unique distinction of being banned in the Yoshiwara district of Tokyo, a place euphemistically called "the nightless city." The story behind this banning is distinctive in itself. The madams and owners of the various houses in the red-light district found that, after prolonged exposure to *shinnaibushi*, their "employees" tended to fall in love and, in many cases, run away, both of which were bad for business. Despite this prohibition, or perhaps because of it, *shinnaibushi* can still be heard today.

*Shinnaibushi* adopts a *shamisen* style somewhat like that of *naniwabushi*. The instrument used is also rather thick-necked, though the plectrum is not as blunt. In *shinnai*, there is often a second *shamisen* which continues to pluck away at a light, high obbligato, adding more sweetness to the overall tone of the music. When *shinnai* is used to accompany theatrical performances, the voice of the singer is penetrating and intense, while in concerts the intensity is retained but the volume is reduced. The most characteristic quality of *shinnai* music is a tendency to start main phrases at an extremely high pitch and then flutter down in tight arabesques until a reciting tone is reached. The formal outline of *shinnaibushi* pieces is similar to that of *naniwabushi* except that there are very few dialogue sections. The pieces that are sung today also tend to be shorter than those of *naniwabushi*.

*Shinnaibushi* has attracted groups of amateur practitioners, for it is not as blatant in its emotional display as *naniwabushi* and yet retains enough eroticism to be appealing. In the past, it was best heard in one of the smaller Japanese theaters in which everyone sat on the mat floor. Here one could smoke, eat, or drink while casually savoring the melancholy of an old love tale sung with great passion—though not too much. Now most of the theaters are gone, but the music lives on.

*Tokiwazubushi*, founded by Tokiwazu Mojidayū (1709–81), is one of the forms of narrative music often found in the *kabuki* theater. This also has a good following among amateurs and *shamisen*-concert devotees. It differs from the styles described above in that it uses a much less intense vocal style and has a less percussive *shamisen* part. Both the neck and plectrum are not as thick, though the tone of the *shamisen* is definitely heavier and throatier than the lyrical instruments to be described later. A wide-based bridge helps to produce this "alto" sound in the *shamisen* family.

*Kiyomoto*, founded by Kiyomoto Enjudayū (ca. 1814), is listed as a *katarimono*, or narrative style of *shamisen* music, but it really stands on the borderline between the lyrical and the narrative. The voice part is very high, and falsetto-like tones are used much more than in most other styles. To abet this quality, the *shamisen*, plectrum, and bridge are all built thinner. The tunings are also generally higher. All these factors do much to reduce the usual percussive quality of the *shamisen*, and the relative sweetness of the sound makes it suitable for accompanying love scenes on the *kabuki* stage. In addition to its firm place in the theater, it has also become popular as a form of amateur music.

The general tendency in the singing of *shamisen* music is to force the voice "naturally" into the musical stratosphere. Any Western-trained voice would find this most unnatural, but it is really only a matter of different preliminary training, and much the same thing can be said of Western opera.

To get some idea of what standard *shamisen* narrative stories are like, let us look at the plot of "Gompachi," a nineteenth-century tale found in both the *tokiwazu* and *kiyomoto* repertoires. It is divided into two parts. In the first half, the hero, Gompachi, has been arrested. Earlier he had fled from his native prefecture to the anonymity of the Yoshiwara. He was forced to do this because he had seriously wounded a man during an argument. He soon found that his money did not last very long in the brothel quarters and resorted to robbery as a livelihood. For this crime he is now being led away to execution. As he travels to his doom, his mistress, Komurasaki, begs the guard to let her exchange a cup of water with her lover as this is the custom in these circumstances. The guard consents, and when they begin to do this, Komurasaki whips out a knife and cuts Gompachi's bonds. At this dramatic point in the story we find Gompachi waking with a start: it has all been a bad dream.

The second half of the story shows that not all of the dream was unreal, for Gompachi is worrying about the reputation of his mistress; he is afraid that her association with him will ruin her business as a geisha in the Yoshiwara. He vows to leave her out of love for her, but as they weep and pledge eternal love, they become aware of some suspicious activity outside. By now it's too late—the police have surrounded the house! There is only one solution left in an authentic *jōruri* piece: a double suicide, of course, in a long, tearful scene of slow dying. An added bit of pathos attaches to this particular tale, in that the actual graves of Gompachi and Komurasaki are apparently to be found today at the Fudōson temple in Meguro, Tokyo. Though their story has been considerably altered for the sake of the drama, their green-mossed memorial pillars are evidence that many of these romantic tales have a basis in genuine human tragedies.

The resemblance between this story and an Italian opera libretto only points up the fact that both countries have a great love of musical melodramas. Indeed, there is a theatricality to some aspects of everyday life in Japan that might be likened to that of Italy, though on a less exuberant scale. The itinerant salesman of Japan has an innate sense of dramatic timing, and often his sales pitch is really an aria, with banging sticks or rolled newspaper for accompaniment. When I first arrived in 1955, life seemed to be lived as if it were on a stage. The very seasons could be marked by the songs of the men with handcarts who sold tofu, sweet potatoes, bamboo poles, laundry baskets, vegetables, and goldfish, or bought junk, newspapers, and old clothes.


## GIDAYŪBUSHI—THE MUSIC OF BUNRAKU

During this discussion of narrative *shamisen* music, no mention has yet been made of the giant of them all, *gidayūbushi* (or just *gidayū*). Founded by Takemoto Gidayū (1651–1714) in the booming commercial city of Osaka, it has all the bluster and drive of the merchant class to which it was directed. At one time, the thoughts and speech habits of some Osaka residents were guided by *gidayū* songs in much the same manner that some Americans are cultural byproducts of the *New Yorker* magazine, *The New York Times*, or movies and musicals. Together with the famous playwright Chikamatsu Monzaemon (1653–1724), Gidayū created a great puppet-play tradition, eventually called *bunraku* after the name of one of the theater owners. Many present-day *kabuki* plays are nothing but a humanization, if you will, of the puppet play. Likewise, the singing of Takemoto Gidayū was so powerful that, from his time onward, the music of *gidayūbushi* was considered to be the epitome of narrative *shamisen* music.

The *gidayū* musicians at a puppet performance (Plate 61) are placed on a rostrum to the right of the stage as seen by the audience (i.e., stage left). From this position, the singer (*tayū*) delivers an extravagant range of vocal expression. His violent exertions are said to instill actual human emotions in the wooden puppets, whose gestures are in fact so lifelike that the movements are often studied by actors—a phenomenon all the more remarkable when one remembers that each principal puppet is manipulated by three men, one for the head and right arm, one for the left arm, and a third for the feet.

Look at Plates 62–73, showing Takemoto Tsudayū (1916–87) in full cry. They clearly demonstrate that *tayū* are as much actors as they are musicians. By connecting these pictures with the following description of a performance, those who have never seen a *tayū* in action may get some idea of the excitement of such an occasion.

After a *shamisen* prelude, the *tayū* begins with a deep rumbling hum not unlike the sound of a two-ton truck in low gear. Slowly his lips part and a rough but very open vowel sound floats over the stage to awaken the puppets and the audience to the electricity that lurks heavily in the atmosphere. The story begins to unfold in a simple line, with the *shamisen* restlessly making short tonal comments between phrases. Gradually, the tension mounts, the *shamisen* interrupts more frequently, and the voice becomes part singing, part speaking, and partly an indescribable mixture of the two. At the same time, the singer's entire body becomes possessed by the characters he is portraying. His legs seem bound to the cushion, but his trunk, head, and arms are a mass of writhing emotion, to say nothing of his face! Look again at Plates 62–73. With scarlet, sweating face and bulging veins in the neck and temple, it is as though the singer were trying to infuse great passions into his wooden counterparts on stage by the sheer heat of his own emotions. The music stand (*marudai*) in front of the singer is a heavy, squat affair and it needs to be, for it is pounded, thumped, and crawled upon as the crises mount higher and higher.

One lone singer will portray every character on stage, from a small child to a warrior or an old grandmother (CD track 14). But never did a villain growl more ferociously nor a heroine simper in such a meek and squeaky tone, for in *gidayū* things are black and white. The confusing grays of many Western dramas are not often found in *bunraku* plays. Right is right, wrong is wrong, and death is the only solution for a single transgression. Thus, no one has ever cried as hard or laughed as heartily as the characters presented by the *gidayū* singers.

When the midway point comes in the series of crises, the singer solemnly closes his book, touches it to his forehead, and the rostrum suddenly revolves, revealing a fresh pair of artists, a *shamisen* player and another singer, who begin all over again the same process until the plot is brought to its conclusion.

*Gidayū* is considered by many to be the most difficult of all Japanese music forms, for the singer must possess a voice of great stamina and be a good melodramatic actor. The stage direction itself is actually in the hands of the *shamisen* player, who must sense the pace of the drama and, by grunts and musical signals, knit the entire production together though neither he nor the singer tends even to look at the stage. *Shamisen* players and singers usually team up and work together for years so that their coordination is perfect. These teams are characteristic of *gidayū* music, though in some finales or dance sections four or five singers and several *shamisen* may be used.

The *shamisen* used in *gidayū* is quite different from other *shamisen* (see Plate 75). The skin is thicker and the general structure of the instrument is heavier. The plectrum, in turn, is thick though very narrow and blunt, and the tortoiseshell bridge contains lead inserts to keep it from bouncing off the head. A professional performer will have a set of bridges of different weights marked to coordinate the string tuning with the desired tone. The net result of all these features is a deeper, harder tone that matches admirably the forceful expression inherent in the entire drama.

To understand the form and structure of the music of *bunraku*, one has to first recognize that it is part of a complex play comprising from three to twelve acts (*dan*).[5] Each act, up to two hours long, is further divided into scenes. With the increasing pace of modern life, one rarely sees a complete play nowadays, but even one scene or merely a concert excerpt from one scene is enough to convey the skill and artistry of the tradition.

Our brief description of a performance given above involved three basic styles: straight text declamation (*kotoba*), lyrical singing (*ji*), and a half-spoken, half-sung parlando (*ji iro*). Unlike Western traditional opera, in which dialogue, recitative, and aria are clearly separated, the performance of *gidayū* remains constantly fluid in style. Even the rendering of dialogue is filled with contour and rhythmic manipulations that make a Shakespearean performance sound almost bland by comparison. As proof of this, listen to the excerpt on CD track 14 from the "Sakaya no dan" scene of the play *Hade sugata onna maiginu*.

Figure 30 represents the flow between and within the three styles. Like any established music, each style has its own characteristic conventions,

5. See Gerstle in Biblio. refs. 8·3 and 8·4 for details.

and there are audible methods of moving from one to another as seen in the terms *iro* and *kakari*. However, there are no specific "themes" such as are common in Western opera (Carmen's tragic motive or Wagnerian leitmotivs). The *shamisen* does have standard preludes to show that the location of the scene is the same as before (*sanjū*) or in a new place (*okuri*). Except in the opening scene of a play, the first words of the singer are the last of the previous scene, to give the play a sense of continuity. Throughout the scene, the functions of the *shamisen* are to set pitch, support the meaning of words, and play interludes relating to stage action.

The texts of *bunraku* plays have been published since the eighteenth century. Many of these printings were intended for devotees who were taking lessons, so special music terms (*kotoba*, *kakari*), pitches (e.g. *kami*, "high"), and performance styles (e.g. *suete*, "strong,") are found alongside the words. This "notation" cannot be sight-read. For example, in Figure 58 (Appendix I) the term *naka* in the fourth line from the right, or *haru*, in the fifth line, can mean either a pitch level, a performance style, or a conventional melodic pattern. Rote learning was and is the best method when combined with frequent listening to performances, preferably by one's own teacher.

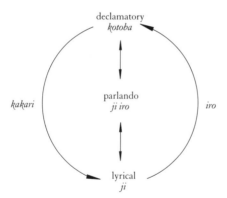

FIGURE 30. The flow of *gidayū* musical styles

The inexperienced listener to Japanese music is often overwhelmed by the melodramatic violence and deep tone of *gidayū* singing and the almost brutal snaps of the blunt *gidayū* plectrum and calls of the *shamisen* player. With a series of such masculine characteristics, it may be surprising therefore to learn that there are also female practitioners of *gidayūbushi* (see

Plate 60). In the early nineteenth century, female (*onna* or *musume*) *jōruri* flourished at small *yose* theaters, where excerpts from famous plays and new works were performed in concert form. The popularity of the tradition by the end of the century is evident in an order from Meiji University that forbade students from spending time in the enthralling presence of these skillful and often good-looking female *tayū*. One fringe benefit of the rise of Japanese feminism in the late twentieth century has been the return of such performances to urban stages.

Like Western opera, occasional new pieces of *bunraku* appear among the standard repertory presentations. During the occupation period (1945–52) after World War II, the most interesting revival was *Ochō fujin*, better known in the West as *Madame Butterfly*. It was not only the Japanese theme and the presence of American sailors that made it seem suitable, it was also the fact that it contained all the essential ingredients of any *bunraku* play, namely, several tearful scenes preferably with a child about somewhere, frustrated love, a sense of obligation, a tragic death, and more tears. Once again, one is forced to call attention to the close similarity between the spirit of *jōruri* and that of Italian opera.

The *bunraku* version of *Madame Butterfly* opens with "Auld Lang Syne" being played on an offstage violin, mixed with the Japanese folk song "Sakura" on the *gidayū shamisen*. The drama ends with the famous death scene and the *gidayū* singer weeping "Pinkerton-san, Pinkerton-san!" by which time there is scarcely a dry eye in the audience. To join in and appreciate the honest, heart-on-the-sleeve melodrama of *gidayūbushi*, all the Western viewer needs is a little orientation (in this case a familiar story). With further listening and a modicum of preparation, any sensitive patron can discover the full theatrical experience that this king of Japanese narrative music has to offer.

Looking back over the entire field of *katarimono*, one can see several distinctive styles classified under this one category. *Naniwabushi* presents the roughest style, with a vocal quality that is highly nasal, at times almost shouting. *Gidayūbushi* is next in roughness of tone, but the vocal and *shamisen* techniques are much more developed and the entire structure of *gidayū* compositions is more sophisticated. *Shinnaibushi* comes next in line, with a tense but more restrained style accompanied by a much softer *shamisen* part. *Bungobushi* is out of the picture today and *katōbushi* is rare, its style being much like *tokiwazu*. *Tokiwazu* is markedly less violent in its vocal technique as well as *shamisen* sound, though its high, tessatura singing may sound strident to some Western ears. *Kiyomoto* is the highest and least percussive of the narrative music. In order to recognize more specific distinctions between various genres, one must simply hear each type many times. The results are well worth the effort.


UTAMONO—LYRICAL SHAMISEN MUSIC

The early use of *shamisen* for accompanying folk songs, mentioned previously, might be called the beginning of *utamono* (also known as *utaimono*), or lyrical music for the *shamisen*. A more direct source is the music of restaurants and brothels in the cities and along the pilgrimage roads of early Edo-period Japan. Generic terms for these ditties were *kouta* (short songs) or *hauta* (regional songs). These were combined into sets of unrelated songs known collectively as *kumiuta*. A collection of the texts is found in the *Shichiku shoshinshū* of 1664, and the notation in the *Ōnusa* of 1685. It was shown in Chapter Seven how this form affected early *koto* music. The general style of these songs is simple and unassuming, while the verses themselves tend to be wistful and romantic. A translation follows of two poems by Rōsai Ryūtatsu, an early seventeenth-century composer of a style of *kouta* called *ryūtatsubushi* or *rōsaibushi*.

> The longer I live in this world,
> The more I think of my love.
> I'd like to disappear with the moon
> Behind the ridge of the mountains.

> I can't seem to write
> The letter I have in mind,
> So let this piece of white paper
> Give you my message.

The Rōsai *kouta*, which was somewhat classical in style, was absorbed into the mainstream of *kouta* found in the geisha world and the *kabuki*, where the concept of *iki*—subtle sensuality—was predominant. CD track 15 demonstrates this quality as well as an ambiguity characteristic of "floating world" music: although a woman is singing, one is not sure who is saying the words. Over time, every geisha district and brothel quarter (there is a difference) developed its own style of *kouta*, the repertoires of the Kyoto/Osaka style (*kamigata kouta*) and Tokyo style (*edo kouta*) remaining distinct to this day.

Under the aegis of brothel employees, one can well imagine that the delicate imagery of the earlier *kouta* songs began to deteriorate. The natural punning capacity of the Japanese language was overworked to the point where the play on words was lost and the erotic meaning became as direct as porno pictures and the comic books (*manga*) that continue to flourish in modern Japan. Here is a *kouta* text that was found on a woodblock print of the late seventeenth century.

> Indeed, indeed! With all their hearts sharing love's pillow—
> Stroking her Jewelled Gate, and taking
> The girl's hand and causing her to grasp his Jade Stalk—
> What girl's face will not change color,
> Her breath come faster?

While pornography moved on to other media, *kouta* went through several reforms. The nineteenth-century *utazawa* form attempted to add dignity and grace to the music and reduce the erotic content, while in 1855 new *kouta* for the *kabuki* appeared. By the late twentieth century, *kouta* came to be considered either a geisha party element or a light concert genre. A good number of amateurs were actually older businessmen for whom skill at performing one *kouta* at a party was as important as being able to play golf. Many a *kouta* recital would show a comely, kimono-clad female *shamisen* player accompanying a slightly rotund gentleman in a somber business suit who may have had to rush from the office in time for the performance. In order to give each patron his ample few minutes, the stage often contained two small rotating platforms so that as one pair of performers disappeared, the next appeared on the adjacent spot—the high-speed Japanese equivalent of an American barbershop-quartet contest.

The intimate quality of *kouta* is enhanced by playing the *shamisen* with the fingertip or small plectrum (*utazawa* uses a larger plectrum). This finger strumming produces a softer tone that matches the equally subtle sounds of the singers. In addition, the *shamisen* is smaller than that of other genres.

Most *kouta*, *utazawa*, and *hauta* re-create the atmosphere and thoughts of the Edo and Meiji periods in much the same manner as do the famous *ukiyoe* woodblock prints of that same era. *Kouta* represents to many

Japanese the "good old days." As long as there is room in the world for a little unabashed sentimentality and subtle sensuality, there will be room for *kouta*.


## NAGAUTA—THE HEART OF *KABUKI* MUSIC

If *gidayūbushi* is the king of the narrative branch of *shamisen* music, then *nagauta* is the ruler of the lyrical domain. *Nagauta*, or "long song," is the product of Tokyo in the same way that *gidayū* is a product of Osaka. The term *nagauta* was applied earlier in history to a different form of music in Kyoto, and the *Matsu no ha* collection of 1703 contains texts of such *nagauta* in *jiuta* music. Now this older music is called *kamigata* (Kansai area) *nagauta*, while the giant of whom we are about to speak is called *edo nagauta*, or simply *nagauta*.

The growth of *nagauta* is intimately connected with the evolution of the *kabuki* theater in Tokyo. When the *shamisen* was first used in *kabuki*, sometime before 1650, the music played was various short songs, but as the theater matured, dances became longer and such music was not appropriate. The term *edo nagauta* is first seen on a *kabuki* program of 1704. By mid-century this genre and the Kineya guild of musicians who composed or performed it spread throughout the *kabuki* theaters. Like many of the narrative *shamisen* genres mentioned earlier, lessons in *nagauta* became popular along with those in *kabuki* dance itself, which came to be known as "classical dance" (*buyō*). Amateur *kabuki* performances occurred in the Edo mansions of feudal lords[6] as well as rich merchants, despite strong government regulations against it. In the early nineteenth century, actual concert (*ozashiki*) *nagauta* compositions appeared along with concert versions of the dance music and new, non-*kabuki* dances. These innovations flourished in the late nineteenth and early twentieth centuries and continued after World War II.

Whether concert or dance music, *kabuki*-derived *shamisen* genres reflect their *kabuki* origins. We can see this in a study of *nagauta* performance practices and musical form. Since *kabuki* itself grew out of the *noh* tradition, it is logical that the *noh* drums and flute (the *hayashi*) should be a normal

---

6. Feudal lords were required to leave family members in Edo as hostages against possible revolt.

part of the ensemble, where the two *tsuzumi* drums are collectively known as the *daishō* (a combination of the other reading of the characters for large [ō] and small [*ko*] in the words *ōtsuzumi* and *kotsuzumi*). In keeping with the gaudier style of *kabuki*, the number of drums as well as singers and *shamisen* may increase, usually by three each (see Plate 77). The flute player may also use the more lyrical seven-hole bamboo flute (the *takebue* or *shinobue*).

The full ensemble could be considered to be an orchestra with strings, percussion, and winds plus a vocal line. The musical results of this combination, however, are very different from those of Western music, as will become apparent in the following paragraphs.

Like almost all the music studied so far in this book, *nagauta* is "through composed"; it does not use specific first or second themes that need to be developed throughout the piece. There are general repertory-wide conventional melodic styles and orchestrations that help one to recognize a specific moment in the music but, like the word-oriented music of the Renaissance, the music changes when the text topic is new. Since *nagauta* was originally used for dance accompaniment, the basic terminology to describe *nagauta* form was called by late nineteenth-century Japanese scholars the *kabuki* dance form, and consists of six standard sections: the *oki*, *michiyuki*, *kudoki*, *odoriji*, *chirashi*, and *dangire*. Keep in mind that *nagauta* is text and dance oriented, so it cannot be easily compared with the abstract Western forms such as a sonata allegro or a rondo. As in Western music, there are many deviations from standard practice in *nagauta*, but a study of the basic terms is an appropriate introduction to the logic of the music. Examples will be taken from the Kineya Rokuzaemon X 1841 dance composition "Gorō Tokimune," heard on CD track 16 from after the *kudoki* to the end.

The *oki* introduces the scene or characters. For example, in "Azuma hakkei" (Eight Views of Eastern Japan), an 1829 piece by Kineya Kisaburō, the *oki* evokes a lovely spring day in old Tokyo. The *oki* of "Gorō Tokimune" announces the name of the main character—Gorō, one of the famous Soga brothers who vowed vengeance on the death of their father[7]—and tells of his mission. In a manner not unlike recitative, the singer imi-

---

7. The Soga cycle in theater is studied in Laurence R. Kominz, *Avatars of Vengeance* (Ann Arbor: Center for Japanese Studies, 1995).

FIGURE 31. *Nagauta ōzatsuma* section in "Gorō Tokimune"

tates the declamatory style of a *kabuki* actor. The *shamisen* accompaniment uses conventional named patterns that are derived from a former *shamisen* genre called *ōzatsuma*. Such patterns (*te*) are seen later in the piece in the first eight measures of Figure 31.

As in *noh* drama, the *nagauta michiyuki* is the name of the section in which actors enter onto the stage. The *kabuki* actor often arrives via the *hanamichi* (Plate 76), a ramp that extends from the back of the theater to the stage. The music of the *michiyuki* varies with the personality of the character and the manner of the entrance (walking, running, emerging from a trap door, etc.), but it usually starts with a full-ensemble instrumental interlude.

The *kudoki* is a softer, lyrical style of singing, usually performed by singers and *shamisen* alone. The forward motion of the music is enforced by frequent pauses on pitches above or below the pitch centers. The singer and *shamisen* are seldom on the same beat. This rhythmic disjunction not only helps clarify syllables of the text from the sound of the *shamisen* but also creates another sense of forward motion.

Figure 31 is from a transition section (*tsunagi*) between the *kudoki* and *odoriji*. The *shamisen* accompaniment of the declamatory opening uses the conventional *ōzatsuma* patterns mentioned earlier. The drum accompaniment of the first phrases is the *noh* drama *mitsuji* pattern (see Figure 15), but thereafter the *tsuzumi* drums play in a *kabuki* style called *chirikara byōshi*, the name being derived from the mnemonics that are used to learn the patterns (see Figure 48). These not only tend to support the rhythm of the *shamisen* line but, in this case, relate to the choreography. In measure ten the actor kicks off a rain clog, and in measure fourteen kicks off the other. The "invisible" assistant (*kōken*) behind the actor catches both and takes them offstage.

The *odoriji* is livelier and often begins with a new *shamisen* tuning. The bamboo flute may appear along with the *taiko*; in fact, the section is sometimes called the *taikoji*. Both the words *odori* (dance) and *taiko* (drum) reflect the influence of *noh*, for the *taiko* in *noh* is usually reserved for the final dance accompaniment (see p. 142). The flute comes in different sizes in order to be able to play an ornamented (*ashirai*) version of the *shamisen* melody. In this context, it should be recalled that Japanese vocal music, like most Western songs, is not composed on a set pitch level. In both traditions the pitch is normally chosen by the singer, though there are conventional tunings for each piece.

*Chirashi* means "scattering," and that is what happens in this section. The pace, though it may vary, eventually picks up, the orchestration thickens, and one feels a definite sense of a finale approaching. One can hear on CD track 16 that the *tsuzumi* are playing eight-beat patterns that rhythmically relate to the *shamisen* line; however, the *taiko* and *nōkan* in Figure 32 play a ten-beat pattern that creates the "sliding door" effect to which we have made periodic reference in this book. This "out-of-synchronization" effect helps propel the music toward the ending. The flute and drum pattern is called *sarashi*, which was originally used to accompany the flapping of silk streamers in a different dance but has since become a standard addition to any section that requires a thicker, more dramatic texture. Like dance music in *noh*, the flute and drum often become one unit whose rhythm

234

**FIGURE 32.** The *chirashi* section of "Gorō Tokimune"

and length does not always match that of the melody, thus creating another form of tension that drives the music forward. Note that the flute line in this passage is unrelated to the *shamisen* melody in both line and tonality. This contributes to its coloristic function as well as its role in what might be called the "third force" in such music. Besides melody and rhythm, in *nagauta* there is no meaningful harmony. Rather, the flute-drum unit assumes the functions (not the sounds) of harmony by adding color and providing a special sense of tension and progression.

The *dangire* is the finale. All the instruments appear, and the dancers strike a final pose (*mie*) or tableau. The standard final cadences are so well known that audiences start to applaud the moment they begin and the curtain is often closed before the last note is played! All this upsets the aesthetic of some twenty or more minutes of fine music. At one time the same discomforting habit applied to Western concerts as well but, fortunately, things have changed, at least in that respect. Since CD track 16 was derived from a recording meant to accompany dance, the final note of the *dangire* is deleted and a *kabuki mie* accompanying pattern is played while the dancer strikes a pose. The curtain closes to the additional sound of the clappers (*ki*), which will be discussed in the *kabuki* chapter.

This, then, is the basic form used in *shamisen*-accompanied dance music. The *jo-ha-kyū* principle mentioned in *noh* drama has sometimes been applied to the form, placing the *oki* and *michiyuki* in the *jo*, the *kudoki* and *odoriji* in the *ha*, and the *chirashi* and *dangire* in the *kyū*. With the increase in concert vis-à-vis dance-accompanying compositions, other formal designs have been used, such as the *jiuta* structure from *koto* music, in which there are more instrumental interludes between vocal sections. Instrumental interludes (*ai no te*) are a study in themselves. There are even recordings in which only these excerpts are heard. Many of them are clever imitations of other styles of music, representations of weather conditions or famous places, or even natural sounds. In the 1845 composition by Kineya Rokuzaemon X, "Aki no irogusa" (The Colors of Autumn Foliage), one interlude is based on the famous *koto* piece "Midare," while another represents the chirping of insects.

This brief survey of *nagauta* illustrates an equally logical but very different approach to both form and structure. The feature most lacking for Western-trained musicians is tertian harmony (chords in thirds, such as C E G) and harmonic progression. Oriental music in general has succeeded in producing much excellent music without chords at all. We have seen in *nagauta* how form has been identified, not by themes that repeat and return at the end, but rather by specific musical conventions and orchestrations that create a strong sense of progression and come to a satisfying ending that does not use the same sounds with which it started. It is not a Schubert song, a Verdi aria, a Chinese opera, nor a sacred song from India, but, like all of them, it can be beautiful to hear once one learns to use different methods of listening and to accept a different aesthetic.

We have concentrated so much on the music that another vital element of the genre has been left out, the text. *Shamisen* texts follow the traditional tendency of poetry to be in seven- and five-syllable units. They are also filled with conventional phrases from poetry, such as "the wind in the pines" or "the rush of the wind in the valley." In dance-related genres, one seldom finds a full story in the text. Rather there are tableaux or short passages that only the dance movements or knowledge of the story can explain. With the influence of *katarimono* genres in later concert pieces, however, complete narratives began to appear in *nagauta*.

Another aspect of *shamisen* music worth commenting on concerns the composer. Along with the name of the composer and the poet in the published announcements (*banzuke*), one will find the date, location, and musicians who participated in the first performance. The composer was usually the lead singer or *shamisen* player of the guild. Composers like Kineya Rokuzaemon X (1800–58) and Kineya Kisaburō II (1820–96) were as well known in Edo as were Robert Schumann (1810–56) and Giuseppe Verdi (1813–1901) in Europe during the same decades. But there is one major difference that must be noted. In *shamisen* music, the named composer is the person who creates the *shamisen* and vocal lines. He then turns to the head of the *hayashi* guild (*hayashigashira*) with whom he works, and asks for the percussion and flute parts to be added. Thus, one can say that it is a communal composition. The conventions are so strong that it is hard for a Western-trained musician to believe that the result is not the work of one mind. If played by the same guild, the piece will not change over time, but if different guilds of musicians perform the same piece it may have different features. This amounts not just to reorchestration but to recomposition.

## TWENTIETH-CENTURY SHAMISEN GENRES

Throughout the twentieth century, new compositions have appeared in all the *shamisen* genres we have discussed, and new styles were established. In 1910, Hiraoka Ginshū (1856–1934) created a new genre derived from *katōbushi*, first naming it *hiraokabushi* in the traditional manner and later, in keeping with the times, using the name *tōmeibushi*; the *tō* is derived from Tokyo and the *mei* from the Meiji era, the place and time in which he lived. Well-known *nagauta* and *kiyomoto* musicians contributed new compositions to *tōmeibushi*. In 1928, the genre became known as the *tōmei ryū* (*tōmei* school). Delicacy of style and some Western influence seem to have been characteristic of this rare genre, and though it is seldom heard today, in the best Japanese tradition there still are performers.

Western-style singing was the unique feature of a genre called *yamato-gaku*, created in 1933 by Ōkura Kishichirō (1882–1963). He accompanied his songs with a mixture of older *shamisen* styles, such as *katō*, *ogie*, *itchū*, and *miyazono*. New poetry and a Western-influenced new end-blown flute (the *ōkurabue*) were part of his experiment, and musicians from other genres joined his efforts, particularly Kiyomoto Eijurō, who used the name Miyagawa Eiji when composing *yamatogaku* pieces. The results were interesting but did not take root in the *hōgaku* world. Still, there remain so many popular and virile *shamisen* genres that a wide vista of new musical experiences awaits anyone who wishes to listen to them and learn what to listen for in them.

# CHAPTER NINE

# KABUKI MUSIC

## 1. The Components of *Kabuki* Music

The basic components of *kabuki* music have already been discussed. It remains for us to tie these elements together and show more precisely how they are used in the theater. It might be wise first to learn something about the history of *kabuki* itself.

*Kabuki* is the great theatrical contribution of the Edo period. As such, it is the inheritor of all the varied forms of theatricals that preceded it. Tradition claims that *kabuki* began in 1596 on the dry bed of the Kamo River in Kyoto with the performance of a Shinto dancer named Okuni of Izumo. She is said to have danced *nembutsuodori*, a form of Buddhist exorcist dance, though her performance was decidedly secular—indeed, the early use of the word *kabuki* had distinctly lascivious overtones.[1] When *kabuki* went on tour, a troupe was formed from the ever-bountiful supply of city prostitutes. Eventually this female *kabuki* was banned and all-male troupes came into existence. These troupes also found governmental resistance strong until they reduced their more obvious homosexual tendencies. Throughout its formative years, the colorful, complicated history of *kabuki* thereafter shows a continuous struggle against prohibitive regulations, until it became a mature theatrical form and the very center of Edo social life.

The crowds that appeared daily in the theater district were comprised of members from every social class. The government had ossified society,

---

1. The present Chinese characters for the word *kabuki* mean "song, dance, and acting."

239

but the theater surreptitiously dissolved some of the social restraints that were felt by men and women of every rank. Perhaps this is one of the major reasons for the popularity of *kabuki*. In a highly restricted society, it provided a safety valve through which some of the pent-up energy of the people could be dissipated. The adulation accorded actors was in excess even of that given to modern movie stars and popular singers. The *kabuki* actor influenced speech, dress, and morals. Under the pressure of advanced communications and marketing propaganda, modern civilization has shown a similar concern with fads, but in that embodiment of frustrated energy known as the Edo man (*edokko*), one finds a preoccupation with fads even more intense. Perhaps without the theater, Edo civilization would have fallen apart sooner, but that is a problem for the sociologist; what concerns us here is the music of this famous theatrical tradition.

Old scroll paintings show that *kabuki* first used a standard *noh hayashi* —a *noh* flute and three drums—for accompaniment. In fact, early *kabuki* was performed on *noh* and *kagura* stages. Such performances were particularly popular during public benefit performances (*kanjin noh*) put on by various ruling houses. As *kabuki* developed its own form of architecture, it also added more instruments. For example, a large drum (the *ōdaiko*) was installed in a tower over the entrance, and if the audience became too rowdy, the drum was used to get the police to come and pacify the spectators. Eventually, this instrument was used to signal the opening and closing of the theater. As will be shown later, it also became a mood-creating device in the plays themselves.

When the *shamisen* made its appearance on the *kabuki* stage sometime between 1620 and 1650, the main genres of *shamisen* music were *kumiuta* and *kouta*. As mentioned in the previous chapter, the *kabuki* found such music too short for dance accompaniment. This led to the creation of *edo nagauta*, the core of present-day *kabuki* music. Many other *shamisen* genres came into being in the *kabuki*, but only *tokiwazu, gidayū, kiyomoto*, and *shinnaibushi* remain along with *nagauta* in contemporary *kabuki* productions.[2]

When the *noh hayashi* and *shamisen* genres appear on stage, the ensemble is called the *debayashi*. This group is usually placed at the back of the stage and set on tiers (Plate 77), with the singers and *shamisen* above and the drums

---

2. *Katōbushi* is still used for one play, *Sukeroku*.

and flute at floor level. Because of this, the members of the *hayashi* are known as the *shitakata*, the "ones below." When a piece is derived from a puppet play, it is common to see the *gidayū* singer and *shamisen* player seated at the lower stage left (see p. 188), as they are in the puppet theater.[3] Sometimes they are placed in a special alcove above the stage-left entrance or in an offstage room at stage left. In such cases, they may be hidden from the audience by a bamboo curtain. In Plate 79, for example, placed even further offstage left, they are only just visible. This set of *gidayū* musicians is known in *kabuki* as the *chobo*. They perform in a manner similar to that heard in the puppet theater, except that their use is more restricted. In the puppet plays, these musicians are the life-giving element in the drama, propelling the plot with their music and narration; in *kabuki*, they are analogous to the chorus in ancient Greek drama, setting and commenting on the scene, sometimes expressing the thoughts of the actor. Such functions, however, are not their exclusive domain, and other forms of music may serve the same purpose.

The use of *tokiwazu* or *kiyomoto* is most frequent in romantic scenes. When they appear on stage, they are usually placed downstage right. The placement of any group of musicians on stage, though, is flexible and will vary according to the scenic requirements of the play. As Earle Ernst (Biblio. ref. 9.3, 125) has pointed out, the physical presence of all these musicians on stage is in keeping with the presentational (vis-à-vis representational) attitude of the *kabuki* theater: that is, the plays do not try to hide their theatricality, but rather exploit it through a thorough stylization of the various contributing elements. One feels it is a symbolic rather than a realistic presentation of these elements, whether they are music, scenery, or acting. This allegorical approach is one of the major contributions of *kabuki* to the world of the theater.

Not all *kabuki* music comes from the stage. The most fascinating sounds emanate from behind the slats of a window in the downstage-right scenery flat. On the other side of the bamboo curtain that hides this room from the eyes of the audience are the performers of *geza ongaku*, the offstage music of the *kabuki* (Plate 78). This room is called the *kuromisu*, or "black curtain," in memory of the black flat that used to be placed in front

---

3. In the theater the directions are given as seen from an actor facing the audience, so stage left is to the right from an audience's point of view.

of it. The term *geza*, "lower place," comes from its original position below the second-floor *chobo* room at stage left.[4]

From the semi-darkness of this room, the *geza* musicians peer out at the stage and the *hanamichi* ramp leading to the back of the theater (Plate 76). Their task is to provide all the necessary music, noise, sound effects, and signals not covered by the musicians on stage. For this purpose, they have a battery of percussion equipment and many other instruments. A study of such *geza* music can best be divided into two sections: the melodic music of the *geza* and the use of the battery.

Although the *koto*, *kokyū*, and *shakuhachi* are required in certain plays, it is the *shamisen* that dominates the music of *kabuki*, offstage as well as onstage. Used offstage, it functions primarily as an indicator of atmosphere. This can be a reminder of a period, place, time, or mood. For example, the melody called "Shinobi sanjū" is played offstage to set the atmosphere of a very dark, mysterious scene. To further evoke a particular mood, the opening phrase of the *shamisen* music imitates the call of the cicada in summer. If the *shamisen* plays *kangen* (see Figure 56, Appendix I), it is to indicate that the scene is set in the court, as the term refers to orchestral *gagaku* music. The double stops of the first bars imitate this "thicker" *gagaku* sound. The tune "Tsukuda" (Figure 33A) is another example of a *shamisen* pattern indicating place, literally the "floating world" of old Edo. Tsukuda is the name of an island at the mouth of the Sumida River in Tokyo. Across from this island was a large geisha district. In order to accommodate their would-be customers, the owners of geisha houses there provided boats to ferry the patrons to and from the district. As patrons passed by Tsukuda Island on the way to their pleasure, they were entertained on the boats by *shamisen*-playing geisha. The jaunty *shamisen* ostinato of "Tsukuda" in the "geisha" *sansagari* tuning evokes the jolly mood of these boat trips and is used whenever the Sumida River is in the plot of a play. In Figure 33, the *geza* drummers are playing the pattern *nami no oto* ("the sound of the waves") beneath "Tsukuda." Singers might use the text of the song "Fukeyo kawakaze" (The River Wind Is Blowing) or some geisha-related piece. The *kabuki* tradition being fairly rigid, how-

---

4. In the Edo period this word was also written 外座, which meant an "outside place," referring to their position offstage. The present version of the word is now more common.

ever, "Tsukuda" cannot be used to indicate any other river except the Sumida.

In that context, songs usually differ according to whether productions are in the Kanto or Kinki area. A good example is the opening of the seventh act of *Chūshingura*, which is set in the (still standing) geisha house called Ichiriki in the Gion district of Kyoto. Figure 33B and C show the subtle regional differences of the *shamisen* introduction to the opening song, "Hana ni asobi," whose first words are "Playing among the flowers that bloom so beautifully in Gion."[5] In Tokyo, there is drum music before the singing, and in Kyoto afterward. When the same *geza* music is used in the play *Ise ondo*, the text places us in the old-town district of Ise.

FIGURE 33. *Geza shamisen* music for the "floating world"

*Geza shamisen* music comes from two sources: borrowed music and original music. In many cases, pieces that are thought to be original *geza* melodies may actually have been derived from one of the many defunct forms of Edo *shamisen* music. Although the *geza* musicians were originally *nagauta* men, they play all kinds of music. For example, the melody of the *koto* piece "Rokudan" is used during the *kabuki* play *Sukeroku*, the only apparent reason for this being that both pieces have the word *roku* (six) in their titles. Usually, however, the reason for using a piece is more directly

5. See Biblio. ref. 9-8, I, which contains Tokyo music, and II for *kamigata* music.

related to the requirements of the drama. Mention was made earlier of the *jiuta* piece "Yuki" (Snow) which is used during winter scenes.

*Geza shamisen* melodies that underlie dialogue are called *meriyasu*. These are purposely rather quiet and, like most music in films or TV dramas, are designed to fade in or out as necessary. This enables such music to accommodate itself easily to the pace of the action on stage. Because of its general background function it does not often involve singing. However, there are *meriyasu* songs that may appear in certain scenes in which the actor is meditating on some deep subject, when a solo voice coming from the *geza* room can be highly effective.[6]

The other two main melodic instruments of the *geza* are the *noh* flute and the bamboo flute (*takebue*). The *noh* flute is heard most often as a reminder that a certain play is an adaptation of a *noh* drama, and is used particularly at the beginning and ending of a play. At other times, it is used to indicate court music because its sound resembles that of the court flute (the *ryūteki*). Played in a low, menacing way, it implies a ghostly presence. The bamboo flute is seldom used alone though it appears in many combinations, especially those imitating folk festival music. Since there are no full-time *shakuhachi* players in a *kabuki* company, the bamboo flute is used as a substitute when the sound is needed.

Like the sound-effects equipment of the radio studio, the percussion department of the *geza* has an eternal fascination for the outsider. In addition to the standard *taiko*, *ōtsuzumi*, and *kotsuzumi*, there are many other types of drums, several sizes of gongs, chimes, bells, and a collection of miscellaneous instruments ranging from castanets to xylophones. But the king of the *geza* percussion section is the *ōdaiko*. Like its temple companion (Plate 18), it is a large drum with two tacked heads. Different sticks are used to hit it, depending on the effect desired. The most common are two tapered pieces of wood, seventy-six centimeters in length; these can be played on the tips or struck flatly in order to produce a much sharper sound. Occasionally one stick is held against the skin while the head is beaten with the other. This creates a dramatic rattle somewhat like that produced on a snare drum.

The *ōdaiko* has a long tradition as part of *kabuki*. Its use as a signal

6. *Meriyasu* songs in Western notation with their functional locations are found in Biblio. ref. 9·8.

instrument in the watchtowers of the old *kabuki* compounds was mentioned. This tradition is still maintained. One hour before curtain time, the pattern *ichibandaiko* ("drum number one") is played on the *ōdaiko*. Originally, this pattern was played early in the morning to indicate that there would be a performance that day, a custom necessitated by the financial and political uncertainty of theaters during the Edo period when managers were never sure from one day to the next if their operation would be able to continue. The government took a very dubious view of popular theater, and there were enough laws already on the books to enable theaters to be closed on very little pretext. This, by the way, is one of the many reasons why one seldom sees a social or political protest play in the *kabuki*, except for dramas written since the Meiji era. Before the late nineteenth century, the existence of *kabuki* was dependent on the favor of a paranoid government. The very fact that it did prosper is proof of the growing strength of the townspeople and the merchants as well as the ingenuity of the theater managers.

In the past, the playing of *ichibandaiko* was followed by "drum number two" and "drum number three." The dedicatory dance "Sambasō" was then performed, and the *kabuki* day had officially begun. Today, only *ichibandaiko* remains. It starts with a gradually accelerating roll executed on the edge of the drum which is meant to represent the sound of a heavy wooden bar unbolting the entrance of the theater.[7]

The principal use of the *ōdaiko* is not for traditional signals but for the creation of atmosphere. For example, the sounds of wind or rain are common effects played on the *ōdaiko*. Rather than being direct imitations of the real sounds, however, the drum patterns are symbolic evocations of the idea of wind and rain, to ensure that the music blends in with the nonrealistic acting style of classic *kabuki* plays. In keeping with this idea, these patterns are sometimes used when the element depicted does not figure in the play at all; on such occasions, it is felt that the quality of that element is present rather than the thing itself. Thus, one may hear the pattern of the sound of the wind in a still, nocturnal scene when a robber is peering surreptitiously into a house. The feeling of a chill wind and the cold eye of the robber are

7. If this tradition is true, it must date from the latter half of the Edo period. Until that time, the entrance of *kabuki* theaters consisted of a "mouse" door which allowed only one person at a time to pass through while the guards checked tickets and weapons.

245

Hyōshigi     Okedo     Daibyōshi     Gakudaiko

Dora     Sōban     Atarigane     Hitotsugane

Rei     Ekiro     Yotsudake     Chappa

Orugōru     Mokkin

similar enough in the *kabuki* musician's mind to warrant the use of the same music for both. One more utilitarian use of the wind pattern should also be mentioned: to keep up the tension and cover the noise of the scenery being moved while the stage is in darkness between different scenes.

It should be obvious by now that a large part of the appreciation of *geza* music depends on previous knowledge of the music and patterns used. In this respect, it is similar to the leitmotiv technique of the Wagnerian operas, though developed about one hundred and fifty years earlier. In Wagner, themes are used to indicate people and situations as well as ideas important to the opera. One may hear the theme of the Rhine maidens when they are not on stage, reminding enlightened listeners of the maidens' connection with the topic under discussion on stage at that moment. A complete appreciation of *kabuki* music, like an understanding of the Wagnerian cycle, is dependent on learning to recognize some of the music's leitmotivs and their significance.[8] Some of this knowledge is simply intellectual fun; for instance, when the *ōdaiko* plays the sound of the ocean, the *shamisen* often joins in with the piece "Chidori," as the *chidori* is a bird (a sandpiper) commonly found along the shores of Japan. But knowledge of many other effects is a fundamental aid to one's appreciation of the entire production.

After the *ōdaiko*, the next best-known percussion instrument is the *ki*, an abbreviation of the term *hyōshigi*. These two rectangular blocks of wood are only struck on the curved side in order to produce the clear, sharp sound needed to reverberate in a large theater. Actually, they are not part of the *geza*. A special stagehand called the *kyōgenkata* bangs them together to alert the entire theater as to the number of minutes remaining before the curtain rises. Then, when the curtain is opened, he produces an accelerating series of clacks (this can be heard on CD tracks 16 and 17). Just before the curtain closes, there is a sharp report from the *ki* to call the audience's attention to the final pose. And as the curtain is pulled across the stage, the *ki* is once more used as accompaniment.

During fight scenes, or with people running, and other rough-style (*aragoto*) acting, a different, larger set of clappers called the *tsuke* is struck on a wooden board placed on the apron of the stage at stage left. The clatter of these beats adds greatly to the power of the episode.[9]

A complete list of all the instruments in the *geza* room together with their various uses would form a separate book and require voluminous illustration.[10] Nevertheless, to help the reader identify some of the sights and sounds

8. There are several books in Japanese that list all the patterns and melodies in *geza* music, and how and when they are played. See Biblio. refs. 9·8 and 9·9.
9. In classical *kabuki*, stage fighting is highly stylized so that it can often appear to be stately dancing accompanied by fierce grimaces. In keeping with this the *shamisen-ōdaiko* piece "Dontappo," used in fight scenes, seems rather leisurely out of context. The *kabuki* explanation is that to put rough music behind such a scene would make it too rough. *Kabuki* may also occasionally use cheerful music behind a sad scene to keep it from being too sad.
10. These are found in Biblio. refs. 1·14 and 9·7 under *geza*.

that may be experienced at a *kabuki* performance, here is a description of the other major *geza* instruments seen in the drawings of this book:

### Drums (membranophones)

*Okedo*, a folk drum with two heads lashed together. It is played with one or two slightly tapered sticks and used primarily in folk scenes.

*Daibyōshi*, a two-headed lashed drum. Unlike the *okedo*, these heads extend beyond the body of the drum (like a *taiko* head), and the binding ropes are lashed around the middle to create tension. Primarily a Shinto-music instrument, it is played with two thin sticks (see p. 58).

*Gakudaiko*, a short-bodied drum with two tacked heads. Played with two thin sticks, it is meant to imitate the sound of the *gagaku* large drum and is also used in war scenes.

*Uchiwadaiko*, a fan drum. This drum, mentioned in Chapter Two (Plate 22), is also found in the *geza*. Its use is not restricted to religious scenes.

### Gongs and Bells (idiophones)

*Hontsurigane*, a temple-style bell hit with a large padded hammer. In addition to its use in temple scenes, it is also a signal device like the *ōdaiko*.

*Dora*, a gong with a knobbed center. This is used in temple scenes in conjunction with the above-mentioned bell as well as for signals.

*Sōban*, a gong with a rough surface. In addition to its use in temple scenes, it accompanies the entrance of various rough characters and represents the sounds of battle offstage. Made of thinner metal than the *dora*, its tone is more percussive.

*Atarigane*, a brass hand gong (Plate 8) played with a small bone hammer on the inside of the gong. Its use in folk music and festival *hayashi* groups has already been discussed. As a rule, its use in the *kabuki* is similar. It is played either held in the hand or suspended by a rope.

*Hitotsugane*, a small gong similar to the *atarigane* but set on three legs and played on the outside. It was originally used in the performance of Buddhist rosaries and hence appears often in religious scenes. It is also used in festival scenes. A smaller version of the same instrument, called the *matsumushi* (pine insect), is used in religious scenes as well as to create the sound of these seasonal insects.

*Orugōru*, a set of bells of varying pitches. Originally Buddhist-style Sanctus bells, they are used most often in *kabuki* to indicate lightness—for example, in scenes containing butterflies. They also evoke horse-sleigh bells (*ekiro*) in certain dances and help create a pleasant effect when desired.

*Rei*, a Buddhist sutra bell used to indicate religious services or the entrance of a priest. The *mokugyo*, mentioned in Chapter Two, is also used in such scenes.

*Chappa*, a pair of small cymbals used for dance accompaniment and temple or Chinese music scenes.

*Yotsudake*, four short pieces of bamboo that are played like castanets. This instrument is found in the old dances of the Ryukyu Islands, and in *kabuki* is used for certain goddess dances. Plate 20 shows a street musician playing them. The two-piece wooden clapper of the court (the *shakubyōshi*) is also used for scenes in which court music is needed, particularly if *imayō* is sung.

*Mokkin*, a xylophone with sixteen keys. The pitches of these keys are not important because it is played in a desultory fashion. The *mokkin* follows the rhythm of a piece rather than the melody. Borrowed originally from the Japanese societies for Chinese music (*minshingaku*),[11] it is used in *kabuki* primarily for blind or comic characters.

This long yet incomplete list does at least give the reader some idea of the variety of sounds that come from the *geza* room. The instruments are combined in a host of different ways so that the ear is constantly assaulted by a plethora of sounds. The choice of these sounds, however, is regulated by the requirements of the play: the *geza* is not used without dramaturgical justification. In order to better understand this process, it might help if we now looked at a specific case. Though each play has its own variety of musical characteristics, the detailed explanation of one production should provide a basis for understanding other performances.

---

11. No such xylophone is found in China. It may have become part of the Nagasaki Chinese merchants' pleasure-house ensembles because some of these Chinese came from Southeast Asia where xylophones abound.

# 2. The Music of One *Kabuki* Scene

*Momijigari* (The Maple-viewing Party) is an excellent example for it uses *nagauta*, *tokiwazu*, and *gidayū* musicians on stage. Such a combination of *shamisen* genres in one piece is called a *kakeai*, literally "mixing together." The play also uses virtually every *geza* instrument offstage.

The story revolves around the encounter of Taira no Koremochi with the demon of Mount Togakushi. The exact plot line and production varies from year to year and troupe to troupe. The following account is based on the Kichiemon-troupe production for November 1956. The first five minutes of a later production can be heard on CD track 17.

The prelude to every play is the sound of the *hyōshigi* that cracks out the minutes before the curtain. When everything is ready, the *noh* flute begins a slow overture called "Issei," after the name of an early section of a *noh* play (see p. 127). The small and large *tsuzumi* join in from across the stage, reinforcing the effect of the introduction to a *noh* play. The reason for this music is that *Momijigari* is in fact based on a drama from the *noh* repertoire. As the curtain rises, however, the deep, menacing tones of the *ōdaiko* are heard, implying a scene deep in the mountains and also removing the *noh*-like serenity from the music and creating a sense of menace.

The first *shamisen* music one hears comes from a group of *tokiwazu* musicians placed on a dais downstage right (Plate 79), which is followed by a comment from a quartet of *gidayū* musicians, seated in a separate niche just above the stage-left entrance. The next music comes from the *nagauta* musicians, who are placed upstage and a little to the left in order to accommodate the tree that forms part of the set (Plate 79). There are no actors onstage at the moment. The music sets the scene, which is in the mountains in the fall. This section corresponds to the *oki* mentioned in the *nagauta* dance form.

It is the *gidayū* singer who begins the actual story by telling how the warrior Taira no Koremochi has been sent by the emperor to kill the demon of Mount Togakushi. From the back of the theater Koremochi and two attendants abruptly appear and come marching down the *hanamichi* ramp that connects with the stage. Their approach is accompanied by the booming of the *ōdaiko*, which gives weight and pomp to the entrance of the hero, while the flute is added again as an echo of the original *noh* drama. This is the beginning of the *michiyuki* section of the *nagauta* form. The *kotsuzumi* and *ōtsuzumi* drums take over in *noh*-drama style, while the *tokiwazu* musicians continue the singing.

Finally, the actors stop at the traditional place just short of the stage and the dialogue begins. Beneath this dialogue, the *nagauta shamisen* play a very light, slow *meriyasu* melody. This backing of conversations with *meriyasu shamisen* is usually the responsibility of the *geza shamisen* offstage, but in this production it is done by the *nagauta* players. While the melody and dialogue are going on, one can hear the occasional beats of the *kotsuzumi*, which are immediately answered by another *kotsuzumi* on the opposite side of the stage. This effect, called *kodama*, has been added to heighten the mountain setting by providing echoes bounding across the make-believe valley.

When Koremochi and his attendants walk onto the stage proper, they are again accompanied by the *ōdaiko*, while the *gidayū* adds comments much like a Greek chorus or the chorus in a *noh* play. Suddenly, a young girl appears, and the music changes to the softer strains of *tokiwazu*. The drums continue to echo across the valley as she informs Koremochi and his men that her lady—a princess—is in the region enjoying the beauty of the maple leaves and would like to have them join in a party. The girl leaves to fetch the princess, and the *gidayū* singers comment again, while the *ōdaiko* lightly taps to mark her hurried steps out. During a discussion about whether to stay or not, the *nagauta shamisen* play a soft background and occasionally the singers come in with commentary. The valley echoes continue and the *ōdaiko* is heard whenever the actors move about the stage.

Koremochi decides that he must not be swayed from his mission and is starting to leave when a court lady appears (to the music of *tokiwazu*) and tries to dissuade him. *Gidayū* music warns of the princess's arrival. When she and her retinue appear, the *nagauta* singers extol her beauty (she, by the way, is a he, as are all the actors of present-day *kabuki*). The bamboo flute and two medium-size drums are added, which give a processional sound to the entrance. *Nagauta* and *gidayū* underline the ensuing conversation between the princess and the warrior. Once again, Koremochi vows to leave, but one court lady tries to detain him with a comic pantomime dance done to *tokiwazu* music. As another girl joins in, the music switches to *gidayū*, then *nagauta*, and finally back to *tokiwazu*; in this way, the various sections of the dance are marked off by actual stylistic changes in the music. The princess persuades Koremochi to stay, saying that their meeting in such a lonely place must have been predestined. The *gidayū* narrator takes note of this.

The bustle in preparation for a picnic takes place to the accompaniment of *tokiwazu*, plus the *taiko* drum and occasional beats with a hard stick on the edge of a gong (the *dora*). This produces a festive mood. *Tokiwazu* and *nagauta* are used as the warrior sits down with the princess and saké is poured. When a flirtation between them begins, the more menacing sound of *gidayū* takes over.

The party starts, and dance interludes interrupt the progress of the plot. First, one of the princess's attendants does a lighthearted dance to the accompaniment of *tokiwazu*, flute, cymbals, and two drums (the *okedo* and *daibyōshi*). This combination gives a bright, festive air to the proceedings. When the dance continues with a flower and a little girl added, *nagauta* is used. The dance ends with *gidayū*.

One of the warrior's men then gets up and does a balancing dance to a mixture of *gidayū* and *tokiwazu*. The percussion includes sleigh bells (*ekiro*) as well as *kotsuzumi* and *ōtsuzumi*. When he changes to a fan dance, the music becomes *nagauta* and the sleigh bells stop. A fellow attendant then dances in competition, the subject of his dance being a blind man. The music is *tokiwazu*, and the percussion uses the *ōdaiko* along with the edge of a cymbal and the xylophone (*mokkin*). These add to the gauche quality required.

The dancing stops, and saké combines with gentle conversation in a quiet matrix of *nagauta shamisen*. In general, whenever there is dialogue in the play there is a *meriyasu shamisen* background (it may not always be mentioned in our description).

Finally, the princess herself consents to dance. In addition to the regular *nagauta* music, the *geza* provides a very clever imitation of a *gagaku* court orchestra. Small double reeds are blown to sound like the *shō*, while the *daibyōshi* drum plays in court style and the hand gong, *noh* flute, and another drum (*gakudaiko*) add characteristic court sounds. When the music changes to *tokiwazu*, the *gagaku* imitation is dropped and normal *kotsuzumi* and *ōtsuzumi* patterns are used.

The next section of the princess's dance is done to *gidayū*, with *noh* flute, *kotsuzumi*, and *ōtsuzumi*. The style then changes to the softer *tokiwazu*, and the *hayashi* is silent, as in a *kudoki* section. Koremochi begins to succumb to the lulling effect of saké, soft music, and gentle dancing. The princess dances on, watching him occasionally to see if he is asleep. The menacing roll of the *ōdaiko* is heard as she dances closer to the warrior. Then suddenly, with a sharp bang on the *ōdaiko*, he awakens and she quickly switches to a fast rhythm set by *nagauta*, bamboo flute, *taiko*, *ōtsuzumi*, *kotsuzumi*, and the silvery-toned *orugōru* bells. When *tokiwazu* takes over, she begins a Japanese fan dance, the *hayashi* maintaining the rhythm and the mood. Then *gidayū* is played (without *hayashi*) as she uses two fans. *Nagauta* and *hayashi* combine while she performs tricks by flipping the fans in various clever ways. The *hayashi* continues as the music styles change at a faster rate. During one of the *gidayū* sections, Koremochi is discovered to be fast asleep. A little more dancing to *tokiwazu* and *taiko* follows, and then a finale with all the *shamisen* joining in with the *hayashi* and the piercing *noh* flute. There is silence as the princess hurls a curse at the helpless warrior and dashes offstage to the sound of *nagauta* and the roar of the *ōdaiko*, the roar subsiding to a menacing rumble as the *gidayū* singers provide a transition.

Next comes a great banging of cymbals, drums, and *ōdaiko* as a boy messenger from Hachiman, the war god, appears on the ramp through a trap door. This is the usual music for the appearance of a god, especially if he arrives by way of the trap door, called a *seri*. The choice of instruments also corresponds to the ensemble associated with temples. During the young messenger's dialogue and dances, the three main styles of *shamisen* music alternate, while *hayashi* is used throughout. The *ōdaiko* becomes particularly loud whenever the boy tries to wake up the warrior. In his final dance, a whole host of drums are used, each played with two sticks to add weight to the sound. Cymbals and the *noh* flute are also present. Finally, he manages to wake Koremochi and his companions and informs them that the lovely princess is really the demon, the object of their mission to the mountains. The messenger gives Koremochi a sacred sword, and to the terrific pounding of the *ōdaiko*, the hero dashes offstage in pursuit of the villain.

While the *ōdaiko* keeps up a steady rumble, the two male attendants do a comic dance to *gidayū*, as they find that their legs are not too steady after so much drinking. Eventually, they too dash offstage. A big blast on the *ōdaiko* brings Act One to an end.

Act Two begins with *nagauta shamisen* music taken from the *ōzatsuma* music patterns. In Chapter Eight, these remnants of an old *shamisen* genre, along with their use as transitional material and for the backing of narrative sections, were introduced. Here, they form a very necessary and flexible kind of transition music, used until the actors are ready to appear again. Then, there is a flash of lightning, the *ōdaiko* is hit with one stick lying against the skin so as to increase the rattle, and the villain comes flying onstage, face hidden by a veil, with Koremochi in hot pursuit. An added effect to the lightning is the grating of a bronze hand gong over the rough surface of a much larger, thinner gong, the *sōban*. This gives the lightning a genuine "ripping" sound. It is also used when the demon reveals herself in all her horror and begins to whirl her long hair about by violently swinging her head.

The music for the big fight is mostly *nagauta* and *hayashi*, with plenty of *ōdaiko* mixed in. The villain blows blinding smoke into the hero's eyes. There is a sudden silence as the villain approaches her now helpless victim. The shouts (*kakegoe*) of the drummers break the silence; the *noh* flute, *taiko*, and *ōdaiko* join in; and a slow, dramatic fight begins in which the magic sword keeps the demon at bay as Koremochi recovers his eyesight. The pace of the fight picks up again with all the musicians and most of the percussion adding to the din of battle until at last the demon climbs a nearby tree, spits out a final load of flame, and poses with fearsome grimaces as the curtain comes across the stage to the beat of the *ki* clappers.

While the actors make a dash for the dressing rooms to change and the set disintegrates under the hammers of the stage crew, the *ōdaiko*, together with the *noh* flute and two *taiko*, bangs out the finale of the drama with the rhythm called *uchidashi* (playing out).

This, then, is the way a *kabuki* drama is constructed musically. What general observations can be made? First, it should be noted that the music proper and the *geza* are arranged by two different people. Though there are separate pieces called *Momijigari* in both the *nagauta* and *tokiwazu* repertoires, the particular version used for the *kabuki* play is a very special pastiche, with different musical materials being used together with the addition of *gidayū*. It is important to observe how this switch from one style of music to another usually indicates a change in action, while helping to add variety to the color and pace of the drama.

The *geza* music of this play shows most of the characteristic uses of offstage effects. Notice how the *ōdaiko* music runs throughout the play, serving many different functions. Though the *geza shamisen* music is produced onstage in this play, its character remains the same, wandering quietly beneath the drama in much the same way as modern film music. The use of the other *geza* instruments indicates certain special conditions but does not reproduce their exact sounds; the ripping of the lightning flashes isn't entirely realistic but is still very effective. The nearest this play comes to direct imitation is the *gagaku* effect at the beginning of the princess's dance. Even then, the sound could never be confused with that of the real court orchestra. It merely gives a hint of the sound. As in most of Japanese art, it is up to the viewer to fill in the rest with his or her own imagination.

The most important observation to be made concerning this play is that it reveals a sense of overall "orchestration." There is a constant awareness on the part of the producers of the need for varied tone colors and the proper psychological timing of theatrical effects such as the sudden switch to the rougher style of *gidayū* when the princess's dance begins to show menacing characteristics.

Even a cursory study of this one *kabuki* play shows that a full appreciation of *kabuki* music is more involved than it would appear on the surface. The use of leitmotivs, signals, varying musical styles, and sound effects has been coordinated in a manner little exploited in the West. Before the late twentieth century, this aggregate of theatrical traditions was passed down from teacher to apprentice by rote methods. *Tsukechō*, books of *geza* music, were cue sheets that contained only the text of the play for the part at which the *geza* entered and the names of the music or patterns to be played.[12] The few books of *geza* notation were considered the sacrosanct property of the various *geza* music guilds. Hence it was difficult, and sometimes impossible, for the researcher to see such material unless he joined the guild and worked his way through the repertoire at the slow pace regulated by the head musician. Modern books and recordings now provide all but the most secret information to all those who wish to know.

For the ordinary *kabuki* fan today, the process of appreciating *geza* music requires no such arduous work. With a sharp ear and some familiarity with the information given in this chapter, one can savor that delicious sensation of being among those "in the know" at a *kabuki* performance.

12. See Biblio. ref. 9·1 for an example of such a page.

. The thunder god appears complete with local raincoat during the
ncient *amegari* rain dance from Kumamoto prefecture.

. The Ainu *tonkori* lute is plucked
ith both hands.

82. Ainu throat game performers create strange effects
by singing into each other's mouths.

83. A 1956 *kamishibai* man selling candy before he illustrates his story with paper pictures in a frame on the back of his bicycle.

84. A 1957 street vendor of hand puppets demonstrating his wares in Kyoto, as was done in ancient times.

85. The Awaji tradition of puppet performances continues, now with female musicians.

6. A performance of Gifu puppets at an outside stage before an interested but chilled audience.

7. Regional *noh* from Mizuumi in Fukui prefecture performing *Takasago* as part of a temple fund raiser. The same play is seen on a *noh* stage in Plate 38.

88. Children's *kabuki* in Shiga in one of several youth troupes in Japan.

89. *Yamabushi kagura* in Iwate prefecture continues to perform old ritual dances in costumes designed centuries ago.

# CHAPTER TEN
# FOLK AND POPULAR MUSICAL ARTS

## 1. Introduction

Fishermen pulling in their nets, farmers planting their crops, a wedding, a festival, a lullaby: these are the inspiration for folk music all over the world. Japan is no exception. Folk-song field workers need only visit any rural area in Japan and, with patience, they can uncover a full repertoire answering these same musical needs in peasant life. The modern urban world is also filled with nostalgic remnants of these traditions as well as new things serving analogous functions. Since the period of feudalism was a long one in Japan and rural districts were relatively isolated, there is great variety in its folk arts. The festivals and songs of one district may be quite different from those of adjacent territories. One cannot hope to cover them all. However, we can try to point out some general musical characteristics and typical forms that give Japanese folk music its special appeal. The picture will be rounded out with references to traditional elements in urban popular music and contrasts in other cultures at the two geographical ends of Japan: Okinawa, to the south, and the Ainu minorities on the northernmost island of Hokkaido. Our final musical route promises to be filled with sights and sounds from the rich heritage of folk traditions and innovations found in the island country of Japan.

The study of Japanese folk musical arts can be divided into two major categories: folk songs (*minyō*) and folk theatricals (*minzoku geinō*). While these two are not mutually exclusive, they emphasize an important characteristic of the field. In addition to the usual folk song tradition, there survives in Japan, as in most Oriental countries, a strong proclivity for folk theatricals. Quite apart from the charm and color of these folk *geinō*, their study provides many excellent clues as to the origins and early styles of the more famous Japanese theater traditions.

## 2. Folk Songs

Historically, Japanese villagers might simply use the word *uta* (song) if asked to classify what they sing. The term *minyō* (people's songs) was created in the late nineteenth century by scholars as a translation of the German term *volkslied*. Since that time, it has become the common term for Japanese folk songs and stands in contrast with *fōku songu*, which refers to all the non-Japanese folk music heard throughout Japan since the mid-twentieth century. The heart of traditional *minyō* is found in work or agriculture-related songs. Thus, the most widespread genres in Japan are songs dealing either with rice production or fishing. As late as the 1960s there were still rice fields in Tokyo, though by the end of the century they were being absorbed by housing as far as Narita airport. Still, *taueuta* (rice planting songs) can be heard at national folk song contests and regional folk song societies. The latter are particularly interesting, for many are part of a "preservation society" (*hozonkai*) in which each club is dedicated to the "correct" performance of one specific song! There are actually national contests in which various clubs compete for the best interpretation of that one song. Such an approach to the subject seems uniquely Japanese, rather like the quest for the perfect brushstroke in calligraphy or the best bowl of *soba* noodles.

Mass communication is often considered the destroyer of indigenous traditions, but it can also have a positive effect where folk music is concerned. Japanese radio broadcasts of folk singers began in the 1920s. Unlike the street musicians and music hall (*yose*) entertainers, radio singers could reach a wider audience and listeners were exposed to music outside their own local traditions. The singers often became "stars" whose records sold well and whose concerts were well attended. At the same time, regional business and government groups began to promote both traditional and new "folk" songs to attract tourism and greater national awareness of their area. Cultural and educational bureaus of the central government joined in by encouraging and supporting studies and collections of regional folk arts, including music.

# 3. Characteristics and Performance Practices

Since folk music is an aural/oral phenomenon, the first step toward understanding its characteristics is to listen to some of it (CD tracks 18 and 19). Then listen again, looking at Figures 34 and 35, and turn to the discussion given below.

FIGURE 34. A *shamisen* opening for "Tsugaru jongarabushi" from Aomori prefecture

FIGURE 35. The folk song "Kawasaki" from Gujō Hachiman in Gifu

TONE SYSTEM

As noted earlier in the book, the *yō* and *in* scales (Figure 21) dominate Japanese folk music and most art music after 1600, with an emphasis on a five-tone (pentatonic) core. Figure 34 contains that core[1] in the *yō* scale, with a sixth pitch, C-sharp, appearing in the vocal line. The vocal line in Figure 35 contains the pentatonic core in the *in* scale with a sixth note, G, added as an ornament. In both cases, as in other *shamisen* and *shakuhachi* pieces, it is often difficult to identify the scale of a passage, because only a few of the seven notes (Figure 21) appear. As seen in Figure 37, some pieces also seem to "modulate" frequently. The challenge is that, unlike its Western counterpart, Japanese music does not require a full scale or harmonic support to establish a tonality. Instead it is oriented more toward moving tone centers (usually a fourth or fifth apart) and supporting each center

FIGURE 36. A Japanese tonal analysis method

with pitches above or below it in whole or half steps. Using the pitch centers B and F-sharp from the transcriptions above, Figure 36 illustrates the way in which Japanese scholars analyze melodies in terms of three-note units.[2] The two white notes, a fourth apart, are pitch centers, and the third (black) note, inside the fourth, identifies the scale. For example, in Figure 34 the "inside" notes are a whole step above or below the pitch centers and, in Figure 35 they are a half step. *Yō* scales are implied by the first and *in* scales by the latter even though a full seven-note scale has not been used. The need to be able to analyze with little data is evident in Figure 37 which contains quick "modulations" between *yō* and *in* scales.

1. The recording starts on F-sharp so one can "play along" on the black notes of the piano. It is transcribed on D to help comparisons with other examples in the book.
2. The system is best discussed in Biblio. ref. 10·4 and summarized in English in Biblio. ref. 8·8. Besides the B and F-sharp basis for the units in Figure 36, E and A can be used.

**FIGURE 37.** Excerpt from the folk song "Ise ondo"

## FORM

Figures 34 and 35 are binary (A-B) and strophic, i.e., the same music is used for each verse of the text. The latter is a common characteristic of many Japanese folk songs. A ternary form (A-B-A) can also be found, though it may have three independent phrases (A-B-C). The text is often in the poetic syllabic order of 7, 7, 7, and 5. In Figure 35, the syllables "*a son de se*" are interjections by a chorus (*hayashi kotoba*), not part of the poem. The first passages for the vocal part of all three examples use a common Japanese folk song opening style, which shifts to a high pitch and is often ornamented before moving on with the melody.

Of course, there are many styles of folk music. One cannot expect a lullaby to contain all the characteristics listed above, but recognizing them should prove useful to those who enjoy being informed listeners.

## RHYTHM

While Japanese folk songs are usually notated in two or four beats, their internal beat, as seen in Figure 34, is often somewhere between duple and triple. Being an oral tradition, even the placing of Western-style bar lines in a transcription of a Japanese folk song (as well as much of its art music) is a distortion of the length of phrases. When a song is not work or dance music, it is often sung in a free rhythmic style with much ornamentation. The rhythmic tension of festival ensembles was discussed in Chapter Two (p. 60).

## PERFORMANCE PRACTICES

Although, as seen in Plate 24, it is quite possible to perform folk music with no accompaniment at all, flutes, *shamisen*, *shakuhachi*, and drums have become common in folk song performances since the Edo period.

Figure 34 is an example of a flashy *tsugaru jamisen* style, derived from a tradition of blind musicians in northern Japan who wandered the villages singing songs and narrations. The particular style of Takahashi Chikuzan[3] (1910–98), from Tsugaru, caught on with younger Japanese toward the end of the twentieth century, becoming an indigenous competitor with the Western banjo or rock guitars and eventually an international fad.

A striking folk vocal style can also be heard on CD track 18. The high, strident tone is ideal for singing outdoors. On a microphone, it competes with rock vocal style though it is actually fairly traditional.

## 4. Other Ethnic Groups in Japan

On the two extremities of Japan there are other forms of folk music to be found. In the far south is the island culture of the Ryukyus, and to the north is Hokkaido, where the influence of the Gilyak people can still be traced, and a reviving Ainu tradition exists.

The outer islands of the Ryukyu chain (Amami and Sakishima groups), being farming and fishing areas, maintain a folk music style similar to that of mainland Japan though, as in every prefecture, there are specific things that identify local arts. The central Okinawan group has a broader cultural background. As far back as the fourteenth century it was an independent kingdom and formed an important link between Japan and the cultures to the west (China) and south (Southeast Asia and the Philippines). Politically it became a Japanese colony in the seventeenth century and was absorbed as a prefecture in the last half of the twentieth century, but it continues to use its arts extensively to define its own identity.

The culture of the former Okinawan court is implicit in surviving dances and their Chinese-style costumes and foot movements. Some of their hand gestures and castanets also suggest a Southeast Asian influence. An interesting example of the marginal survival of a style that changed in mainland Japan itself is the Okinawan *koto* tradition, which probably came from

3. See *The Autobiography of Takahashi Chikuzan: Adventures of a Tsugaru-Jamisen Musician*, trans. by Gerald Groemer (Warren, MI: Harmonie Park Press, 1991), and Suda Naoyuki, K. Daijo, and A. Rausch, *The Birth of Tsugaru Shamisen Music* (Aomori: Aomori University Press, 1998).

Japan in the eighteenth century. But the best-known Okinawan instrument is the *sanshin* or *jamisen* (Plate 59), mentioned in Chapter Eight as a source for the *shamisen* and a relative of the Chinese *sanxian*. With heads made of large snakeskins, it is plucked with a horn pick attached to the middle finger and is tuned like the *shamisen* (see Figure 28).

The pentatonic scale creates in Okinawan melodies a Chinese sound, but their jaunty rhythm (somewhat like Figure 34) gives them a distinctly Okinawan lilt. The *taiko* drumming is also noteworthy, for the drummers lift the sticks away from the head quickly after each stroke and fill the rhythm with lively vocal interjections that are a long way from the *kakegoe* of *noh* drama, though they have many relatives in Japanese folk *hayashi*.

In northern Japan, the few Gilyaks or Orochon people who survived traced their origins to Siberia and the steppes of Manchuria. Their mouth harp (jew's-harp), one-stringed fiddle, and pan drum were much like those found throughout the so-called circumboreal region, from northern Canada through Siberia. Another continental North Asian root is found in the use of the pan drum by shamans (nowadays female), who drive away evil spirits and cure the sick. These features persist in the culture of the Ainu people in Hokkaido.

Like Native Americans, the Ainu were driven from their hereditary lands, in their case ending up in the far north, where they were left to die out through cultural starvation. However, they are a tough, ethnically distinct people and have maintained much of their tradition tenaciously. There are many songs and dances imitating birds, bears, and other creatures, as well as epic narrations (*yukar*) of Ainu mythology. The grunts of male sword dancers, the trills of female bird dancers, and the annual ritual bear sacrifice adumbrate an ancient, tribal origin. For one trained in Japanese music, the sound of an Ainu song comes as a real shock: it is like meeting a grizzly bear in a pet store.

There are only two instruments of importance in Ainu music. One is the *tonkori*, a two- to five-stringed plucked zither (Plate 81), played as a drone accompaniment for singing or dancing. Only the open-string sounds are used, and it is plucked with both hands to create a basic rhythmic effect. The second is the *mukkuri*, a type of jew's-harp. Both of these instruments traditionally are played by women. In the late twentieth century, new Ainu music, like that of Native Americans, brought traditional instruments together with popular music electronics in an effort to receive ethnic recognition in the modern world.

The most unusual sound in Ainu music is a duet style called *rekukkara* (Plate 82), in which two women perform "throat games" that create tunes and percussive sounds by singing into each other's mouths. Similar performances are found in Siberia, Alaska, and Northern Canada.

## 5. Folk Theatricals

From the first page of this book's prologue onward, the theatricality of Japanese lifestyles has frequently been made apparent. Chapter Two was particularly rich in religious processions (*gyōretsu*), festivals (*matsuri*), Shinto theatricals (*kagura*), and lion dance genres (*shishi mai*). All are found throughout the country. Folk forms of Buddhist celebrations (*ennen*); large, costumed dance forms (*fūryū*); and the popular *bon odori* are equally varied. The roots of *noh* drama are latent in "field dances" (*dengaku*) and "monkey music" (*sarugaku*) performances, and there are local variants of court dances (*bugaku*) as well as *noh*, *bunraku*, and *kabuki*. Musical storytelling (*katari-mono*) is another exponent.

Before turning to the folk versions of the professional theatricals, we should pay tribute to one of Japan's more charming street presentations, the *kamishibai* (Plate 83). Up until the late twentieth century, one could hear the sounds of a small set of clappers announcing the arrival of the paper-play (*kamishibai*) man. Like the bells of the old Good Humor ice cream trucks in America, the sound of the clapper's clicks summoned the children of the neighborhood to his bicycle. After they had bought enough of his candy, he would show them his paper slides in a small theater box set on the back of his bicycle, above the tempting drawers of candy, accompanying the pictures with a narration done with all the flourish of a country *kabuki* actor. Television has seriously damaged this delightful brand of children's theater though, as we have noted before, in the best Japanese tradition it may still survive in some obscure neighborhoods. After all, television sets do not sell penny candy. In Tokyo, *kamishibai* can still be seen demonstrated at the Shitamachi ("lower city") Museum in Ueno Park, where it had once flourished for many years.

Other larger clappers are commonly used by the leaders of portable shrine (*omikoshi*) processions during local festivals. Even at night, the sounds of clappers can sometimes be heard. Guests in older Japanese inns can lie down peacefully to the reassuring sound of the fire patrols that pass through the hallways, and there are still neighborhood associations, even in Tokyo, that share the nightly fire watch, strolling through the streets and signaling "All's well" with the sound of the clappers.

Among the various folk theatricals, the puppet tradition is particularly interesting. Edo-period prints sometimes feature one-man puppeteers on the streets (Plate 84 shows that the tradition persisted). The simplest puppets consisted of a head on a stick and a crosspiece for arms from which costumes were draped, though legs eventually were used. Such puppetry was called *ayatsuri ningyō* to differentiate it from ordinary doll (*ningyō*) puppets.[4] A variety of simple puppet shows are found in several villages, with plots and actions from the historical to the comic and salacious. The more complex puppets of the *bunraku* theater are said to have begun as village traditions on Awaji Island[5] (Plate 85). Other folk versions, in turn, were derived from *bunraku* itself. In Gifu, for example, there is a barn whose side wall is opened in the agricultural off-season to become a stage on which classical plays are performed by local farmer puppeteers and *jōruri* musicians to an audience seated on straw mats in the adjacent cold and barren field (Plate 86). It is an impressive if chilly experience. This *makuwa bunraku* has some puppet heads older than those in Osaka and thus is an important historical source.

Perhaps the most ancient theatrical events in Japan are the purification dances "Sambasō" and "Okina," which can be seen annually in nearly every village, city, and professional theater. Their earth-pounding movements reflect primitive origins far from later Japanese dances. Regional *noh* performances and surviving folk *dengaku* traditions are usually shrine- or temple-related. The local *noh* productions are standard plays based on published texts, with local versions of the music and costumes. Plate 87

---

4. In Aomori prefecture in northern Japan such dolls are called *oshirasama*, as they are considered household gods. A new layer of cloth is added to the doll every year, thus allowing one not only to judge its age but to trace the development of local fabrics for decades.

5. Scenes involving that tradition are found in Tanizaki Jun'ichirō's novel *Some Prefer Nettles*, trans. by Edward Seidensticker (New York: Knopf, 1955).

shows a production of the play *Takasago* in the village of Mizuumi, in Fukui prefecture. The papers that festoon the stage are financial pledges. Country theatricals generally take place in the farmers' slack season, and are connected with shrine or temple fund drives.

Traveling professional *kabuki* (*tabi shibai*) was common up until the early part of the twentieth century.[6] This, as well as farmers' visits to the big cities, inspired regional *kabuki*. The *kuromori kabuki* held at Sakata in Yamagata prefecture as part of an annual festival on February 15 is another entertaining but freezing experience.

Of particular interest is the *hikiyama kabuki* at Nagahama, in Shiga prefecture (Plate 88). There, *kabuki* stages are built on floats. Well-known plays are produced, often with complex stage devices, but the actors are all children! Both this and the Awaji puppet tradition, mentioned earlier, have remained viable through local and national government support as well as international tours.

Plate 89 is an example of *yamabushi kagura* from Iwate prefecture. Between agricultural seasons, the men and boys of the town used to supplement their meager incomes with performances at local villages. The tradition suffered after the Meiji Restoration period when all boys had to attend school during the traditional performance season, but it has since been revived and enjoys notice in both national and international theatrical contests. The music consists of the large drum, seen in the picture, and a pair of cymbals. The dancer in Plate 89 is wearing a devilish *tengu* mask, one of the many types that not only enrich the folk festivals but provide excellent data for the study of ancient court and country traditions. Other folk theatrical masks have been noted (see Plate 16), as well as a variety of different drums. To this we could add the many plumes, poles, and other appendages that tower in the air above dancers (Plate 25). There are also umbrellas and flower hats (Plate 12), some of which completely hide the face of the performer. In all, Japanese regional theatrical events are communal activities that delight the mind and the senses of all who see and hear them.

---

6. A mixture of *kabuki*, popular music, and dance is still seen at the Mokubakan in Asakusa, Tokyo. This *taishū engeki* (popular theater) and its clientele maintain some of the spirit of the Edo traveling troupes.

# 6. Urban Music

The growth of what is called civilization has always been related to the movement of rural populations into new urban centers. Folk songs are sung nostalgically while new music is created reflecting new environments and occupations. Given the oral nature of such music we know little about it in Japan before the Edo period except for the street music and theatricals that have been referred to elsewhere in this book. The *sekkyō* performances in Plate 20 provide an example of "before-the-doorway arts," ensembles that played and sang stories, ditties, or blessings door to door, particularly during the New Year or local festival seasons. Plate 21, taken in 1956, shows a *chindonya* trio standing in front of a Tokyo gate with advertisements on their backs. Their title comes from the sounds of the drum and *kane* combination that accompanies whatever melodic instrument is available—whether *shamisen* or clarinet. Present-day performances seem limited primarily to the opening of *pachinko* pinball parlors, but one such *chindonya* ensemble entertained me in April 1998 as it moved through the cherry blossom viewing parties along the banks of the Sumida River, and again in March 2000 at a Japanese parade in Honolulu. The tradition of musical performers and hawkers obviously still colors the sounds of Tokyo streets even though recorded songs on portable cassette players have usually replaced the live voices of most baked sweet potato and bamboo pole sellers. Occasionally, from a night noodle stand one can hear the piercing tone of the *charumera* oboe, another instrument whose origin may be either Chinese or Portuguese, though its name clearly relates to the Portuguese word *charamela*.[7]

The Edo-period word for popular music was *hayariuta* (known in the following period as *ryūkōka*). Among its many genres was *kudokiuta*. The term *kudoki* was noted earlier in *biwa*, *noh*, and *shamisen* music, where it denoted a lyrical or dramatic excerpt that could be performed separately from a longer narrative. The street *kudoki* generally dealt with local events, romantic or scatological tales, or counting songs which were a more elaborate and entertaining version of children's chanted lists. The *kudoki* texts were often published in much the same way as eighteenth-century

7. The CD Soundscape of Japan (KICH 2029, King Record Co., 1991) contains the sounds of one day in Tokyo. It is sonic proof that the oboe, street calls, and even *rōkyoku* (see p. 219) survive in modern Japan.

English broadsheets. Similar to this was the *yomiuri* genre, in which news was sung and printed.[8] All these traditions continued to flourish well into the Meiji era where, in the new music halls, patter songs called *oppekepē* were also heard, commenting on the social and political issues of the day, like Western talking blues or rap. Most long-lasting of the popular music-hall genres was *enka*, which is still going strong. Here, as in popular music elsewhere in the world, the major topic of love was coupled with issues of concern to the specific generation for whom it was composed ("Thinking of Far-Off Manchuria," 1936; "Tokyo Boogie Woogie," 1946).[9]

We have already shown how traditions tend to survive in Japan and how mass communication actually contributed to the expansion of folk music. While you may not see many street performers today, you can always buy a CD or a tape of them somewhere. Occasionally, Western musicians take to Tokyo streets, playing either Japanese or Western music. Groups of young Japanese can also be seen playing the latter for tips placed in a cowboy hat or guitar case. Until recently, the ultimate youth experiences occurred on Sundays in Tokyo's Harajuku, where large troops of groupies performed their particular version of Western popular genres. Like the old *fūryū* traditions of Edo, they usually performed complete with proper costumes for the decade and style of the music.

The Japanese tradition of being able to perform music at a party has been noted before in this book. This has been carried over into the contemporary international pop music world in the form of *karaoke*: musical accompaniment to which anyone can sing. Computers can adjust pitch and tempo, and videos may enhance things, but the microphone does little to improve the singing except in volume. Still, we should remember that a villager singing in a folk song doesn't have to sound "good," though being loud helps; the real goal is participation. While the literal meaning of the term *karaoke* will seem perfectly appropriate to those who are not too fond of this "empty music," one can at least admire the dogged practice that devotees put in to improve their performance.

8. One of the major newspapers of today in Japan is the *Yomiuri Shimbun*.
9. Among the many studies of popular and *enka* music are Fujisawa Morihiko's *Hayariuta hyakunenshi* (Tokyo: Daiichi Shuppansha, 1951) and his *Enka no Meiji Taishōshi* (Tokyo: Kansui Shobō, 1983).

# 7. Summary

Even such a brief journey through the world of Japanese folk and popular music is exhausting. Studying the subject is like stepping into a lush jungle, but within the tangle of known and unnamed forms are hidden treasures. The last few pages are merely pointers toward trails that one should explore for oneself. Increasingly, foreign scholars have been attracted to these trails, whether they lead to caches of pop music, jazz, or traditional ballads.

The art music of Japan has contributed many beautiful and significant moments to the world of sound, but it is the steady stream of folk music that has always irrigated the fields in which both art and popular music grow.

EPILOGUE

In the past ten chapters, we have seen the music of Japan grow out of a Chinese, word-oriented tradition into a multiplicity of forms. The ceremonials of antiquity were preserved by the court musicians and dancers, while the message of Śākyamuni was memorialized through the music of the Buddhist temples. The storytelling tradition flourished under the aegis of the *heikebiwa* bards and was carried on by later *biwa* schools and by the exceptional *jōruri* singers. At the same time, a host of folk theatricals combined to create one of the world's unique dramatic forms, the *noh*. This, in turn, joined with the *jōruri* tradition to produce the *bunraku* and *kabuki* theaters. The instrumental orientation of *gagaku* was carried on in *koto* music, which joined with the *shamisen* and *shakuhachi* to form the basis of the music of the Edo period. Thus we find in the finest products of Japanese music today the residue of centuries of musical mixtures and refinements.

One might call folk music the catalyst that periodically accelerated the fusion of styles. At present, these folk arts are still a matter of local pride, but history has shown that such arts, though important stimuli for other forms, are themselves very susceptible to influence and change. In modern folk music, the new factor is mass communication. It is impossible to calculate the extent to which this medium is capable of helping or damaging things . The communication centers may take over the functions of storytelling and entertainment, while advertising may usurp education. Nevertheless, the ordinary person's need for self-expression and a close connection with the basic forces of nature will prove, perhaps, an antibiotic for this virulent infection which seems to be decimating the folk arts of the world. It is still too early for any firm theories. The best we can do is learn to appreciate the wonderful Japanese folk tradition as it is, encourage it whenever possible, and hope that history will treat it kindly.

Traditional art music has been shown to be dominated by the three-part *jo-ha-kyū* concept of form and the tendency to be "through composed," where a piece moves forward without repeating or developing previous themes. This so-called open form (A, B, C, etc.) contrasts with the Western preference for closed forms (ABA) with first and second themes, developments and recapitulations. In keeping with a similar inclination found in all the arts in Japan, a compositional penchant for repertory-wide conventional melodic patterns has been noted frequently. It was pointed out that such a need for conventional sonic signals is common to all musics, including that of the West. What makes the Japanese signals different is the concentration and nature of the rhythmic patterns and a strong emphasis on melodic (not harmonic) modulation, tension, and release through small patterns around pitch centers.

We should emphasize again the basic chamber-music concept of Japanese music. Though *gagaku* and *kabuki* music can be considered as orchestral, the fundamental compositional orientation is toward a subtle refinement of a deliberately limited tonal and instrumental spectrum.

We have also seen the strong guild structure, the rote teaching methods, and the concomitant notation systems that are specific to the genre and the instrument used. When postwar plans were made for the founding of the Tokyo National University of Fine Arts and Music, the deliberate multiplicity of notations and the differences in guild interpretations of a piece were two reasons given for the exclusion of traditional Japanese music from the curriculum, except as history. It was said that, unlike Western art music, it could not all be written in one notation and always played the same way.[1] The effort failed, and students can now major at that institution in several forms of Japanese music. In addition, by the end of the twentieth century, important dissertations had been written on the topic at both Japanese and Western universities, and by both Japanese and foreign students. Unfortunately, Western music continues to dominate Japanese music education; singing Japanese folk songs in indigenous style is suppressed, and it was only recently that traditional Japanese art music could be heard —after Bach, Mozart, and Beethoven—in middle or high school music appreciation courses.

In the epilogue of the first edition of this book, the twenty-nine-year-old author pontificated about the need to preserve the basic orientation of Japanese music. The same sort of opinion has continued to be asserted periodically though, at one recent conference in Japan, I was told that it was none of my business. Now over seventy, I tend to agree. Still, it pains me to hear *hōgaku* orchestras or violent new sounds on a *koto*, *shakuhachi*, or *shamisen*.

1. This fascinating battle of musical wills is discussed in Kikkawa Eishi's *Shamisen no bigaku to Geidai hōgaku-ka tanjō hiwa* (Tokyo: Shuppan Geijutsusha, 1997).

At the same time, some of the electronic compositions of Takemitsu Tōru (1930–96) seem to have successfully captured the essence of the Japanese sonic aesthetic without using a Japanese instrument at all. By the same token, Benjamin Britten's very Western opera *Curlew River* successfully evokes the spirit of the *noh* drama *Sumidagawa*.

Buddha has taught us that all life is change. *Hōgaku* cannot be like a handsome but fossilized fish, set in stone. May it continue to swim in the eddies and currents of modern life so as to share the old and new beauties of its shape, color, and movements with all generations. To use a traditional Japanese saying, "May it live ten thousand years."

# APPENDIX I

## JAPANESE MUSIC NOTATION SYSTEMS

The fact that the topic of notation is complicated does not lessen its importance as regards a general understanding of the entire music culture. The following discussion has therefore been appended so that the reader with a more technical bent will not be left without any information about Japanese notation.

## 1. Vocal Notation

The history of the notation of early Christian chant is a story of several centuries of evolution through a series of vague contour symbols to systems of relatively greater accuracy. The earlier systems grew out of a Greek tradition of contour notation known as neumes, symbols that stand for more than one note. Early Japanese Buddhist music also began with a neumatic notation (*hakase* or *bakase*). However, in its evolution toward a more precise script, theology and Chinese systematics got in the way of practicality. The net result was the *goinbakase*, credited to Kakui (b. 1236), a priest of the Shingon sect of Buddhism.

The *goin* system divides a range of fifteen notes into three "layers" of five notes each. Hence, the system is known also as the *goinsanjū*, the "five sounds and three layers." In actual practice, only eleven notes are used: the bottom "layer" (*shojū*) comprising two notes, the middle (*nijū*) five notes, and the top (*sanjū*) four notes. The notation consists of short strokes that indicate specific pitches by means of the angle at which they are tipped (see Figure 38). The first layer is notated by the symbols 1–5; the second layer begins at 6 and goes through 10; and the symbols 11–15 are used for the top layer. The symbols in white are the notes not used, and, of course, Arabic numerals do not appear in the original system. The dot on the end

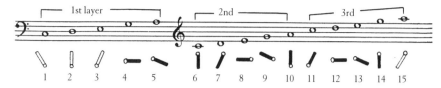

FIGURE 38. *Goinbakase* symbols

of the stroke establishes which way the stroke is pointing. Thus, for example, if we apply this system to a standard *ryo* scale, the strokes can be transcribed into Western notation in the way shown in Figure 38.

It should be noted that some of the symbols point in the same direction (look at 4 and 12), but since the music (*shōmyō* chant) is very diatonic, there is seldom any doubt as to which pitch is meant. However, the system is really efficient only when there are a very few notes to each word. As the direction of the symbols has no relation to the contour of the melody, the notation is very confusing to the Western eye (see Figure 39). An additional complication is that special vocal melismas, dynamics, and tempo indications are written around the symbol in a direction dependent on that of the notation.[1]

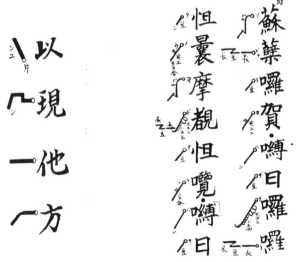

FIGURE 39. *Goinfu*            FIGURE 40. Modified *goinfu* (*meyasu*)

1. Japanese can be written left to right, right to left, or straight down. It is possible to find all three systems in use within one publication. When I first arrived in Japan I was confused by many signs that read "*ko-ba-ta*" until I reversed the reading to "*ta-ba-ko*," that is, tobacco.

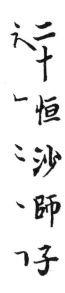

FIGURE 41. *Kōshiki gomaten* notation

*Goinfu* (*fu* means notation) underwent many modifications. The simplest change was a reversing of directions so that the notation always led away from words (Figures 39 and 40). However, few of the modifications ever approached a real visual representation of the contour of the melody.

The other prevalent style of Buddhist notation is called *meyasu*, literally "easy on the eyes." This style is open to the greatest variation. A twentieth-century version of *meyasu* is shown in Figure 40, which is the notation of the chorus section on CD track 4. If you listen to the track carefully while looking at Figure 40, the meaning of many of the exotic signs will become evident. For example, the little loops clearly stand for vocal ornamentation (*yuri*), and symbols that look the same are performed the same way. Reading any notation improves once one has knowledge of the style of the music.

The above notations were intended primarily for the writing of *shōmyō* chant. The notation of the music of *wasan*, *kōshiki*, and other short, more rhythmical forms derived from a simple style of neumatic notation for *gagaku* vocal music. Historically, the most important development in these simpler notations was *gomafu* (or *gomaten*),[2] in which teardrop-shaped strokes were placed to the left of the words (Figure 41), marking longer

2. Six different examples of the evolution of this style are found in Biblio. ref. 1·3, p. 698.

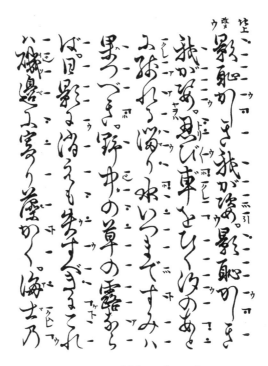

FIGURE 42. *Noh* vocal notation

conventional patterns and rhythms. This type of notation was impractical for any involved melodic style. It was further simplified by the *heikyoku* narrators into a form known as *sumifu*, where strokes were put on the right and certain marks were added concerning the *biwa* part (Figure 49).

The most important outgrowth of these earlier systems, however, was the notation of *noh* singing. Early *noh* notation used signs to indicate stereotyped melodies, rhythms, or special singing styles. The system was vague and could not be read in any detail. In the Edo period it was subjected to greater regimentation so that each mark was given a rather definite meaning. Unfortunately, the various schools of *noh* applied different meanings to the same symbols, making any study of *noh* notation, like Buddhist script, inevitably sectarian. This style of *gomaten* notation is used today without any basic change (the passage shown in Figure 42 can be heard on CD track 6). Again, one should note that this sort of system is designed for a music that is highly conventional in melodic and rhythmic style.[3]

3. Think how little notation is used for popular music songs.

# 2. Instrumental Notation

The first important forms of instrumental music in Japan came from the Asian continent. Thus, the notation systems were also based on continental models, particularly Chinese. As in early European instrumental notation, a majority of the systems used were types of tablatures, indicating either a string, a fingering position, or, in the case of woodwinds, a hole or fingering. Percussion notation became a more specialized field in early Japanese music than in Western music because of the greater variety of instruments used. In the following discussion, emphasis is placed on present-day systems, for it must be remembered that notation in Japan has always been primarily a supplement to rote teaching methods and, as such, often seems vague to the Western eye. Part of the contrast is that the West emphasizes notation as a visual phenomenon and thus has a tendency to use one style (the five-line graphic) for all music, inserting diacritical additions for the special needs of individual instruments. Most Asian notations are based on the premise that music is an oral/aural event. In Japan, they are designed with the sounds and styles of one specific instrument in mind. Different guilds of players may also develop their own graphic memory aids. Thus, we will have to look at instrumental notation one instrument at a time.

## GAGAKU NOTATION

The earliest notation for the *wagon* was modeled after the Chinese zither system. It consisted of the number of the string to be played while accompanying a song, written to the right of the words, the rhythm being remembered by its connection with the vocal line (which was rote learned, not notated). Later, when the *wagon* and the *gakusō* were used in the *gagaku* ensemble, their notation became even simpler. Since these two instruments usually play stereotyped patterns with occasional notes added, the notation only needed to list the name of the pattern and have numbers interspersed for any added notes plus explanations for any special playing techniques that might be required. Rhythm was indicated by dots (see Figure 43). The basic rhythmic unit was also indicated in a style much like the Western time signature at the start of a composition (see under the title in the lower right of Figure 43).

The *gakubiwa* also inherited a Chinese notation, but one based on a separate symbol script for each of the four fret positions on the four strings (in some cases five). In addition to indicating the single positions (the actual pitch will depend on the tuning), these symbols also represent arpeggios, of which the given symbol is the top note. Such arpeggios are the basic style of *gakubiwa* music in the *gagaku* ensemble.

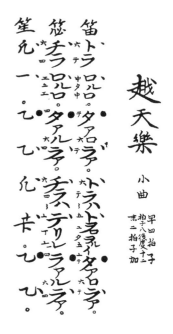

Figure 43 shows the notation of the *ryūteki*, the *hichiriki*, and the *shō* for the beginning of the piece "Etenraku" in the *hyōjō* mode (CD track 5). The column to the right is the *ryūteki* notation. It is based on two separate systems. The larger symbols are syllables (*kana*) which the player uses when first learning the music by singing it. These mnemonics (*shōga*) are not a solfège, i.e., they do not represent specific pitches within a tone system like the Western *do*, *re*, *mi*, though they do imply ranges and

FIGURE 43. *Gagaku* wind notation from "Etenraku," *hyōjō* mode

conventional melodic patterns. Most of the characteristic melismas are learned while singing the mnemonic, so that they are seldom apparent to the eye. The smaller figures to the left of these syllables in Figure 43 represent fingerings on the instrument, thus guiding the performer to specific pitches. Most fingering or pitch symbols are derived from earlier Chinese notations. The black dots to the right of the line represent time units, often (though not always) four beats apart. The meter and tempo of the music are listed below the title of the piece. The tiny rings in the column itself are breath marks.

FIGURE 44. *Ryūteki* and *hichiriki* notation symbols

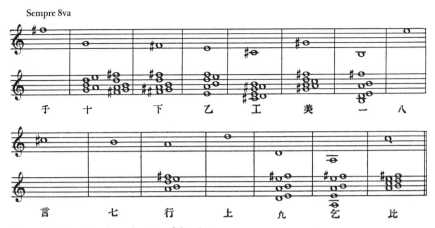

**Sempre 8va**

FIGURE 45. The chords and notes of the *shō*

The next column in Figure 43 is the music for the *hichiriki*. It is organized on exactly the same principle as the notation of the flute[4] except that the mnemonics and fingering symbols are different. Figure 44 gives the pitches produced by the various fingerings on the *ryūteki* and the *hichiriki*. Since more than one note can be produced by a single fingering, further explanation is to no avail; one must either know the piece or find a teacher.

The left-hand column of Figure 43 is the notation for the *shō*. Each symbol represents the bottom pitch of one of the eleven chords of the *shō* or, in some cases, the note itself. These notes and chords can be seen in Figure 45. Rhythm is shown in the same method as mentioned above for the *ryūteki*. (As a rule, *gagaku* music is not written in score form as shown in Figure 43;[5] rather, there is a part book for each instrument which contains the basic repertoire organized according to the music of each mode.)

Lastly, we come to the notation of the percussion instruments in *gagaku*. The notations for all three instruments are normally combined in a single column. Japanese numbers mark the beats. The *taiko* left-hand beat (*zun*) is indicated by a dot to the right of the column. The symbol *chin* (金) is placed to the left or right of the numbers to indicate the proper strokes on the *shōko*. When the sticks are used together, a *chin* is placed on both sides of the number. The *kakko* notation consists of two symbols: the first, *sei* (正), indicates a stroke with the right stick; the symbol *rai* (来), placed to the left

---

4. The same notation is used for all three flutes in *gagaku* ensembles.
5. This score was published for use in Tenrikyō religious ceremonies, not the court.

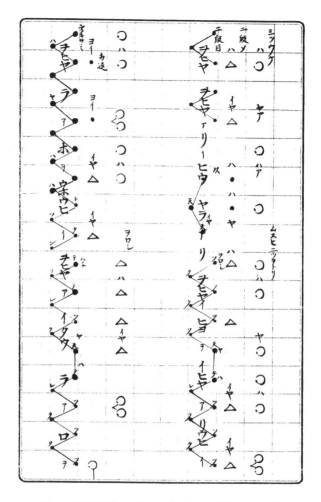

FIGURE 46. *Noh hayashi* notation from "Chū no mai"

of the numbers, indicates a left-stick roll, while a *rai* on both sides of the numbers indicates a two-stick roll. *Rai* never appears by itself on the right.[6]

## HAYASHI NOTATION FOR *NOH* DRAMA

The three drums of the *noh* orchestra and the *noh* flute have developed notation systems based on the eight-beat phrase (*yatsubyōshi*). The nota-

6. For details see Harich-Schneider, Eta, "The Rhythmical Patterns in Gagaku and Bugaku," *Ethno-musicologica*, Vol. 3 (Leiden: E. J. Brill, 1954).

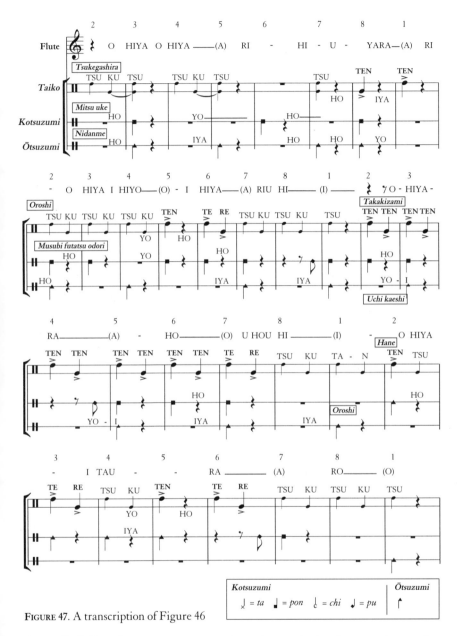

FIGURE 47. A transcription of Figure 46

tions of all four instruments are written in vertical columns. As a rule, each instrument has its own part book, in which one occasionally finds (as in Figure 46) the half beats represented by the line and the beats by the space, though the normal procedure is to place the beats on the line.

Figure 46, containing the first thirty-two beats of the second section (*dan*) of the dance music for "Chū no mai,"[7] is from a rare score that notates all the instruments together. It places the beat in the middle of each square. The first column to the right is the *kotsuzumi* part, the second the *ōtsuzumi*, and the third contains both the *taiko* and the flute music. In the original score, both the *kotsuzumi* and the *taiko* parts are printed in red.

In the right-hand column a circle is used for the sound *pon* and a triangle for *ta*. A dot, used for *chi* and *pu*, is not shown in this notation,[8] though the first of the two closely joined circles is usually a *pu*. The drummer's calls (*kakegoe*) are seen between the symbols, and the names of patterns appear along the right-hand side of all the drum columns. Though the two most frequent calls are written *ya* (ヤ) and *ha* (ハ), the actual sounds are closer to "yo" and "ho," and neither can really be described as "singing" or "calling," the voice being literally otherworldly.

In the *ōtsuzumi* notation (the second column from the right), the triangle represents the strongest beat, *chon*, while a circle is the deader tone, *don*, and the dot indicates the light tone, *tsun* or *chin*. The drummer's calls are also marked between the symbols.

The *taiko* part (third column from the right) involves three types of symbols: (1) those showing the rhythm and strength of the beat, (2) mnemonic syllables to further clarify the beats and aid memory, and (3) drummer's calls. All three are transcribed in Figure 47. The strengths are indicated by the size of the dots used. When played quietly (small dots), the sticks deaden the sound (*osameru*), but they let the skin sound (*kesubi*) for all other strokes (large dots).[9]

Only the mnemonics of the flute part are transcribed in the top line of Figure 47, for the resulting melody varies from school to school as well as in different pieces.[10] Since flute music consists of many standard melodies (see Figure 16) played in a given order (Figure 17), the four patterns played,

7. From the eighth page of "Taiko chū no mai" in Biblio. ref. 4.9.
8. In other notations it is often written with the *kana* プ.
9. Modern notation differs. See Komparu Sōichi, *Komparuryū taiko zensho* (Tokyo: Hinoki Shoten, 1953).
10. Biblio. ref. 4.9 lists the guild sources as follows: flute, Morita; *kotsuzumi*, Kō; *ōtsuzumi*, Ōkura; and *taiko*, Komparu.

though not named in the score, are those of a second *dan* opening: *dan no fu*, *ryo no chū*, *ryo*, and *oroshi*.

The *taiko* transcription on line two of Figure 47 places the mnemonic above the drum part and the drummer's calls below it. The four eight-beat *taiko* patterns played are named in boxes above the mnemonics, starting with *tsukegashira*. The two *tsuzumi* parts appear on the third and fourth lines along with the names of the patterns they play. Note that the name of the sixteen-beat *ōtsuzumi* pattern is *nidanme*, or "second *dan*." Like the flute part, it sonically marks the beginning of this section of the music. The second *kotsuzumi* pattern is sixteen beats long and named *musubi futatsu odori* ("*musubi* followed by two *odori*"). Note also that the final *tsuzumi* pattern, *oroshi*, is rhythmically unrelated to the *oroshi* pattern played by the *taiko* earlier.

This *noh hayashi* score clearly shows the characteristic orientation of *noh* rhythm away from the first beat. In all separate part books the notation begins with the second beat, as it does in our example. The effect, musically speaking, is to keep the flow of rhythm always "off balance." Patterns never seem to lose their dynamism but continue to push forward. It is somewhat like the effect Bach achieves by ending melodic phrases on the first beat of a measure instead of the last. If the *hayashi* parts are played separately, their natural phrase accent seems to fall elsewhere; when they are played together, this simultaneous combination of varying rhythmic phrases produces one of the most distinctive qualities of *noh* music—the "sliding door" effect often mentioned in this book.

When this same *hayashi* is added to *kabuki* music, the independence of the *ōtsuzumi* and *kotsuzumi* is more restricted. While they sometimes play straight *noh*-type rhythmic patterns, more often than not they play *chirikara byōshi*. This usually is an imitation of the rhythm of the *shamisen* melody. The *taiko* and flute, however, tend to continue with their *noh*-oriented patterns. As was explained in Chapter Eight (p. 235), these two separate kinds of rhythm in combination with the *shamisen* melody create a system of tension and release similar to that produced in Western music by harmony, melody, and rhythm. The *taiko* and flute serve a function analogous to that of harmonics in Western music, though the sound they produce is totally different.

The notation of *kabuki* and *shamisen* music drumming is similar to that of the *noh*. However, since the patterns are often much faster and syncopated, the *ōtsuzumi* and *kotsuzumi* parts are written together, as shown in Figure 48, heard on CD track 16, and transcribed in Figure 31 (measures 19–22).[11] The *ōtsuzumi* is on the right side and the *kotsuzumi* is on the left of Figure 48. For the *ōtsuzumi*, the black triangles are the lighter sound *tsu*, and the white ones represent the stronger *chon*. The black triangles for the *kotsuzumi* are the dry, side sound *ta*; and the circles, the deep, center sound *pon*. The single-finger *pu* sound would be noted by the *kana* ツ and the sound *chi* with a dot. In both *noh* and *kabuki* drumming, a professional book will usually carry only the names of the various patterns to be used in a specific piece, but not all *kabuki* drum patterns have specific names, as their rhythms often match those of the *shamisen* line. In *kabuki tsuzumi* cue sheets, the passage might be written only in the short-hand symbols shown above the column in Figure 48. In lessons, the mnemonics for the sounds of Figure 48 are *chiri kara, chiri popo, tsu ta tsu ta, tsu, pon*. This is such

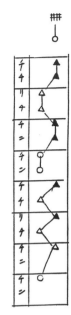

FIGURE 48. *Chirikara* drum notation from "Gorō Tokimune"

a common pattern that the drumming style is called *chirikarabyōshi* ("*chirikara* rhythm"). The *kana* along the left-hand side of Figure 48 are the mnemonics of the *shamisen* line (*kuchijamisen*, or "mouth *shamisen*").

## BIWA NOTATION

The early *heikebiwa* style of notation was relatively simple. It used the above-mentioned short strokes (*sumifu*), placed to the right of the text, as a general indication of the vocal line. Since the *biwa* usually played only between the sung phrases, there was no need to develop a notation that could be superimposed on the existing vocal script. Instead, words and symbols were inserted between the phrases to indicate which conventional pattern should be used. This type of notation has remained the basis of the Satsuma and Chikuzen music that followed. As used by these schools, each phrase of the poem is separated by a space. At the head of each col-

11. The notation is derived from mimeographed scores in the author's collection.

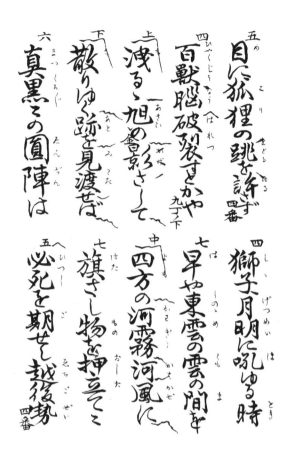

**FIGURE 49.** Traditional *biwa* notation (Chikuzen school)[12]

umn of the text, the name of the *biwa* or vocal pattern to be used may appear, though in Figure 49 the notation (Chikuzen) basically shows only the number of a reciting tone pitch. Along the side of the text are found other symbols and wiggly lines that remind the musician of patterns to be used at that point (see the third and fourth columns from the right). At the end of the phrase, any special *biwa* interludes are marked by name (see the end of the initial phrases of the first and second lines from the right and the last line at the bottom).

During the early twentieth century there were attempts to create a more

12. From Tachibana Kazusada, "Kawanakajima" (Tokyo: Tachibana Chikuzen-biwa Sōka, 1917).

FIGURE 50. A modern *chikuzenbiwa* instrumental notation

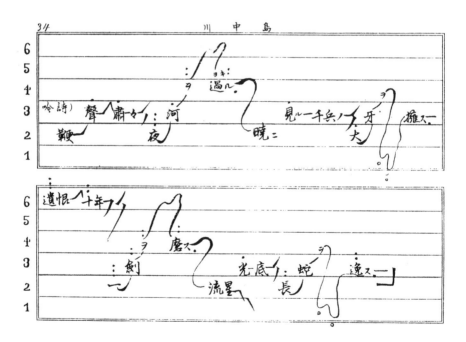

FIGURE 51. A modern *satsumabiwa* vocal notation

accurate notation. Figure 50 is the *chikuzenbiwa* notation of two instrumental patterns (*toboso* and *shigure*).[13] The three lines represent the *biwa* strings (the fourth top string being the same pitch as the third), with up and down plectrum strokes being shown by the black triangles. The white triangles are open strings, and the frets are indicated with Japanese characters. The dots show the degree of pressure on the string (for half steps, whole steps, etc.), and additional marks refer to other performance techniques.

Another system adopted in the twentieth century is seen in Figure 51, which is an excerpt from a *satsumabiwa* version of "Kawanakajima."[14] The lines represent the basic pitches of the scale. The text is written on the line corresponding to the correct pitch, and wiggly strokes indicate the melismatic movement. In all the *biwa* notations mentioned above, the signs for vocal ornamentation or patterns are usually printed in red, while the text is in black.

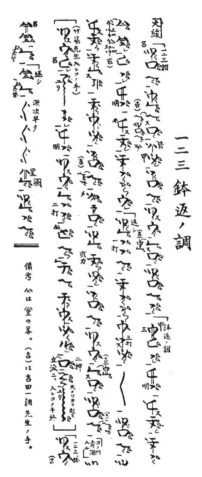

FIGURE 52. *Shakuhachi* notation from "Hifumi hachigaeshi"

## SHAKUHACHI NOTATION

Figure 52 is the Kinko school notation of the piece transcribed in Figure 24. To the Western eye, this system seems the clearest notation style studied so far, since basically the symbols consist of the names for the different holes on the *shakuhachi*, which corresponds to the Western fixed *do* system in which each

13. From *Chikuzenbiwa hikofu* (Tokyo: Gansandō Sōka, 1917), Vol. 1.
14. From *Satsumabiwa uta* (Tokyo: Miyata Bunkadō, 1919), Vol. 1. Being a narrative tradition, there are different texts and performance practices for one piece in different schools of *biwa* music. Thus, the text in Figures 49 and 51 is not the same.

syllable stands for a specific pitch.[15] The *merikari* system of microtonal changes in pitch (see p. 172) is indicated by separate marks in the notation.

Since rhythm is usually varied in *shakuhachi* music, it is not a major concern in notation. One or two vertical lines down the middle of a pitch symbol indicate the length of a tone, as do wiggly strokes at the end of phrases. There are also special signs and short comments referring to performance techniques and melismas. For those who might want to put *shakuhachi* music into Western notation, there are now instruction books on this process,[16] but many of the subtle glides and graces that are so characteristic of *shakuhachi* music remain unwritten and must be learned from a teacher.

KOTO NOTATION

Until the nineteenth century, collections of Edo popular and art music contained mostly text. The *Shichiku shoshinshū* of 1664 has notation for tunes to be played on the *koto*, *shamisen*, or *shakuhachi* yet there are no performance or rhythm details. The growth of purely instrumental pieces made the invention of instrument-specific notation essential. Since the *koto* was of Chinese origin, it was logical to turn to the Chinese notation system, which consisted of a number for each string and dots of various sizes indicating rhythm, with the names of special playing techniques written in or indicated by special signs. Today this system is no longer used, though its basic plan has been retained.

| 1 | 2 | 3 | 4 | 5 | 6 | 7 | 8 | 9 | 10 | 11 | 12 | 13 |
|---|---|---|---|---|---|---|---|---|----|----|----|----|
| 壹 | 貳 | 參 | 四 | 五 | 六 | 七 | 八 | 九 | 十 | 斗 | 爲 | 巾 |

FIGURE 53. *Koto* notation symbols

FIGURE 54. Yamada school *koto* notation and transcription

15. Details are found in Biblio. refs. 6·1 and 6·7.
16. One is Biblio. ref. 6·8.

There are two main types of *koto* notation in use today, one for the Ikuta school and the other for the Yamada school. They both employ a common number system, shown in Figure 53, to indicate strings. As used by the Yamada school, the arrangement of these symbols more closely resembles Western notation (on which it is based) than its counterpart. Figure 54 shows the opening phrase of the piece "Chidori" in Yamada and Western notation. The use of vertical lines to represent bar lines is another Western adaptation. The *koto* tuning and number of beats in a measure (usually two) are shown at the beginning of a piece and do not appear in Figure 54. The beams used to indicate short notes in Western notation are clearly applied to the Japanese score (second bar, second beat). Rests can be seen as short lines (first bar, second beat) or as circles. Special playing techniques (e.g. left-hand string pressure) are indicated by such signs as the square and triangle in bar six. The symbols above the notation are a form of solfège (*shōga*) by which the composition is learned. When there is text, it is written below the notation. Though the vocal line differs somewhat from the *koto* melody, there is no separate notation for it, as it is memorized during *koto* lessons.

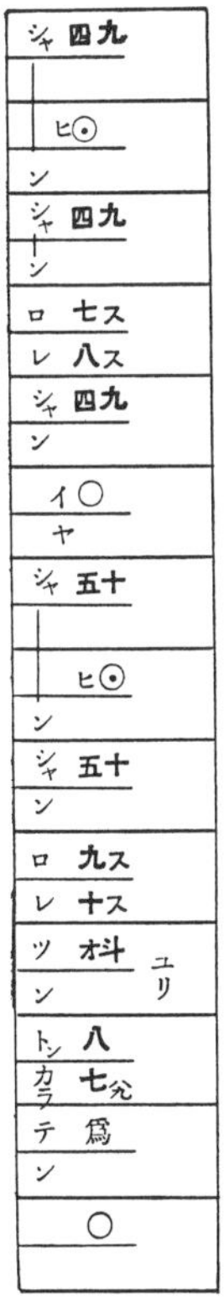

The Ikuta school notation for the same phrase from "Chidori" is seen in Figure 55. Although essentially the same as the Yamada notation, it is written Japanese-style in vertical columns. Half beats are indicated by short horizontal lines, the solfège is to the left of the notation, and special fingerings and techniques are noted to the right. Modern Ikuta pieces come in special editions with traditional notation in one part of the book and a Western transcription in another (Biblio. ref. 7·4).

FIGURE 55. Ikuta school *koto* notation of the same passage

## SHAMISEN NOTATION

There are a vast number of styles of *shamisen* music. Clever attempts at devising a notation were made during the Edo period,[17] but it was in the

17. See Biblio. ref. A·3, 197–226.

late nineteenth century that *shamisen* notation became common. Before this, one merely purchased the text and memorized the music in reference to the words. With the rise of amateur lessons and printed collections of popular music, *shamisen* mnemonics (*kuchijamisen*) involving a syllabary for finger positions on each string appeared. This was called the *i-ro-ha* system after the first three syllables of a poem with which children learned to write *kana* syllables. It worked well in the rote teaching method, but the oral tradition is fragile, and many songs have disappeared with the loss of memory and performers. In this relation, recordings have become a vital means of preservation.

In the twentieth century, two forms of *shamisen* notation have proven to be equally useful for both the performance of the music and the study of it. One is sometimes called *kosaburōfu*, after Yoshizumi Kosaburō of the Kenseikai branch of the Kineya school of *nagauta*. This notation, shown in Figure 56 (the *kangen* passage from the *nagauta* piece "Tsuru kame"), is rhythmically like the *koto* notation in Figure 54 except that it is written in vertical columns. The Arabic numbers represent diatonic pitches, the number ·7 being the lowest note. The exact pitch of this note will depend on the tuning of the instrument. If this note were B, then the number 7 would be the B an octave higher and the number 7· would be the B an octave above that. The string on which to play is marked in Roman numerals (I, II, III). The Japanese numbers (一, 二, 三) tell one which finger to use. Special playing methods are marked to the side (for example, the left-hand pizzicato in the seventh bar). The small writing on the left of the music is the mnemonic aid mentioned earlier: *ton chi ten*, for example, would correspond to "B c b" or any other pitches that move from lower open string to upper fingered string to open upper string. The words for the music are written to the right of the *shamisen* line, and the music of this vocal line appears to the right of the words. Note that it does not line up with the *shamisen* notation: this reflects the correct performance practice in which the vocal line usually floats freely over the *shamisen* part.

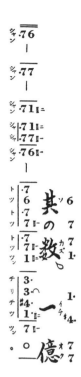

FIGURE 56. *Kosaburōfu shamisen* notation

Figure 57 shows the same music written in the so-called *bunkafu* notation. This is read like Western music, from left to right. The Arabic numbers

FIGURE 57. The same music in *bunkafu* and Western notation

in this case represent finger positions on the fingerboard. The three horizontal lines indicate the strings. The disadvantage of this system is that the
actual pitch of these symbols and their interval relations change if a different
tuning is used. For example, the 4 in the first measure is the note A in
*honchōshi* but B in *niagari*. Since the strings are shown by the three lines,
only the fingers need be noted. These are represented by Roman numerals.
Rhythm is shown as before with short lines, derived from the beams of
Western notation. Since circles represent open strings, this symbol is not
used for a rest; instead, you will see large black dots, as in measure one, or
a dash as seen in measure two. The major drawback of both systems is the
use of Western meter. Japanese music, like that of the Renaissance, is rich
in long-lined phrases. These are represented poorly, trapped within bars
of two-four time.

The *bunkafu* system is used in the notation of *nagauta*, *kouta*, *kiyomoto*,
and several other forms, including folk music, and has become the most
widespread system in use today, with sets of music or separate pieces readily
available.[18] Among the other systems still followed is one that combines
elements of the two discussed above, in which the vertical style and Arabic
numbering of the first notation are allied with the three lines of the second.[19] But with knowledge of the two main systems, the various offshoots
of them can be read with a modicum of practice.

Finally, mention should be made of the notation for *gidayūbushi* (Figure
58). Its traditional notation is similar to that used for the *biwa* (compare with
Figure 49). The rise of amateur interest in performing led to further vocal
notation, somewhat like that of *noh*, with even *shamisen* mnemonics incorporated. Excerpts of famous *gidayū* sections have appeared in the full *bunkafu*

18. A complete catalogue can be ordered from Hōgakusha, 1–19–14 Toranomon,
Minato-ku, Tokyo.
19. One version is the Kineya Yanotsuke notation found in the series *Nagauta
kenkyū keikobon*, Aoyagi Shigezō ed. (Tokyo: Tōwa Shuppansha, 1987).

FIGURE 58. *Gidayūbushi* notation

notation. But professional performers use books in the style shown in Figure 58. (Like the vellum pages from old church hymnals in the West, they have become collectors' items, prized for their decorative appeal.)

## 3. Summary

During the last few pages we have discussed a vast number of disparate notation systems. It is hard to make a general statement about so many different methods. In the first edition of this book, the author (then twenty-nine) was irritated that Japanese notation seemed so inaccurate and diverse; it wasn't unified, like its Western counterpart. But in retrospect it seems better to look at it in the context of the functions notation fulfills in the kind of music it is used for. Early Buddhist and Western chant notation shared linear goals, though the text was written in different directions—the Buddhist from top to bottom, the Western from left to right. Each tradition developed independent, ingenious ways of handling further ornamentation of single lines. In due course, though, the two notation traditions split. Western notation evolved into a highly specific style as the music became more vertical in its orientation; lines had to be written accurately so that harmonies came out correctly. But, throughout this book, we have emphasized how aharmonic Japanese music is. Horizontal lines coordinate only at specific moments, and each line must have its special characteristics, so that it doesn't necessarily mix with other parts. This is particularly evident when we turn to instrumental music. Each instrument developed a notation specific to its needs and to the characteristics of the school of players using it. Until the late nineteenth century, the function of such notation was not so much to be read as to be used as a memory aid for things learned orally. We have noted the later development of Western-style notations for *koto* and *shamisen*, which did indeed "modernize" teaching, but only at the expense of a loss of performance information.

Buddha has always said that all life is change. Each moment of notation is true to the needs of those who use it.

# APPENDIX II

## CD CONTENTS AND TEXT TRANSLATIONS

TRACK 1: First line of *kagura* song "Sakaki"
Performers: Tokyo Gakusō ensemble.
Text translation: Adapted by Edward Seidensticker and William Malm.

[Throngs of people are enthralled by the fragrance of the] *sakaki* leaves
[That flourish in front of the mountain home of the Gods....]

TRACK 2: *Matsuri bayashi* music from Tokyo
Performers: Wakayama Taneo ensemble.

TRACK 3: Dance music from snow festival in Niino, Nagano prefecture

TRACK 4: Buddhist "Shichi no bongo" chant
Performers: Priests of the Buzan school.
Content: The second phrase of the opening words of the "Sanskrit Hymn to the Four Wisdoms" from the Diamond Sutra, praising a principal figure in Shingon mythology.
Text translation: David M. Rosenfeld and Steven Nelson.

[Through receiving the teachings of Kongōsatta (Vajrasattva),] we obtained the diamond treasure

TRACK 5: *Gagaku* "Etenraku" excerpt
Performers: Shigenkai ensemble.

TRACK 6: *Noh ageuta* in lyrical style from *Matsukaze*
Composer: Zeami Motokiyo (1363–1443).
Performers: *shite*, Noguchi Kanesuke; *tsure*, Tatsumi Takashi; flute, Sadamitsu Yoshitsugu; *kotsuzumi*, Takeda Toshirō; *ōtsuzumi*, Sannō Fumio; chorus, Takeda Kōun and others.
Plot: Two women who had loved Lord Yukihara have only his cap and robe as memories as they gather brine along the Suma beach.
Text translation: Adapted by William Malm.

> Our reflections in the water shame us.
> Our reflections in the water shame us.
> Carefully we pull the cart of brine,
> Though our destiny is like a stagnant pool
> Left by the low tide on the beach;
> How long is it our lot to live?
> If it were the dew on the grassy field,
> It would be gone with the rising sun;
> We are but unwanted weeds
> Thrown on the shore by fishermen.
> With sleeves wet with dew, we waste away,
> With sleeves wet with dew, we waste away.

TRACK 7: *Noh* dance music and strong style of singing in *Takasago*
Composer: Zeami Motokiyo.
Performers: *shite*, Takeda Takashi; flute, Terai Masakazu; *kotsuzumi*, Kō Enjirō; *ōtsuzumi*, Kamei Toshirō; *taiko*, Kakimoto Toyoji; chorus, Kanze Hisao and others.
Plot: A priest travels to the Sumiyoshi shrine at Takasago. He meets the gardeners, who are the spirits of the pine trees that stand for longevity in the shrine compound. The shrine spirit then dances.
Text translation: Adapted by William Malm.

> Myōjin (the spirit): Plucking a plum blossom, I deck my hair,
> Chorus:    And petals, like spring snow, fall over my robes.
> ["Kami mai" dance in *kakari* and 3 *dan* with *hayashi* accompaniment]
> Chorus:    O blessed vision, O blessed vision!

Under the lovely moon
The God is dancing before the Sumiyoshi shrine!
Awe fills our hearts,
Myōjin:     The voices of the female dancers rise clear,
The waters of the bay
Reflect the Pines of Suminoe.
This dance is called "The Blue Sea."
Chorus:     The way of the Gods and the Sovereign is as straight
As the road to Miyako
Myōjin:     By which the traveler "Returns to the Imperial City."[1]
Chorus:     Dressed in an auspicious
Myōjin:     Shinto ritual robe
Chorus:     Dread spirits quelling, arms are stretched out,
Life and treasure gathering, arms are inward drawn.
"A Thousand Autumns"[2]
Rejoices the people's hearts;
And "Ten Thousand Years"[3]
Endows them with new life.
The murmur of the wind in the Twin Pines
Fills each heart with joy,
Fills each heart with joy.

TRACK 8: *Mōsōbiwa* Buddhist "Kannonkyō" chant
**Performer**: Kitada Meichō.
**Content**: A passage from Chapter 25 of the Lotus Sutra in which Buddha replies to a bodhisattva's question about the Goddess of Mercy (Kannon). Though Buddhist divinities are generally hermaphroditic, Kannon is female to the Japanese people for whom the performer is singing. Thus, the standard translation found in "The Scripture of the Lotus Blossoms of the Fine Dharma" by Leon Hurvitz (New York: Columbia University Press, 1976, 316–17) has been adjusted to properly reflect the message intended for a peasant audience.

1. The name of a *bugaku* dance ("Genjōraku").
2. A Shinto piece played at imperial enthronement ceremonies.
3. *Manzai*, a congratulatory dance still surviving in folk forms.

O World-Honored One, fully endowed with subtle signs!
Now again I ask you about that Child of the Buddha.
Why is it named the One Who Observes the Sounds of the World?
[the Buddha's reply]
Listen you to the conduct of the Sound-Observer (Kannon),
The one who responds well to all places in all directions
With broad vows as deep as the ocean. Throughout time beyond reckoning or discussion, Kannon has served many thousands of millions of Buddhas, uttering great and pure vows.
I will tell it to you in brief.
Hearing Kannon's name, seeing Kannon's shape,
Or remembering Kannon in thought are not done in vain,
For Kannon can extinguish the woes of existence.
Even if someone whose thoughts are malicious should be pushed into a great pit of fire,
Thanks to Kannon's constant awareness, the pit of fire would turn into a pool.
Or, one might be afloat in a great sea in which there are dragons, fish, and various ghosts,
Thanks to Kannon's constant awareness
One could not drown in the waves....


TRACK 9: *Heikebiwa* opening of "Gion shōja"
**Performer:** Takeyama Kōgo (Maeda school).
**Plot:** The opening lines of the medieval *Tale of the Heike* about the strife between the Genji and Heike forces (1183–85) in which the Heike lost.
**Text translation:** Helen Craig McCullough (*Tale of the Heike*, p. 23). The CD is from "The sound" to "all things"; Figure 20 notates only from "echoes" to "all things."

The sound of the Gion Shōja bells echoes the impermanence of all things; the color of the sala flowers reveals the truth that the prosperous must decline. The proud do not endure, they are like a dream on a spring night; the mighty fall at last, they are as dust before the wind.

TRACK 10: *Satsumabiwa* excerpt "Atsumori"
**Performer**: Tsuruta Kinshi.
**Plot**: In a battle against the Heike clan, Kumagai kills Atsumori, a youth the age of his own son.
**Text translation**: The first paragraph is the same text as translated in Helen Craig McCullough, *Tale of the Heike*, except for the new word "phantasm," which is used with permission. The second paragraph is translated by Lili Selden. (Figure 20 transcribes from "echoes" to "all things.")

> The sound of the Gion Shōja bells echoes the impermanence of all things; the color of the sala flowers reveals the truth that the prosperous must decline. The proud do not endure, they are like a dream or a phantasm on a spring night.
>
> During the battle of Suma between the Genji and Heike clans, the fortunes of the Heike sank like the evening sun. The height of pathos was embodied during this time by one who was known as "The Rankless Official, Atsumori."

TRACK 11: *Chikuzenbiwa* excerpt from "Ōgi no mato"
**Performer**: Sasagawa Kyokukō.
**Plot**: During the Dannoura battle in the *Tale of Heike*, the brave Genji warrior, Munetake, shoots a fan off the mast of a Heike boat offshore.
**Text translation**: Lili Selden. The prayer translation is used with permission from Helen Craig McCullough, *Tale of the Heike*, p. 368.

> Munetake Yoichi closed his eyes in the saddle and prayed, "Great Bodhisattva Hachiman and ye gods of my province at Nikkō, Utsunomiya and Nasu Yūzen! Vouchsafe that I may hit that fan. If I miss, I will smash my bow and kill myself; I will never show myself to others again. But if you deign to view me now with merciful compassion, still the wave and wind to provide me a moment of divine protection."
>
> His heartfelt prayer reached the heavens, for the wind and waves quieted down. The fan on the boat seemed easier to hit. Munetaka steadied his heart, firmly drew his arrow back, and held his breath. As he let fly the humming-bulb arrow, the cry of a plover echoed in

the bay. Before the bird could flutter its wings, the arrow pierced through its target, diving into the sea as the fan danced in the sky.

TRACK 12: Excerpt from solo "Hifumi hachigaeshi"
**Performer:** Yamaguchi Gorō (1933–99).

TRACK 13: Opening song and interlude from Yamada *koto* piece "Matsukaze"
**Performers:** *koto*, Nakanoshima Keiko, Nakanoshima Kin'ichi, Ichimura Ayano; *shamisen*, Shinagawa Shōzō; *shakuhachi*, Notomi Haruhiko.
**Composers:** Yamaki Kengyō (1838–73), Nakanoshima Kengyō (1838–94).
**Text translation:** From Tsuge Gen'ichi, *Anthology of Sōkyoku and Jiuta Song Texts* (Tokyo: Academia Music Ltd., 1983).

> The shadow of the judas tree in the moon lengthens.
> Wind blows along a sandy path
> Which is so polished in the bright moonlight
> It seems like day.
> The spreading vista has neither cherry blossoms nor fall foliage.

TRACK 14: *Gidayū* excerpt from "Sakaya no dan," 7th *dan* of the play *Hade sugata onna maiginu* (1772)
**Performers:** *tayū*, Toyotake Yamashironoshōjō; *shamisen*, Tsuruzawa Tōzō.
**Plot:** The father, mother, and wife (Osono) of Hanshichi and her father (Sōgan) wait for his return to the family saké store. The child of Hanshichi and his mistress (Sankatsu) also appears. Hanshichi mistakenly believes he has killed someone.
**Text translation:** Karen Brazell.

> Wife: Early tomorrow I will be taken back to Tenma by my father. If I should happen to hear sad news of Hanshichi's death, I think I will surely die of a broken heart. Yet I make a resolve now not to remain in this world of sorrow. Though I am hated, if it were this house, my husband's house, in which I die perhaps it will be a bond which will connect us in the world hereafter.

Narrator: This devotion which thus sought to hurry death is pitiable even to the eyes of outsiders. Perhaps awakened by her crying, a child who knows nothing of her misery comes out of a room and clings to her knees.

Child: I want milk, I want some milk, auntie, auntie.

Narrator: Looking at the child's face Osono is startled.

Wife: Oh, aren't you Otsū of the Minoya? How did you come here?

Narrator: Puzzled she picks up the child in her arms, at which moment Hanbei, Sōgan, and her mother-in-law come rushing out of their room.

Mother: Oh, daughter-in-law, each time we heard you through the paper door we were filled with gratitude for your gracious heart. There are many things for which I must express my gratitude to you, but what set my heart beating fast was the matter of this child. You said it was Otsū of the Minoya? Hanshichi and Sankatsu's child?

Wife: Yes, this child is that Otsū whom they brought into this world.

Mother: Oh, did you hear?

Father: I heard, I heard. But why have they abandoned Otsū and sent her here? There must be some explanation for this. Mother, isn't there a note in her bodice or somewhere else? Try to find one quickly!

Narrator: Even as he is saying this she hurriedly opens the child's amulet case from inside of which a note tumbles out. In a frenzy of haste she tears open the seal.

Mother: Well, what's this? It says it's a farewell note.

Father: Here, daughter-in-law, read this quickly with your good eyes.

Wife: Yes, of course. But what is it?

Note (read by wife):

I too am aware of the teachings of the world which say that becoming parent and child after the tenfold vow, the obligation of a child to his father is higher than a mountain. But, without repaying this kindness properly, I became entangled in other unexpected obligations and, against my

will, committed a crime against my filial duties. I pray
that you will forgive me for this. The gracious upbringing of my mother ...

Wife:      Oh, it's about you. Listen well.

Mother:    Oh, daughter-in-law, I am listening well. I'm listening well.

Narrator:  Though the moonlight streaming through the ever-listen-
ing paper screen doors is clear and bright, it cannot pierce
the darkness of their hearts.

Father:    At a time like this they have to practice music!...[4] And
what is written after that?

Note (read by wife):

The gracious upbringing of my mother is a blessing deeper
that the sea. When Father was in a bad temper, she always
managed to help me in some way or other. This immea-
surable solicitude of hers has been in vain. It is the tor-
ment of my life that I am in the position of one who has
killed a man. I must bid an unexpected farewell.

Wife:      Oh, in that case Hanshichi really...

Father:    Yes, daughter-in-law, he killed Zenemon.

Wife:      Oh!

Father:    That rascal called Zenemon is not the only one at fault.
Even with a villain like that, in a fight, both sides are to
blame. To think that my son is to be executed as a murderer.
Sōgan, the more I think of it, the more terrible it seems.

Narrator:  [Hanshichi] is like a lonely mandarin duck limping with a
crippled wing; a night plover anxious for its child. How
tragic.


TRACK 15: *Kouta* piece "Tomete mo kaeru"
**Performers**: singer, Tade Komaki; *shamisen*, Tade Koshizu.
**Plot**: A Yoshiwara brothel patron remembers the standard geisha farewell
as he departs. In Edo times, the Yoshiwara was located among rice fields.

4. Note that at this moment on the CD track a two-*shamisen* interlude is heard.
The seemingly irrelevant line about music practice now becomes theatrically important, for it makes the background (*meriyasu*) music that follows a logical sound
behind the reading of the sad note.

The word *furu* means either "raining" or "rejection" (implying failure in his case). Double meanings and ambiguity are characteristic of *kouta* texts.
**Text translation**: David M. Rosenfeld and Lili Selden.

> Even if I hold you, you leave me;
> Even if I coax you,
> You hop away, nervous as a frog;
> And wet as one too,
> Through the dreary rice fields in the night rain
> [or]
> She holds him, yet he leaves her;
> She coaxes him, yet he leaves her, leaves her
> Hopping home like a frog, through the paddy fields.
> What a silly mess for him—alone and wet in the night rain

TRACK 16: *Nagauta* excerpt from "Gorō Tokimune" (1841)
**Performers**: singers, Kineya Gosaburō, Kineya Kichijūrō; *shamisen*, Naka-yama Kojūrō, Matsushima Jutarō; flute, Fukuhara Hyakunosuke; *kotsuzumi*, Mochizuki Tazaemon; *ōtsuzumi*, Mochizuki Sakichi; *taiko*, Katada Kisaku.
**Composer**: Kineya Rokuzaemon X.
**Plot**: A well-known *kabuki* dance based on the Soga story in which two brothers seek revenge for the death of their father.
**Text translation**: David Hughes. (Section names shown.)

> *Tsunagi* (after *kudoki* section)
> "Hey! What am I doing?
> I must clear this thing up soon and avenge my father!"
> The winds of eighteen years ago blow once again, strengthening his
>     determination not to let the enemy escape.
> Dauntless, lusting for blood, he cuts a brave and manly figure with
>     peonies and wings-spread butterflies on his kimono.[5]
>     [instrumental interlude]
> *Odoriji*
> The bush warbler sings self-indulgently in the mountain thicket,
>     envying the plum tree in the garden.

5. These auspicious symbols are revealed by an assistant who holds out his sleeves as he poses.

Gently the spring breeze spreads rumors of love.
Along the earthen dikes, the violet and the knotweed are together
  drenched by the sympathetic dew, a true meeting of desire and love.
In gay Nakanochō all is well.

*Chirashi*
For his matchless deed of filial piety he will be praised in awe like a
  god in man's form until the end of time.
This year too in flowery Asakusa in Edo.

*Dangire*
We bring out the god's image and honor him merrily.


TRACK 17: *Kabuki* opening of *Momijigari*
**Performers**: singers (*tokiwazu*), Tokiwazu Chitosedayū and others, (*naga-uta*) Yoshimura Gorōji and others, (*gidayū*) Toyotake Okadayū, Takemoto Fujidayū; *shamisen* (*tokiwazu*), Tokiwazu Kikusaburō and others, (*naga-uta*) Kineya Eiji and others, (*gidayū*) Tsurusawa Genjirō, Toyosawa Isaburō; *hayashi*, Mochizuki Chōsaku and others.
**Plot**: Members of the nobility go for maple leaf viewing in the mountains and meet a beautiful woman who turns into a demon.
**Text translation**: Richard Winslow. (*Shamisen* genres listed.)

> (*Tokiwazu*): In Shinano stands the famous Mt. Togakushi amidst the drizzle.
> (*Gidayū*):   Colorful evening maple leaves
> (*Nagauta*):  Grow on the branches and enhance the scene in every direction.
> (*Gidayū*):   Now it is the end of September, a man named Koremochi of the Taira family goes maple viewing with his attendants.
> (*Nagauta*):  Anxious to go, they make their way through a grassy field.
> (*Tokiwazu*): Trudging along a steep road, they pass into the deep recesses of a mountain.
> Koremochi: It is said that plants have no heart, but without fail they signal the seasons. In spring the flowers bloom; in autumn again the mountain maples display their autumn colors. Viewers forget to go home.

Jūsha:       Just as they say, the whole area, east and west, is red.
             What a beautiful sight!


Track 18: Folk song "Tsugaru jongarabushi" from Aomori prefecture
Performers: singer, Asari Miki.
Text translation: Lili Selden and William Malm.

Ah, the local pride of *jongarabushi*
When the young ones sing and the oldsters play the drums
While the girls dance and the ears of rice dance too.

Ah, Tsugaru is a good place with high mountains,
The water's clear and the women fair,
Their voices the pride of *jongarabushi*.


Track 19: *Bon odori* song "Kawasaki" from Gujō Hachiman in Gifu prefecture
Performers: Society for the Preservation of *Gujōbushi*.
Text translation: Lili Selden and William Malm.

When leaving Gujō (no) Hachiman
I squeeze dry my drenched sleeves though it hasn't rained.
The moon in the sky is so round, without corners, that
I could embrace it.

## Audio-Visual Materials

Nothing is more impermanent in life than a list of audio-visual materials, particularly if they involve Japanese companies and recordings of Japanese music.

The major producer of cassettes of old recordings of Japanese music is Nippon Columbia. The first four letters for such products, as well as those of other companies whose products are probably no longer available, are shown below. The letters thus serve as clues as to where, among the myriad Beethoven and pop CDs, new traditional Japanese music may exist. The Japanese CDs used for dance practice and performance tend to stay in print the longest.

The two best shopping grounds for such materials remain the Bunkadō Record Store (14–1–5 Ginza, Chūō-ku, Tokyo) across from the Kabukiza, or the Yamano Store near the main Ginza intersection. The impressive sets of LP albums that were produced in the 1960s as part of annual national arts contests survive in foreign university libraries and the Archive of Traditional Japanese Music at Ueno Gakuen University. Foreign CD titles listed below were available in 1999. Happy hunting!

## Audio

World Music Library WML 2001-11 contains ten CDs with English titles. Their contents are: (1) *gagaku*, (2) *noh*, (3) *kabuki*, (4) *biwa*, (5) *shaku-*

*hachi,* (6) chamber music, (7) *sankyoku,* (8 & 9) *shamisen* music, and (10) percussion. WML 2023-20 are CDs of various Japanese folk musics.

The UNESCO series had several LP recordings of Japanese music. Among UNESCO CD listings in 1999 are:

D 8036    *Shōmyō Buddhist Ritual*
558657    *Shōmyō*
559018    *Gagaku*
559005    *Shakkyō, Noh Drama*
559067    *Satsuma Biwa*
560114    *The Art of Shakuhachi*
D 8047    *Chants of the Ainu*

Japan Victor Company releases are: JVC 5354 *Gagaku,* 5355 *Noh,* 5356 *Bunraku,* 5357 *Shakuhachi,* 5358 *Koto,* 5360 *Okinawan Folk Songs.*

Another Victor CD set is: *Taikei Nihon no dentō ongaku,* 1990, KCDK 1100-1127. It is without romanization or English captions. CD 1100 contains fourteen excerpts from different genres. Each of the remaining CDs concentrates on a single genre, from Buddhist chant to contemporary music, with excellent performers.

The Victor CDs in the VICG-2000 and 1300 series contain hundreds of examples of all the major *shamisen* genres. The prefatory letters VZT tend to be traditional music. In 1967 Victor produced two brilliant LP albums on *kabuki* music complete with long studies and examples in Western notation. One was *Kabuki geza uta shūsei* (SJL 2071-50), which dealt with all the major songs used in Tokyo *kabuki.* The other, *Kamigata geza ongaku shūsei* (SJL-101-106), did the same for Kyoto/Osaka productions. A Victor CD series is VZCG-8055-56, titled *Kabuki geza ongaku shūsei.* Three CDs of excerpts of *kabuki* drama dialogue are available through the Bunkadō store mentioned above: *Kabuki meiserifu,* produced by Shinseisha.

The Toshiba TOCF 4000 series has sixty Japanese music CDs. Both Toshiba and Columbia are primarily dubbings from older recordings. They seldom have romanization or English.

Nippon Columbia labels COTN and CAK tend to be *shamisen* or *koto.*

Nippon Columbia CDs COCF 1211-1214 are *Vocal Court Music*. Their CTV cassette series contain unaccompanied *noh* plays sung by professionals and used primarily for practice by amateurs. The text is in *noh* notation. No English or romanization.

The King *Seven Sea Series* KICH 2001–2010 contains Japanese music with English titles. Another King preface is KITX.

*Koto* and *shakuhachi* CDs with English notes abound, so only a few easily available in European/American markets are listed:
*The Koto Music of Japan*. Nonesuch 72005
*Shakuhachi*. Nonesuch 72076-1
*Offerings*, Ralph Samuelson. Music of the World MOW 105
*Shakuhachi* playing methods demonstrated, MOW 104

*Traditional Folk Songs of Japan*, Smithsonian/Folkways cassette 4534, is a reissue of an old Japanese set that contains examples from many regions and islands. English text translations are included.

For *matsuribayashi* see cassette in Biblio. ref. 2·14
For Buddhist chant on CD see Biblio. ref. 2·10

## Video

*The Tradition of Performing Arts in Japan*, Tokyo National Theater VHS NTSC. Excerpts from *noh*, *bunraku*, and *kabuki* with English commentary.

*Early Music Television*, University of Oklahoma Center for Music Television. English language tapes for classroom use.
Gagaku Court Music of Japan (1989)
Music of Bunraku (1991)
Shinto Festival Music (1994)
Nagauta, the Heart of Kabuki Music (1994)
Music of Noh Drama (1997)

*Taikei Nihon no dentō ongaku video*, Victor PVTK 10.
A set of videotapes of traditional music and theater. No English.

*Oto to eizō ni yoru Nihon koten geinō taikei*, Victor/Heibonsha VTMV 100–125.
A set of twenty-five videotapes and two books on theater-related music.
No English.

*Nihon rekishi to geinō*, Victor/Heibonsha VTMV 81–95.
A set of fourteen videotapes each with two books boxed together on the
subject of theatricals and ceremonies of historical or cultural interest.
No English.

# A SELECTIVE ANNOTATED BIBLIOGRAPHY

The following list of recommended reading is so organized that those desiring to pursue the topic of a specific chapter further can quickly learn which sources are most germane. While many of these works are rather specialized, I have tried to include materials of use to the general reader whenever they are available. Both Japanese and European-language books are included. The works listed for Chapter One are those I consider to be part of a basic reference library on Japanese music. References to any of these materials within the text of this book are indicated by the use of their chapter number and number in the Bibliography for that chapter. Thus, Biblio. ref. 1·10, II, 206 refers to page 206 of Volume 2 of *Koji ruien*. These numbers are also used to cross-reference the Bibliography itself. Acronyms are used for series publications (see items 1·16 and 1·22). But the list is by no means comprehensive, and those wishing a broader selection can refer to items 1·4 or 1·22 in this Bibliography or to the Internet. Japanese characters have not been added to authors' names or book titles since they can now be searched for on computers in romanized form.

## CHAPTER ONE: GENERAL REFERENCES

1·1 Harich-Schneider, Eta. *A History of Japanese Music*. Oxford: Oxford University Press, 1973.
A scholarly work emphasizing court and Buddhist music.

1·2 *Hōgaku hyakka jiten*. Kikkawa Eishi, ed. Tokyo: Ongaku no Tomosha, 1984.
"Encyclopedia of Japanese Traditional Music," edited by one of Japan's best *hōgaku* scholars.

1·3 Iba Takashi. *Nihon ongaku gairon*. Tokyo: Kōseikaku Shoten, 1928.
"An Outline of Japanese Music." An extensive discussion of scales, instruments, and forms. Reprint 1938.

1·4    *K.B.S. Bibliography of Standard Reference Books for Japanese Studies.* Tokyo: Kokusai Bunka Shinkōkai, 1960.
Vol. 7 (B) lists basic Japanese publications on theater, dance, and music up to that date.

1·5    Kikkawa Eishi. *Nihon ongaku no bitekikenkyū.* Tokyo: Ongaku no Tomosha, 1984.
"Studies in the Aesthetics of Japanese Music." A fine book on this important topic.

1·6    _____. *Nihon ongaku no rekishi.* Osaka: Sōgensha, 1965.
"The History of Japanese Music." The best Japanese-language music history book in print.

1·7    *Vom Charakter der japanischen Musik,* Vol. 2 (1984) STMJ (see 1·16).
A translation of *Nihon ongaku no seikaku* (Tokyo: Ongaku no Tomosha, 1979, orig. Wanya, 1948). An English summary is included.

1·8    Kishibe Shigeo. *The Traditional Music of Japan.* Tokyo: The Japan Foundation, 1984.
A convenient short survey of the topic.

1·9    Koizumi Fumio. *Nihon no oto: sekai no naka no Nihon ongaku.* Tokyo: Seidosha, 1977.
"The Sounds of Japan: Japanese Music in a World Context." An insightful study by Japan's best ethnomusicologist.

1·10   *Koji ruien,* Vols. 43, 44 (marked as Part I and II). Gotō Ryōichu, ed. Kyoto: Koji Ruien Kankōkai, 1931.
"Selected Ancient Texts." Ancient writings on music and dance. Reprint 1998, Yoshikawa Kōbunkan.

1·11   Konakamura Kiyonori. *Kabu ongaku ryakushi.* Tokyo: Yoshikawa Hanshichi, 1888. 2 vols. Reprint Iwanami Shoten, 1964.
"A Short History of Song and Dance Music." The first historical outline of Japanese music.

1·12   Malm, William. "Practical Approaches to Japanese Music" in *The Garland Library of Readings in Ethnomusicology,* Vol. 2. Kay Kaufman Shelemay, ed. New York: Garland, 1990.

A reproduction of a 1965 article. See also "Interlude" in ref. 8·8.

1·13 *Nihon no ongaku (rekishi to riron)*. Tokyo: Kokuristu Engeki Geinō Kanshō-za, 1974.
"Japanese Music (History and Theory)." Excellent articles by experts written for the educational program of the National Theater.

1·14 *Nihon ongaku daijiten*. Hirano Kenji, ed. Tokyo: Heibonsha, 1989.
"Encyclopedia of Japanese Music."

1·15 Piggott, Francis. *The Music and Musical Instruments of Japan*. London: B. T. Batsford, 1893. Reprint DaCapo Press, 1971.
The first English-language introduction to the field.

1·16 *Studien zur traditionelle Musik Japans*. Robert Gunther, ed. Basel: Baren-reiter, 1979– . (Henceforth STMJ.)
A series of scholarly studies or translations of Japanese studies concerning traditional music. Volumes are listed under topics.

1·17 Takano Tatsuyuki. *Nihon kayōshi*. Tokyo: Shunjūsha, 1926. Reprint 1938.
"The History of Japanese Vocal Music." A work of basic research on the history and texts of Japanese vocal music.

1·18 Tanabe Hisao. *Hōgakuka no tame no ongaku riron*. Tokyo: Hōgakusha, 1977.
"Music Theory for Japanese Musicians." A very useful glossary of basic terms in traditional music practice by the founder of Japanese music research (1883–1985).

1·19 _____. *Hōgaku yōgo jiten*. Tokyo: Tokyōdō Shuppan, 1975.
"A Dictionary of Japanese Musical Terms." A small but very useful reference book.

1·20 _____. *Nihon gakki jiten*. Tokyo: Sōshisha Shuppan, 1964.
"Japanese Musical Instruments." A convenient guide, indexed Western-style.

1·21 _____. *Nihon no ongaku*. Tokyo: Bunka Kenkyūsha, 1954.
"Japanese Music." One of the last of Dr. Tanabe's many books on the subject.

1·22 *Tōyō ongaku sensho*. Tokyo: Tōyō Ongaku Gakkai. 1950– . (Hereafter TOS.)
"Selected Writings on Far Eastern Music." A series of publications on

Asian music, and particularly Japanese genres, sponsored by the Society for Research in Asiatic Music. Volumes are listed under topics. The society also publishes a journal, *Tōyō ongaku kenkyū* (1937– ).

1·23   Tsuge Genichi. *Japanese Music: An Annotated Bibliography*. New York: Garland, 1986.
A guide to European-language sources on the topic.


## CHAPTER TWO: RELIGIOUS MUSIC

2·1   Ashkenazi, Michael. *Matsuri*. Honolulu: University of Hawaii Press, 1993.
A survey of Japanese festivals.

2·2   *Bukkyō ongaku no kenkyū*. TOS, Vol. 12, 1954.
"Studies in Buddhist Music."

2·3   Giesen, Walter. *Zur Geschichte des buddhistischen Ritualgesangs in Japan*, STMJ, Vol. 1, 1977.
Translations and commentary on basic historical treatises from the Tendai *shōmyō* tradition. Includes notation and transcriptions, with English and Japanese summaries.

2·4   Hoff, Frank. "Shinto and the Performing Arts" in *Cornell East Asia Papers*, No. 15. Ithaca: China-Japan Program, 1978, 139–223.
A survey of the basic theories of Honda Yasuji concerning folk *kagura* (see below).

2·5   Honda Yasuji. *Dentō geinō no keifu*. Tokyo: Kinseisha, 1986.
"The Lineage of Traditional Theatricals." A survey of historical records on the growth of Japanese theatricals.

2·6   _____. *Kagura. Nihon no minzoku geinō I*. Tokyo: Mokujisha, 1966.
"Japanese Folk Forms of *Kagura*."

2·7   _____. *Nihon no matsuri to geinō*. Tokyo: Kinseisha, 1974.
"Japanese Festivals and Theatricals."

2·8   Iwahara Teishin. *Shōmyō no kenkyū*. Kyoto: Fujii Sahei, 1932.
"A Study of *Shōmyō*." A detailed study of the Nanzan school of Buddhist chant.

2·9    Matsudaira Makoto. *Gendai Nippon matsuri kō*. Tokyo: Shōgakukan, 1994.
"Thoughts on Contemporary Japanese Festivals."

2·10   Nelson, Steven G. "Buddhist Chant of Shingi-Shingon: A Guide to Readers
and Listeners" in *Shingi shingon shōmyō shūsei gakufuhen*. Tokyo: Shingi
Shingonshū Buzan-ha Bukkyō Seinenkai, 1999.
Scholarly commentary for a two-volume set of original notations and transcriptions of *shōmyō* that includes CD recordings.

2·11   *Nihon matsuri to nenjū gyōji jiten*. Kurabayashi Shōji, ed. Tokyo: Ōfūsha, 1983.
"A Dictionary of Japanese Festivals and Yearly Processions."

2·12   Ōyama Kōjun. *Bukkyō ongaku to shōmyō*. Osaka: Tōhō Shuppan, 1989.
"Buddhist Music and *Shōmyō*." Music history plus details of chant music
theory, with an index. Some notation.

2·13   Sakaki Taijun. *Nihon bukkyō geinōshi kenkyū*. Tokyo: Kazama Shobō, 1983.
"Research in the History of Japanese Buddhist Theatricals."

2·14   *Wakayamaryū edobayashi tsukechō*. Tokyo: Hōseidō, 1996.
A collection of all the basic pieces of the Wakayama school of Edo festival
music in traditional notation plus cassettes of both beginner and professional
performances. A second set, *Kotobuki shishi tsukechō*, contains dance music.

See also 1·1


CHAPTER THREE: GAGAKU

3·1    Garfias, Robert. *Music of a Thousand Autumns*. Berkeley: University of California Press, 1975.
An excellent doctoral thesis on the *tōgaku* style of Japanese court music.

3·2    *Gosenfu ni yoru gagaku sōfu*. Shiba Sukehiro, ed. Tokyo: Kawaigakufu,
1968–72. 4 vols.
"Gagaku Instrumental Music in Western Notation." The basic *gagaku*
instrumental and vocal repertoire in Western notation plus extensive notes,
charts, and some original notation.

3·3    Hayashi Kenzō. *Gagaku*. TOS, Vol. 10.

Studies of instrumental notation from the eighth to the tenth century by the founder of *gagaku* research.

3·4 Markham, Elizabeth. *Saibara*. Cambridge: Cambridge University Press, 1983. 2 vols.
Research and attempted transcriptions of notations from Heian period sources.

3·5 Murasaki Shikibu. *The Tale of Genji*, trans. by Edward G. Seidensticker. New York: Knopf, 1978.
A book filled with musical events in an excellent translation.

3·6 *Musica Asiatica*. Laurence Picken, ed. Oxford: Oxford University Press, 1977–.
This series of publications contains many articles on ancient Chinese music as reflected in Korean and Japanese sources. Studies by Alan Marett, R. F. Wolpert, and Steven G. Nelson are included.

3·7 Nelson, Steven G. "Gagaku: Its Past and Present" in *Gagaku no dezain*. Ōno Tadamaro, ed. Tokyo: Shōgakukan, 1990.
This excellent essay is part of a folio-sized "The Design of Gagaku" publication with color plates of *bugaku* dances and costumes.

3·8 Ogi Mitsuo. *Nihon kodai ongaku shiron*. Tokyo: Yoshikawa Kōbunkan, 1978.
"Historical Theory of Ancient Japanese Music." A more sociological study of *gagaku*.

3·9 *Shōsōin no gakki* and *Shōsōin no men*. Tokyo: Nihon Keizai Shimbunsha, 1967.
"Shōsōin Instruments" and "Shōsōin Masks." Two stunning books of photographs, with measurements and documentation, on the instruments and masks surviving in the Shōsōin.

3·10 Yamada Yoshio. *Genji monogatari no ongaku*. Tokyo: Hōbunkan, 1969.
"Music in *The Tale of Genji*." All the music-related passages organized by genre or instrument.

See also 1·1

4·1    Bethe, Monica, and Brazell, Karen. *Dance in the Nō Theater*, Vol. 29. Cornell East Asia Papers. Ithaca: Cornell University China-Japan Program, 1982.
Three volumes of wonderful details on the tradition. Vol. 16 of the same series gives the choreography, vocal and drum music, and text for the *kuse* of *Yamamba*. A videotape is also available.

4·2    Bethe, Monica, and Emmert, Richard. *Noh Performance Guide*, Vol. 1. Tokyo: National Noh Theater, 1992.
The first of a set of *noh* play guides which includes Japanese text, romanization, interline English, and a full translation plus the formal markings of the play. This volume is *Matsukaze*. More of these exceptional play guides are published regularly.

4·3    Emmert, Richard. "Hiranori" in *Musical Voices of Asia*. Tokyo: The Japan Foundation, 1980.
A detailed study of *noh* rhythm performance practices.

4·4    _____. "The Maigoto of Nō—a Musical Analysis of the Chū no Mai" in *Yearbook for Traditional Music*, Vol. 15, 1983.
An informative study of one *noh* dance piece.

4·5    Komparu Kunio. *The Noh Theater*. Tokyo: Weatherhill, 1983.
An interesting general book by the architect son of a *noh* musician.

4·6    Miyake Kōichi. *Fushi no seikai*. Tokyo: Hinoki Shoten, 1955.
The three publications listed are textbooks meant to help amateur performers. This one, "A Detailed Commentary on Melody," explains *noh* singing.

4·7    _____. *Jibyōshi seikai*. Tokyo: Hinoki Shoten, 1954.
A textbook on *noh* rhythm.

4·8    _____. *Shidai kara kiri made no utaikata*. Tokyo: Hinoki Shoten, 1952.
A discussion of musical problems in singing each section of *noh* drama with examples.

4·9    Morita Misao. *Yōkyoku mai hyōshi taisei*. Osaka: Yoshida Yōkyoku Shoten, 1914.
One of the few books in which *hayashi* music is written in score.

4·10    *The Noh Drama: Ten Plays, Selected and Translated from the Japanese*, Vol. 1.

Tokyo: Charles E. Tuttle, 1955. Vols. 2 and 3 are entitled *Japanese Noh Drama*. Tokyo: Nippon Gakujutsu Shinkōkai, 1959, 1960.
A special series of thirty *noh* plays prepared by the Japanese UNESCO Committee.

4.11   *Yōkyoku hyakuban*. Nishino Haruo, ed. Tokyo: Iwanami Shoten, 1998.
One of many scholarly editions of *noh* drama texts with notes.


CHAPTER FIVE: *BIWA*

5.1   De Ferranti, Hugh. "Composition and Improvisation in Satsuma Biwa" in *Musica Asiatica*, Vol 6. Cambridge: Cambridge University Press, 1991, 102–27.

5.2   Guignard, Silvain. "Structure and Performance of a Melodic Pattern, *Haru Nagashi*, in Chikuzenbiwa" in *The Oral and the Literate in Music*. Tokumaru Yoshiko and Yamaguchi Osamu, eds. Tokyo: Academia Music, 1986, 273–87.

5.3   *Heikebiwa katari to ongaku*. Kamisangō Yūkō, ed. Tokyo: Hitsuji Shobō, 1993.
"The Narration and Music of *Heikebiwa*." A good series of articles on the topic including one in English, "Orality and Textual Variation in the Heike Monogatari," by Eric Rutledge.

5.4   Kimura Rirō. *Higo biwahiki Yamashika Yoshiyuki yobanashi*. Tokyo: Sanichi Shobō, 1994.
"The Autobiography of Yamashika Yoshiyuki, a Blind *Biwa* Player."

5.5   Kishibe Shigeo. "The Origin of the P'ip'a" in *The Transactions of the Asiatic Society of Japan*, second series, Vol. 19 (December 1940), 261–304 and plates.
A detailed study of the three types of lutes that entered Japan.

5.6   McCullough, Helen. *Tale of the Heike*. Stanford: Stanford University Press, 1988.
A full translation of the entire epic on which a large part of the *biwa* narrative tradition is based.

5.7   Ruch, Barbara. "Medieval Jongleurs and the Making of a National Literature" in *Japan in the Muromochi Age*. John Hall and Toyoda Takeshi, eds. Berkeley: University of California Press, 1977.

An excellent essay on the oral roots of Japanese literature, from nuns through *biwa* narrators.

5·8 Schmitz, Heinz-Eberhard. *Satsumabiwa*. STMJ, Vol. 7, 1994.
A two-volume dissertation on the instrumental sections of this narrative tradition. It include photographs, original notation, transcriptions, and analysis with English and Japanese summaries.

5·9 Tateyama Zennoshin. *Heike ongaku shi*. Tokyo: Kimura Anjū, 1910. Reprint 1978.
"The History of Heike Music." The classic study of the history and performance.

5·10 Ōtsubo Sōjirō. *Chikuzenbiwa monogatari*. Tokyo: Asahishinbunsha, 1929. Reprint 1983.
"The Story of the *Chikuzenbiwa*." The history and practice of the tradition as heard from its founder, Tachibana Kyokuō.


CHAPTER SIX: SHAKUHACHI

6·1 Berger, Donald Paul. "The Shakuhachi and the Kinko Ryū Notation" in *Asian Music*, 1–2, 1969.
Useful details on fingerings and the meanings of notation symbols.

6·2 Blasdel, Christopher. *The Shakuhachi: A Manual for Learning*. Tokyo: Ongaku no Tomosha, 1988.
A useful English guide to playing the *shakuhachi*. Includes a translation of a historical survey by Kamisangō Yūkō.

6·3 Fritsch, Ingrid. *Die Solo-Honkyoku der Tozan-Schule*. STMJ, Vol. 4, 1979.
Research on solo *honkyoku* pieces in the Tozan school.

6·4 Gould, Michael, and Taniguchi Yoshinobu. *How to Play Classical Shakuhachi*. Willits, CA: Tai Hei Shakuhachi, 1996.

6·5 Gutzwiller, Andreas. *Die Shakuhachi der Kinko-Schule*. STMJ, Vol. 5, 1983.
Research on the Kinko school style of performance.

6·6 Kōzuki Enzan. *Shakuhachi seisakuhō taizen*. Tokyo: Takeda Tōshadō, 1933. 2 vols. Reprint 1977.

"A Complete Guide to Making a *Shakuhachi*." A rare book dealing with the actual making of the instrument.

6.7  *Shakuhachi Encyclopedia of Musical Instruments*. Tanimura Kō, ed. Tokyo: Ongakusha, 1990.
A book of photographs and articles about the *shakuhachi*.

6.8  Tanaka Inzan. *Gosenfu kara shakuhachi no torikata*. Tokyo: Ongaku no Tomosha, 1956.
"Transcribing *Shakuhachi* Music into Five-Line Notation."

6.9  Toya Deiko. *Komusō shakuhachi shinan*. Fukuoka: Komusō Kenkyūkai, 1984.
"Instructions for *Komusō Shakuhachi*." A history and playing methodology for both concert and street performances, including how to play under a basket hat.

6.10  Ueno Katami. *Shakuhachi no rekishi*. Tokyo: Kyōwa Shuppansha, 1983.
"The History of the *Shakuhachi*." A scholarly book with a good bibliography.

6.11  Weisgarber, Elliot. "The *honkyoku* of the Kinko-ryū" in *Ethnomusicology*, Vol. 12, No. 3, 1968.
A transcription and discussion of the tradition.


CHAPTER SEVEN: *KOTO*

7.1  Ackermann, Peter. *Studien zur koto-musik von Edo*. STMJ, Vol. 6, 1986.
A study of Edo period *koto* music.

7.2  Adriaansz, Willem. *The Danmono of Japanese Koto Music*. Berkeley: University of California Press, 1973.
A study of traditional solo instrumental *koto* music.

7.3  Gunther, Robert, and Mabuchi Usaburo. *Quellen zur Kammermusik der Edo-Zeit*. STMJ, Vol. 3, 1985.
A study of chamber music in the Edo period.

7.4  *Ikutaryū sōkyoku zenshū*. Tokyo: Hōgakusha, 1983–84. 4 vols.
"A Complete Collection of Ikuta School *Koto* Music." Ikuta and Western music notation are included.

7.5 Kikkawa Eishi. *The History of Japanese Koto Music and Ziuta*, with two CDs. Trans. with supplements by Leonard C. Holvik, ed. by Yamaguti Osamu. Tokyo: Mita Press, 1997.
Studies by one of Japan's *koto* experts translated by one of America's devotees.

7.6 Matsuda Tōshū. *Sōkyoku kashi kaimei*. Tokyo: Hōgakusha, 1983.
"An Elucidation of the History of *Koto* Vocal Chamber Music."

7.7 *Sōkyoku to jiuta*. TOS, Vol. 3, 1967.
"*Koto* Music and *Jiuta*." Scholarly articles on these topics.

7.8 Tsuge Genichi. *Anthology of Sōkyoku and Jiuta Song Texts*. Tokyo: Academia Music, 1983.
A fine collection of the texts and history of the *koto* tradition. Includes original Japanese.

7.9 Wade, Bonnie C. *Tegotomono*. London: Greenwood Press, 1976.
A study of five traditional *koto* compositions including Western transcriptions.

7.10 *Yamadaryū sōkyoku gakufu*. Tokyo: Hōgakusha, 1957– .
"Yamada School *Koto* Music Notation." The standard collection of the Yamada school performance repertoire.

7.11 Yamazaki Shinko. *Yatsuhashiryū koto kumiuta no kenkyū*. Kikkawa Eishi, ed. Tokyo: Zenongakufu Shuppansha, 1988.
"A Study of *Kumiuta* in the Yatsuhashi *Koto* School." The history of the tradition and its thirteen basic pieces in both traditional and Western notation.

7.12 Yoshida Bungo. *Nihon no koto*. Hiroshima: Keisuisha, 1984.
"The Japanese *Koto*." A historical study with good bibliographic notes.


CHAPTER EIGHT: SHAMISEN

8.1 Atsumi Seitarō. *Hōgaku buyō*. Tokyo: Fuzambō, 1956.
"A Dictionary of Classical Dance Music." A basic reference book.

8.2 Crihfield, Liza. *Ko-uta: "Little Songs" of the Geisha World*. Tokyo: Charles E. Tuttle, 1979.
A short history and text translations of *kouta* in Kyoto.

8·3    Gerstle, C. A., Inobe, K., and Malm, W. *Theater as Music.* Ann Arbor: Center for Japanese Studies, 1990.
A interdisciplinary study of the "Imoseyama no dan" act from *Imoseyama onna teikin.* It contains text, structure, and musical analysis, plus a complete translation and cassettes of complete scenes.

8·4    Gerstle, C. A. *Circles of Fantasy.* Cambridge, MA: Harvard University Press, 1986.
A detailed study of the form of *bunraku* plays and of the writings of Takemoto Gidayū.

8·5    Keene, Donald. *Bunraku.* Tokyo: Kodansha International, 1965.
A handsome book on the plays and puppets of *bunraku.*

8·6    Malm, William. *Nagauta: The Heart of Kabuki Music.* Tokyo: Charles E. Tuttle, 1963.
A doctoral thesis on the topic.

8·7    _____. "The Rise of Concert Shamisen Music in Nineteenth-Century Japan" in *Recovering the Orient: Artists, Scholars, Appropriations.* Bob Haddad, ed. Reading, U.K.: Harwood, 1994.
A comparison of rising middle class music in Europe and Japan.

8·8    _____. *Six Hidden Views of Japanese Music.* Berkeley: University of California Press, 1986.
Selective studies of drum and *shamisen* music.

8·9    *Shamisen to sono ongaku.* TOS, Vol. 7, 1978.
"The *Shamisen* and Its Music." A series of scholarly articles on the subject.

8·10   Tokita, Alice. *Kiyomoto-bushi: Narrative Music of the Kabuki Theatre.* STMJ, 2000.
A major study of narrative *shamisen* music.


CHAPTER NINE: *KABUKI*

9·1    Brandon, James. *Kabuki: Five Classical Plays.* Honolulu: University of Hawaii Press, 1992.
Translations including music cue sheets.

9.2   Brandon, James, Malm, W., and Shively, D. *Studies in Kabuki*. Honolulu: University of Hawaii Press, 1978.
Studies in the social history, acting styles, and music of *kabuki*.

9.3   Ernst, Earle. *The Kabuki Theater*. Honolulu: University of Hawaii Press, 1956.
A standard early study of *kabuki*.

9.4   Gunji Masakatsu. *Kabuki*. Tokyo: Kodansha International, 1969. Revised 1985.
A standard introduction to the topic.

9.5   Halford, Aubrey. *The Kabuki Handbook*. Tokyo: Charles E. Tuttle, 1956.
Useful summaries of play plots.

9.6   *Kabuki*. TOS, Vol. 12, 1980.
Articles on *kabuki* music.

9.7   *Kabuki Encyclopedia*. Samuel Leiter, ed. London: Greenwood Press, 1979.
An English adaptation of *Kabuki jiten*. Yamamoto Jirō and others, eds. Tokyo: Heibonsha, 1979. Reprint 1984.

9.8   Kineya Eizaemon. *Kabuki ongaku shūsei*. Tokyo: Kabuki Ongaku Shūsei Kankōkai, 1976.
"A Compilation of Kabuki Music." All the basic *geza shamisen* pieces in Western notation, with uses in specific plays described.

9.9   Mochizuki Tainosuke. *Kabuki no geza ongaku*. Tokyo: Engeki Shuppansha, 1975.
"Kabuki Offstage Music." Reference to *geza* patterns and melodies, as well as their positions in specific plays.


CHAPTER TEN: FOLK AND POPULAR

10.1   Fujisawa Morihiko. *Hayariuta hyakunenshi*. Tokyo: Daiichi Shuppansha, 1951.
"A Hundred Years of Popular Music." Texts and information on Meiji popular music.

10.2   Groemer, Gerald. *Bakumatsu no hayariuta*. Tokyo: Meicho Shuppan, 1995.
An excellent study of popular music in the last half of the nineteenth century. It includes transcriptions.

10·3 Hughes, David. " 'Esashi Oiwake' and the Beginnings of Modern Japanese Folk Song" in *The World of Music*, Vol. 34, 1992.
A rare study of modern folk song.

10·4 Koizumi Fumio. *Nihon dentō ongaku no kenkyū*. Tokyo: Ongaku no Tomosha, 1957.
"A Study of Japanese Traditional Music." A basic contemporary interpretation of tone systems in Japanese folk music.

10·5 Kojima Tomiko and Fujii Tomoaki. *Nihon no oto no bunka*. Tokyo: Daiichi Shobō, 1994.
"The Culture of Japanese Sound." Ethnomusicogical studies on many aspects of Japanese music, but mostly folk.

10·6 Misumi Haruo. *Minzoku no geinō*. Tokyo: Kawade Shobō, 1964.
"Folk Theatricals." An introduction to Japanese folk theatricals.

10·7 *Nihon minyō daijiten*. Asano Kenji, ed. Tokyo: Yūzankaku, 1983.
"An Encyclopedia of Japanese Folk Songs." A good reference book.

10·8 *Nihon minyō taikan*, Tokyo: Nihon Hōsō Shuppan Kyōkai, 1953– .
"A General Survey of Japanese Folk Songs." Several volumes of Western transcriptions and commentaries by NHK music staff on the music of each prefecture in Japan.

10·9 *Nihon no minyō to minzoku*. TOS, Vol. 1, 1967.
"Japanese Folk Songs and Folk Culture." A collection of folk music studies.

10·10 Nishiyama Matsunosuke. *Edo Culture: Daily Life and Diversions in Urban Japan, 1600–1868*, trans. by Gerald Groemer. Honolulu: University of Hawaii Press, 1997.
A charming and valuable study filled with musical references.

10·11 Philippi, Donald. *Songs of Gods, Songs of Humans*. Tokyo: Tokyo University Press, 1975.
The texts of *yukar* and other Ainu songs.

10·12 Soeda Tomomichi. *Enka no Meiji Taishō shi*. Tokyo: Tōsui Shobō, 1982.
"A History of Meiji and Taishō Period Theater Songs." Song texts and history plus some notation.

10·13 _____. *Ryūkōka Meiji Taishō shi*. Tokyo: Tōsui Shobō, 1952.
"A History of Meiji and Taishō Popular Music." Song texts and history of
period pieces.


# APPENDIX I

A·1 *Musical Notation of Japan*. Steven G. Nelson, ed. Tokyo: Ueno Gakuen
University, 1983.
Collection of rare Japanese notations with English notes.

A·2 *Nihon ongakushi kenkyū*. Fukushima Kazuo, ed. Tokyo: Research Archive
for Japanese Music, 1996– .
"Japanese Music History Studies." A series providing the English-language
versions of research on notation found in the special Japanese music archive
at Ueno Gakuen University, the most comprehensive collection in the world
on this subject.

A·3 *Sources of Early Japanese Music*. Hirano Kenji and Fukushima Kazuo, eds.
Tokyo: Benseisha, 1978.
One volume of facsimiles of Japanese vocal notation and one of instrumental notation from the Ueno Gakuen University archive. English and Japanese commentaries.

# GLOSSARY / INDEX

This glossary/index is designed to be of use to both the general reader and the researcher. All major music terms have been defined and musicians identified. Many terms have several meanings and extensive ramifications, but they are defined here only as used in this book. Alternative pronunciations or terms are included. Waseda Minko, Nagahara Tomo, and Dana Buck are thanked for their help in compiling this document, and John Stewart for computer assistance.

Letters in parentheses after a page number refer to the following: "pl." is a plate, "fig." is a figure, "d." is a drawing, and "fn." is a footnote. The letter "f." means that there is a further reference to the subject on the following pages, and "ff." implies that there are references for several pages. "tr." is followed by track numbers on the CD of related examples.

Azuchi-Momoyama (安土・桃山) period
(1568–1600), 39, 42
*azuma asobi* (東遊, a *mikagura* dance genre),
49, 50, 54 (fig. 4), 82 (pl. 4)
"Azuma hakkei" (吾妻八景, a *nagauta* piece),
232

Bach, Johann Sebastian, 50, 289
*bachi* (撥, generic term for a plectrum or
drumstick), 57, 103, 106, 126, 160, 163, 190
(pl. 75), 215, 218
*bachigawa* (撥皮, a patch on a *shamisen* that
protects the front skin from plectrum
stokes), 214
*bachimen* (撥面, material or lacquer protect-
ing the *biwa* soundboard from plectrum
strokes), 156
*bai* (唄, a Buddhist chant in Sanskrit), 72
*bakase*: *see hakase*
bamboo instruments: *see* flutes, *hitoyogiri,
paixiao, sasara, shakuhachi, takebue, tempuku, xiao, yotsudake*
*ban* (番, a class of *biwa* melodic patterns), 163
*bangi* or *hangi* (盤木or板木・版木, Buddhist
wooden idiophone), 73 (d.)
banquet songs: *see* party music
*banshiki* (盤渉, the pitch B in ancient music
theory), 114 (fig. 12)
*banshikichō* (盤渉調, a Japanese mode built
on B), 114 (fig. 13), 115 (fn. 6)
*banzuke* (番付, theater performance ads), 237
bass *koto*: *see jūshichigen*
bells, 70 ff., 248; *see also bonshō, ekiro, hanshō,
hitotsugane, ōgane, orugōru, rei, suzu*
*binzasara* (びんざさら・編木, a folk idiophone), 62 (d.), 87 (pl. 14)
*biwa* (琵琶, a plucked lute), 35 f., 41, 45, 93
(pl. 30), 106, 112, 116 f., 127, 149–164, 183
(pl. 51), 193, 195, 196, 197 (fn. 6), 207, 214,
215, 271, 275, 282, 290–293, 297, trs. 8–11
*biwahōshi* (琵琶法師, blind *biwa* players), 41,
149, 151, 217
blind musicians, 41, 149, 151, 182 (pl. 48), 187
(pl. 58), 197 f., 200
Boccaccio, Giovanni, 169

*bon odori* (盆踊, a type of folk dance), 27, 77,
90 (pl. 24), 268, tr. 19
*bonsan* (梵讃, Buddhist chant in an ancient
Indian dialect), 67
*bonshō* (梵鐘): *see ōgane*
bridges, 204, 207; *see also koma, ji*
Britten, Benjamin, 277
Buddhism, 33, 35 ff., 48, 62, 65, 66 ff., 80, 128,
151, 168, 217, 268
Buddhist music, 35, 66–78, 99 f., 106, 121, 122,
129, 159, 175, 249, 275, 279, 298, tr. 4
*bugaku* (舞楽, court dances and their music),
74, 91 (pl. 26), 94 (pl. 33), 95 (pl. 34), 97, 103,
112 f., 268
*bungobushi* (豊後節, a narrative *shamisen*
genre founded by Miyakoji Bungonojō),
219 (fig. 29), 221, 228
*bunkafu* (文化譜, a modern *shamisen* notation), 296 f., 297 (fig. 57)
*bunraku* (文楽, a generic term for Japanese
puppet theater), 40 f., 188 (pl. 61), 206,
224, 228, 268, 269, 275
*bushi* (節, a generic term for song; used as a
suffix), 76
*buyō* (舞踊, Japanese classical dancing), 231

Calypso, 76
Canada, 268
*cantus firmus*, 72
*Cantus Gregorianus*, 79
Catholicism, 66, 67, 73,
Central Asia, 106
ceremonies, 47, 49, 71 f., 120, 121; Ainu, 267;
Christian, 79; Buddhist, 121; Shinto, 49 f.
chamber music, 41, 102, 209, 276; *see also
jiuta, sankyoku*
*chappa* (チャッパ, small cymbals), 246 (d.),
249
*charumera* (チャルメラ, noodle seller's
double-reed horn), 271
*chi* (徴, a pitch in old Japanese scale systems), 68
"Chidori" (千鳥, a *koto* piece also used in
*geza* music), 210, 247, 295
Chikamatsu Monzaemon (近松門左衛門,

a famous playwright for the puppet and *kabuki* theaters), 41, 224

*chikuzenbiwa* (筑前琵琶, a genre of lute music and its instrument), 151 f., 155 (d.), 156, 161, 162, 163, 182 (pl. 49), 291 (fig. 49), 292 (fig. 50), tr. 11

*ch'in* (琴): *see qin*

China, 31ff., 38, 42 f., 66, 80, 97 f., 106, 109 f., 113, 150, 163, 168, 174, 194, 199, 213, 236, 266

*chindonya* (チンドン屋, street music ensemble), 89 (pl. 21), 271

Chinese music, 51, 100, 165, 196, 211, 249, 275, 283, 294

*chirashi* (チラシ, a closing section in *shamisen* music), 232, 234, 235 (fig. 32)

*chirikara byōshi* (チリカラ拍子, *kabuki*-style drum rhythms), 234, 289, 290 (fig. 48)

*chō* (丁, a class of *biwa* melodic patterns), 163

*chobo* (チョボ, *gidayū* musicians in a *kabuki* performance), 241

Chōkei (長恵, a Buddhist music theorist), 67

*chōnin* (町人, Japanese merchant class), 40, 123

chordophones: *see biwa, gakusō, gogenbiwa, ichigenkin, jamisen, jūshichigen, kokyū, koto, kugo, nigenkin, pipa, qin, sanshin, sanxian, shamisen, shichigenkin, sō, taishōgoto, tonkori, wagon, yakumogoto*

chorus, 35, 51, 70, 73, 76 f., 97, 104, 117 f., 119, 124, 126 ff., 129, 146, 281

*chōshigami* (調子紙, tuning paper for the *kotsuzumi* drum), 138

Christianity, 39, 67, 78–80, 168, 279; *see also* Catholicism

*chū, chū osae, chū uki* (中, 中オサエ, 中ウキ, pitches in *noh* scales), 130 (fig. 14)

"Chū no mai" (中の舞, a *noh* dance piece), 286 (fig. 46), 287 (fig. 47), 288 f.

chūnori (中乗り, a *noh* rhythm category), 131

Chūai (仲哀), Emperor, 49

*Chūshingura* (忠臣蔵, a *bunraku* or *kabuki* play), 243

composers, Japanese, 29, 30, 99, 102, 112, 171, 200, 211, 237: *see also* Fujiwara, Ikuta, Jōjuin, Kenjun, Kineya, Kishimoto,

Kiyomoto, Mamiya, Manshōin, Miyagi, Nakanoshima, Shōbutsu, Takemitsu, Takemoto, Yamada

composition, 102, 147, 211, 232, 237

Confucianism, 33, 51 (fn. 7), 100 (fn. 2), 194, 196

counterpoint, 210

court music, 33 f., 35, 37, 43, 55, 66, 93 (pl. 31), 195 ff.; *see also gagaku*

cue sheet, 144 (fig. 18), 255

Curlew River, 277

*dadaiko* (大太鼓, largest *gagaku* drum), 96 (pl. 36), 103, 113

*daibiro* (台広, a special *shamisen* bridge used in *sankyoku*), 207 (fn. 17)

*daibyōshi* (大拍子, a drum used in the *geza*), 57, 85 (pl. 10), 246 (d.), 248, 252

*daishō* (大小, abbreviation of *tsuzumi* names), 232

*dan* (段, a generic term for a section of music in various forms); in *noh*, 125 f., 136, 143, 288; in *koto* music, 208; in *gidayū*, 226

*dan no fu* (段の譜, *noh* flute pattern), 136, 289

*dan'awase* (段合, a special duet technique in *koto* music), 209

dance, 24 (pl. 1), 32 f., 35, 49, 50, 54 f., 63, 77, 80, 97 f., 103, 110, 113, 116, 120, 122, 124, 127 f., 135, 143, 152, 154, 199, 200, 202, 231, 234, 239, 268

dancing religion, 65

*dangire* (段切, the final section in *nagauta* music), 232, 236

*debayashi* (出囃子, the musicians on stage in *kabuki*), 191 (pl. 77), 240

deer dance: *see shikaodori*

*deha* (出端, *hayashi* prelude to acts in *noh* and beginning sections in *kabuki* and dance music), 127

Dejima (出島), 39

*dengaku* (田楽, a folk theatrical and predecessor of *noh*), 37, 56, 86 (pl. 12), 120 f., 268, 269

devil dances, 63, 64 (fig. 6)

*Digest of Music Matters: see Gakusho yōroku*

Fujiwara no Yukinaga (藤原行長, supposed author of *Heike monogatari*), 152

Fukeshū (普化宗, a Zen Buddhist sect containing *shakuhachi* players), 168

"Fuki" (富貴, the traditional first piece of *tsukushigoto* music), 197 f.

Fukui (福井) prefecture, 259 (pl. 87), 270

Fukuō (福王, a guild of *waki* actors in *noh*), 146 (fig19)

*fūryū* or *furyū* (風流, street parades and fancy clothes), 121, 268, 272

*fushi* (節, generic term for melody), 130

*fushō* (鳬鐘, the note G-sharp in ancient music theory), 114 (fig. 12)

*gagaku* (雅楽, court orchestra music), 35, 65, 67, 74, 94 (pl. 32), 97–118, 114 (fig. 13), 125, 133, 150, 153, 165, 195, 198, 204, 242, 248, 252, 255, 275, 281, 283–286, tr. 5

*Gagakuryō* (雅楽寮, the ancient Imperial Music Bureau), 99

*gaikyoku* (外曲, *shakuhachi* music borrowed from *shamisen* or *koto* music), 173, 175

*gakubiwa* (楽琵琶, the lute used in *gagaku*), 106 (d.), 150, 156 f., 181 (pl. 46), 283

*gakudaiko* (楽太鼓, an offstage drum in *kabuki*), 103, 246 (d.), 248, 252

*Gakusho yōroku* (楽書要録, Chinese music books brought to Japan in 735), 99

*gakusō* (楽箏, a *gagaku* zither), 112, 117, 194, 204, 283

*ge* (下, a pitch in *noh* scales), 130 (fig. 14)

*ge osae* (下オサエ, an alternate pitch in *noh*), 130 (fig. 14)

*geinō* (芸能): *see minzoku geinō*

geisha (芸者), 42, 213, 223, 229, 230, 242

*gekibushi* (外記節, an early *shamisen* narrative genre founded by Satsuma Geki 薩摩外記), 219 (fig. 29), 220 (fn. 4); *see also* Fujiwara no Naomasa

Genji (源氏) clan: *see* Minamoto

*Genji monogatari* (源氏物語): *see* Tale of Genji, The

Genji (源氏), Prince, 195 f.

"Genjōraku" (還城楽, a *bugaku* piece), 98

Genroku (元禄) era (1688–1704), 40

*gendai hōgaku* (現代邦楽, late twentieth century compositions for traditional instruments), 211

*genzaimono* (現在物, "present-day" plays in *zatsu noh* category), 124

*geza, geza ongaku* (下座, 下座音楽, offstage *kabuki* music), 191 (pl. 76), 241 ff., 254 f.

*gidayūbushi* (義太夫節, major narrative *shamisen* genre founded by Takemoto Gidayū), 163, 188 (pls. 60, 61), 190 (pl. 75), 219 (fig. 29), 223–229, 240 f., 250 ff., 297, 298 (fig. 58), tr. 14

Gifu (岐阜) prefecture, 259 (pl. 86), 263 (fig. 35), 269

*gigaku* (伎楽, an ancient Chinese theatrical used in Japan; now a folk form), 98

Gilyaks, 266

Giō (祇王・妓王, a heroine in *Tale of the Heike*), 55

Gion shrine (祇園神社), 96 (pls. 36, 37)

*gō* (号, a class of *biwa* melodic patterns), 163

*goeika* (御詠歌, Buddhist congregational music; often a folk hymn), 76, 90 (pl. 23)

*gogenbiwa* (五弦琵琶, a defunct Chinese court lute surviving in the Shōsōin warehouse), 92 (pl. 29), 106

*gohei* (御幣, Shinto wand), 59, 62

*goinfu* (五音譜, a Buddhist chant notation), 280 (figs. 39, 40), 281

*goinhakase* or *goinbakase* (五音博士, Buddhist chant notation), 279, 280 (fig. 38)

*goinsanjū* (五音三重, Buddhist chant notation), 279

*gomafu* or *gomaten* (胡麻譜 or 胡麻点, Buddhist chant notation), 281 (fig. 41), 282

gong, 47, 71 ff., 76, 77, 248; *see also dora, kane*

"Gorō Tokimune" (五郎時致, a *nagauta* piece), 232, 233 (fig. 31), 235 (fig. 32), 290 (fig. 48), tr. 16

"Goshōraku" (五常楽, a *gagaku* piece), 116

Greece, 66

Gregorian chant, 33, 67

Guido d'Arezzo, 67

guilds, 53, 133, 135, 143, 145, 146 (fig. 19), 153,

*Jōrurihime monogatari* (浄瑠璃姫物語, an early narrative, source of the term *jōruri*), 217

*jushi* (呪師, old form of temple entertainment), 121

*jūshichigen* (十七弦, seventeen-string bass *koto*), 204

*kabuki* (歌舞伎, the main popular Japanese theatrical), 40 f., 77, 122, 138, 145, 154, 169 f., 190 (pl. 74), 191 (pls. 76, 77), 192 (pl. 79), 213, 222 f., 224, 231, 232, 234, 239–255, 260 (pl. 88), 268, 270, 275, 289, tr. 17

Kadono (葛野, guild of *ōtsuzumi* drummers), 146 (fig. 19)

*kaede* (替手, a second or obbligato part in *koto* or *shamisen* music), 200, 209

*kagura* (神楽, generic term for Shinto music, also specific genres of it), 38, 48 ff., 52 f., 54, 56 ff., 80, 109, 240, 260 (pl. 89), 268

*kagurabue* (神楽笛, flute for formal Shinto and court music), 54 (d.), 95 (pl. 35), 109, 110

*kaguraden* (神楽殿, a Shinto shrine stage), 62, 87 (pl. 14)

*kagurauta* (神楽歌, a type of Shinto song), 49, 51 (fn. 6), tr. 1

*kakari* (掛・懸・カカリ・かかり, opening section of *noh* dance music and music style in *gidayūbushi*), 136, 143, 227 (fig. 30)

*kakeai* (掛合), 250

*kakegoe* (掛声, drum calls), 132 (fig. 15), 141, 142, 254, 288

*kakko* (鞨鼓, small, horizontal drum used in court music), 112, 116 f., 285

*kaku* (角, a note in the old Japanese scale system), 68

Kakui (覚意, creator of a thirteenth-century Buddhist notation system), 279

*kakure kirishitan* (隠れキリシタン・隠切支丹, secret Christian sects during the Edo period), 79

Kamakura (鎌倉), 45, 153

"Kamakura" (鎌倉, a festival ensemble piece), 59

Kamakura (鎌倉) period (1185–1333), 36, 66, 101, 120, 151, 152, 153

"Kami mai" (神舞, *noh* dance), 135, 136 (fig. 17)

*kami noh* (神能, congratulatory *noh* plays), 124

*kamigata nagauta* (上方長唄, *nagauta* from the Kyoto/Osaka area), 231

*kamimu* (上無, the note G-sharp in ancient music theory), 114 (fig. 12)

*kamisama* (神様, a spirit or god), 61

*kamishibai* (紙芝居, paper picture narrations), 258 (pl. 83), 268

*kan* (甲, highest pitch in *noh* singing): *see kanguri*

*kan* and *kan no chū* (甲 and 甲ノ中, *noh* flute melodic patterns), 135 (fig. 16)

*kandabayashi* (神田囃子, festival ensemble in Kanda, Tokyo), 58

*kane* (鉦): *see atarigane*

*kangen* (管絃, *gagaku* term for purely instrumental musics), 97, 113, 242, 296

*kanguri* (甲グリ, highest pitch in *noh* tone system), 130 (fig. 14)

*Kanjinchō* (勧進帳, a *kabuki* play), 191 (pl. 27)

*kanjin noh* (勧進能, public subscription *noh* performances), 240

*kankanjōshi* (カンカン調子, Chinese-style tone system), 210

*kanname* (鉋目, patterns carved in drum bodies for tone), 138

Kan'ami Kiyotsugu (観阿弥清次, a founder of *noh*), 38, 122

Kannon (観音, Buddhist goddess of mercy), 62

*kansan* (漢讃, Buddhist chant in Chinese), 67

Kanze (観世, a school of *noh*), 123, 146 (fig. 19)

*karaoke* (カラオケ, popular songs in music-minus-one format for customer singing), 272

*kase* (枷, cappo for *shamisen* neck), 216

*kashira* (頭, cadence pattern for drums), 141, 143, 144 (fig. 18), 180 (pl. 45)

Kasuga shrine (春日大社), 62, 86 (pl. 12)

*katarimono* (語物, generic term for narrative

music), 217 ff., 219 (fig. 29), 222, 228, 237, 268

*katōbushi* (河東節, a *shamisen* genre created by Masumi Katō 十寸見河東), 199, 219 (fig. 29), 221, 228, 237

*kawa* (皮・革, a drum skin), 137

"Kawanakajima" (川中島, a *biwa* composition), 293

"Kawasaki" (川崎, a folk song), 263 (fig. 35)

*kazura noh* (鬘能, female *noh* plays), 124

*kei* (磬, a Buddhist, fish-mouthed bronze chime), 71 (d.)

*kembu* (剣舞, a form of samurai sword dance), 162

*kengyō* (検校, a term like *maestro* used in blind musicians' names), 198 (fn. 7)

Kenjun (賢順, founder of *tsukushigoto*), 197 f.

*kesubi* (消すび, a muffled stroke on the *taiko*), 228

*ki* (木・柝): *see hyōshigi*

Kibi no Makibi (吉備真備, eighth century ambassador to China), 99

*kibigaku* (吉備楽, music for the Kurozumi religious movement, founded in 1814 by Kurozumi Munetada 黒住宗忠), 65

Kichiemon (吉右衛門, a *kabuki* troupe named after Nakamura Kichiemon 中村吉右衛門), 250

*kin* (磬, a bowl-shaped Buddhist bell), 71 (d.)

Kineya (杵屋 or 稀音家, names of two major *nagauta* guilds), 296

Kineya Kisaburō (杵屋喜三郎, *nagauta* musician), 232, 237

Kineya Rokuzaemon X (十世杵屋六左衛門, famous *nagauta* composer), 232, 236, 237

Kinko (琴古, school of *shakuhachi*), 170, 173 (fn. 7)

Kinshin (錦心, early twentieth century school of *satsumabiwa*), 155, 162

*kiri* (キリ・切, ending section of a *noh* drama), 128

*kiri noh* (切能, ending of supernatural *noh* plays), 124

Kishimoto Yoshihide (岸本芳秀, creator of *kibigaku* music), 65

Kita (喜多, school of *noh*), 123, 146 (fig. 19)

*kitsune* (狐, masked fox in dance), 59, 85 (pl. 10)

*kiyomoto* (清元, a *shamisen* genre founded by Kiyomoto Enjudayū 清元延寿太夫), 219 (fig. 29), 222 f., 229, 238, 240, 241, 297

Kiyomoto Eijurō (清元栄寿郎, twentieth century performer/composer), 238

*kizami* (刻み, a *taiko* drum pattern), 145 (fn. 17)

Kō (幸, guild of *kotsuzumi* drummers), 146 (fig. 19)

*kodama* (こだま, mountain echo drum sounds in *kabuki*), 251

Kodō (鼓童, a drum ensemble from Sado Island), 60 (fn. 17)

*Kojiki* (古事記, history, legend, and song textbook dated 712), 31 f., 49, 57

*kojime* (小締, a rope used on the *kotsuzumi*), 138, 140

*kōjinbiwa* (荒神琵琶, a *biwa* and blessings played on it by itinerant traveling priests), 151

*kōken* (後見, stage assistant in *noh*, *kabuki*, and dance), 234

*Kokon chomonshū* (古今著聞集, a thirteenth century collection of tales), 108

"Kokūreibo" (虚空鈴慕, a *shakuhachi* piece), 174

*kokyū* (胡弓, Japan's only bowed lute), 153, 187 (pl. 58), 199, 206 (d.), 242

*koma* (駒, a bridge on a *shamisen* or *kokyū*), 207, 215

*komai* (小舞, *kyōgen* dance), 124

Koma no Chikazane (狛近真, author of *Kyōkunshō*), 99

*komabue* (高麗笛・狛笛, a flute used in *gagaku*), 95 (pl. 35), 109 (d.)

*komagaku* (高麗楽, Japanese court music of Korean origin), 98, 100, 109, 111 f., 116

*komosō* (薦僧, beggar priests of the Muromachi period), 167, 176; *see also komusō*

Komparu (金春, a school of *noh*), 123, 146 (fig. 19)

*komusō* (虚無僧, wandering *shakuhachi*-

playing priests), 167 f., 185 (pl. 54), 167

Kongō (金剛, school of *noh*), 123, 146 (fig. 19)

Korea and Korean music, 31, 33, 39, 43, 45, 51, 98 f., 100 109

Kōsei (幸清, guild of *kotsuzumi* drummers), 146 (fig. 19)

*kosaburōfu* (小三郎譜, a modern *shamisen* notation), 296 (fig. 56)

*kōshiki* (講式, a form of Buddhist chanting), 67, 281

*koten ongaku* (古典音楽, "classical music"), 221

*koto* (箏, thirteen-stringed plucked zither), 30, 35, 41, 42, 45, 52, 65, 114, 153, 155, 170, 175, 186 (pls. 56, 57), 193–211, 204 (d.), 208 (fig. 26), 229, 236, 242, 266, 294 (figs. 53, 54), 294–295, 295 (fig. 55), tr. 13

*kotoba* (詞, heightened speech in *noh* and dialogue in *gidayū*), 127, 130, 226 f., 227 (fig. 30)

*kotsuzumi* (小鼓, an hourglass-shaped drum), 137 (d.), 137–139, 146 (fig. 19), 179 (pls. 43, 44), 190 (pl. 74), 232, 244, 286 ff., 290 (fig. 48)

*kouta* (小唄, genre of short *shamisen* songs), 27, 30, 38, 124, 167, 219 (fig. 29), 229 f., 240, 297, tr. 15

*kouta* (小歌, short songs in *kyōgen*; earlier *shamisen* songs), 124, 229

*ku* (句, episode in narratives), 158

*kuchijamisen* (口三味線, mnemonic version of *shamisen* lines), 296

*kudaragaku* (百済楽, court music from the ancient Korean kingdom of Kudara), 98

*kudoki* (口説, common term for lyrical sections in vocal musics), 127, 159, 232 f., 252, 271

*kudokiuta* (口説歌, a type of Edo period popular music), 271

*kugo* (箜篌, ancient harp), 93 (pl. 30), 106

Kumamoto (熊本) prefecture, 257 (pl. 80)

*kumeuta* (久米歌, ancient *kagura* songs), 32, 49, 50

*kumiuta* (組唄, *shamisen* and/or *koto* suites of songs), 197, 208, 219 (fig. 29), 229

*kumoijōshi* (雲井調子, a *koto* tuning), 205 (fig. 25)

*kuri* (クリ・繰リ, a formal section in *noh*; a high pitch in *noh* and in narrative tone systems), 127, 130 (fig. 14)

*kuromisu* (黒御簾, a screen that hides *geza* musicians from the audience in *kabuki*), 241

*kuromori kabuki* (黒森歌舞伎, outdoor *kabuki* in Sakata, Yamagata prefecture), 270

Kurozumikyō (黒住教, a neo-Shinto religion) 65; *see also kibigaku*

*kuse* (曲, the dance section in the first act of a *noh* play), 127

*kuzure* (崩れ, a *biwa* melodic pattern), 162

*kyōgen* (狂言, comic interludes in *noh*), 122, 124, 125, 127, 146 (fig. 19)

*kyōgenkata* (狂言方, the *hyōshigi* player backstage in *kabuki*; also *kyōgen* performers in *noh*), 247

*Kyōkunshō* (教訓抄, a 1233 book on *gagaku*), 99

*kyōmai* (京舞, dances from Kyoto), 200

*kyōmono* (京物, music from Kyoto), 200

*kyōranmono* (狂乱物, madness plays in *zatsu noh* category), 124

"Kyorei" (虚鈴, a basic *shakuhachi* piece), 174

Kyoto (京都), 36 f., 40, 45, 54 f., 84 (pl. 9), 96 (pls. 36, 37), 101, 121, 122, 149, 151, 152, 168, 177 (pl. 39), 231, 243, 258 (pl. 84)

*kyū* (宮, first note in the ancient Japanese tone system), 68

*kyū* (急, last section of the tripartite formal division), 115 f.; *see also jo-ha-kyū*

Kyushu (九州) Island, 31, 45, 49, 150, 196 f., 218

"left music": *see tōgaku*

lion dances, 25, 48, 59, 63, 85 (pl. 11), 98, 268

lute, 35, 150, 162; *see also biwa, gogen, kokyū, pipa, shamisen*

*machifū* (町風, townspeople style), 161

*machiutai* (待謡, waiting song near start of second act in *noh* drama), 127

*Madame Butterfly*, 228

*shirabe* (調べ, a set of ropes used on drums), 137

"Shirabe" (調べ, warm-up music in *noh*), 123, 178 (pl. 41)

*shirabemono* (調物, the main type of instrumental *koto* music), 208, 210

*shirabyōshi* (白拍子, female temple and palace dancers), 55, 83 (pl. 6), 100

*shiragigaku* (新羅楽, court music from ancient Korea), 98

*shishi mai* (獅子舞): *see* lion dances

*shitakata* (下方, the *hayashi* on the *kabuki* stage), 241

Shitamachi (下町, "lower city" in Tokyo) Museum, 268

*shite* (シテ, the principal actor in a *noh* drama or *kyōgen*), 125–128, 146 (fig. 19)

*shite bashira* (シテ柱, *shite*'s pillar on *noh* stage), 126

*shizugaki* (閑掻・静掻, a pattern on the *gakusō*), 105

Shizuka (静, mistress of Yoshitsune), 55

*shō* (笙, an organ-like wind instrument), 93 (pl. 30), 94 (pl. 33), 110 (d., fig. 11), 110–113, 116 f., 252, 285 (fig. 45)

Shōbutsu (生仏, supposed composer of the first *heikebiwa* narration), 153

*shōga* (唱歌, mnemonic singing of instrument parts), 58, 109, 136, 201, 284

*shōgi* (床几, seats used by *noh tsuzumi* drummers on stage), 124

shogun (将軍), 36, 39 f.

*shojū* (初重, lower notes of *goinfu* notation), 279

*shōko* (鉦鼓, bronze gong used in *gagaku*), 96 (pl. 37), 103 (d.), 112, 117, 285

*Shoku Nihongi* (続日本紀, eighth-century history book), 33

Shōmu (聖武), Emperor, 102

*shōmyō* (声明, Buddhist chant), 66 ff., 74, 80, 122, 153, 280, 281, tr. 4

*Shōmyō yōjinshū* (声明用心集, basic chant codex of Tendai Buddhism), 67

*shōsetsu* (勝絶, the note F in ancient music theory), 114 (fig. 12)

Shōsōin (正倉院, ninth century warehouse in Nara), 92 (pl. 29), 102, 106, 150, 165, 194 f.

"Shōten" (正天, a festival drum piece), 59

*shura noh* (修羅能, ancient warrior *noh* plays), 124

*shūshinmono* (執心物, obsession plays in *zatsu noh* dramas), 124

Siberia, 267

"sliding door" effect, 60 f., 234, 235 (fig. 32), 289

snow festival: *see yuki matsuri*

*sō* (箏): *see gakusō*

*sōban* (双盤, a gong used offstage in *kabuki*), 246 (d.), 248, 254

Society for Contemporary Music, 29

*sōga* (早歌, Kamakura-period party songs), 101

*sōjō* (双調, the note G and its mode in ancient music theory), 114 (figs. 12, 13)

*sōkyoku* (箏曲, a generic term for *koto* music), 197

solfège, 101, 109, 295; *see also shōga*

*sonohachi* (薗八, a genre of *shamisen* music founded by Miyakoji Sonohachi 宮古路 薗八), 219 (fig. 29), 221

*sōshidai* (僧次第, priest entrance music): *see shidai*

Southeast Asia, 31, 98

spies, 154, 169

stage positions, 191 (pl. 77), 192 (pl. 79), 224, 241 (fn. 3), 242, 247, 250, 259 (pls. 86, 87), 260 (pls. 88, 89)

stages, 24 (pl. 1), 62, 94 (pl. 32), 119, 123 f., 126, 133, 177 (pls. 38, 39), 188 (pl. 61), 191 (pl. 76), 224, 230, 233, 240 ff.

storytellers, 38, 152, 163, 218

Stravinsky, Igor, 26

street musicians, 76, 89 (pls. 19–21), 262, 271 f.

stringed instruments: *see* chordophones

Suitō Kinjō (水藤錦穣, female founder of Nishiki *biwa* school), 155

*Sukeroku* (助六, a *kabuki* play), 169, 243

*Sumidagawa* (隅田川, a *noh* drama), 277

*sumifu* (墨譜, *biwa* notation), 282, 290

*surigane* (摺鉦, a small hand gong), 58, 84 (pl. 9)

sutras, 66